# THE ROAD TO
# PROSPERITY

## The 21st Century Approach
## to Economic Development

# THE ROAD TO PROSPERITY

## The 21st Century Approach to Economic Development

Edited by

## Marc A. Miles

Published by Heritage Books

an activity of The Heritage Foundation
214 Massachusetts Avenue, NE
Washington, DC 20002-4999
(202) 546-4400 • heritage.org

Library of Congress Control Number:
2004113691

Printed in the United States of America

Distributed to the trade by
National Book Network
Lanham, Maryland

ISBN 0-9743665-1-x

*Cover design by Elizabeth Brewer*

# Table of Contents

# Preface

THE INDEX OF ECONOMIC FREEDOM is more than a measurement of economic freedom; it is an instruction manual, a road map to prosperity, describing how poor nations can achieve growth. Developing countries continue to exist from day to day despite receiving over $1 trillion in foreign aid.

Many of these countries have a list of problems that include corruption, weak property rights, excessive regulation, high barriers to trade, and numerous state-owned enterprises. Their current policies have sentenced generations of their future citizens to live in poverty. But by using the *Index* as a guide, these same countries could redirect their economies onto the road to prosperity.

Developed nations have subsidized this poor behavior by repeatedly giving foreign aid with no strings attached. Taking a new approach, the Bush Administration has introduced a new foreign aid initiative, the Millennium Challenge Account (MCA), to reward countries that have pursued sound policies. According to Secretary of State Colin Powell, Chairman of the Board of the Millennium Challenge Corporation, the MCC "will only support poor countries that have adopted growth-promoting governance and economic policies and countries which invest in their people."[1]

This initiative should serve as a model for institutions such as the World Bank. In his chapter on the World Bank, Adam Lerrick notes that

---

1. Secretary of State Colin Powell, transcript of MCC Board Meeting, February 2, 2004, at *www.mca.gov/Documents/board_transcript_020204.html*.

42 of the recipient nations with a per capita income of $1 a day are growing poorer and have suffered a 25 percent decline in per capita income since 1980. Lerrick proposes that the World Bank be transformed by issuing results-based grants, by requiring recipient countries to pay for a portion of their project, and by having the Bank invest its own resources in international capital markets.

Reforming foreign aid will make it more effective and will force countries to implement sound policies in order to qualify. Ideally, the reformation of foreign aid will lead to its elimination. If foreign aid achieves its intended goal, it will no longer be needed.

The key to achieving this goal lies in the road to prosperity. Countries must have low barriers to trade, a low cost of government, a low level of government intervention in the economy, a low level of inflation, low barriers to capital flows and foreign investment, a low level of restrictions in banking and finance, a low level of intervention in wages and prices, strong property rights, low regulation, and a low level of activity in the informal market. For the past 10 years, the *Index* has revealed that countries that take these steps have higher GDP per capita.

If they fail to take these steps, countries will also fail to attract investment, which is essential for growth. Despite this fact, countries often limit investment in certain sectors or impose other restrictions, such as capital controls. Capital controls are a tax on foreign investment. As Sebastian Edwards notes in his chapter, many leaders have erroneously assumed that capital controls will reduce the vulnerability of the economy. For instance, countries that increased controls on outflows during the 1980s debt crisis experienced long declines in growth.

Moreover, countries often apply this erroneous assumption to trade by refusing to open their markets. Mercantilism even lurks within organizations committed to advancing trade. The World Trade Organization's Doha Round has moved slowly because of varied agendas within its membership despite the fact that this round is focused on the needs of developing countries. Developing countries would benefit significantly from expanded trade, but without an agreement through the WTO, significant trade liberalization is unlikely to occur.

Countries should not depend solely on the WTO for liberalization. A Global Free Trade Association (GFTA) should be formed to advance liberalization. This would be a voluntary association of countries that have embraced free trade, strong property rights, low regulation, and investment-friendly policies. Historically, countries that have opened their markets have enjoyed significantly higher levels of growth than those that have shunned global competition. The mounting benefits accruing to members of this association should therefore motivate other countries to implement sound economic policies in order to join. Moreover, countries seeking to qualify for GFTA membership would benefit simply from implementing other market reforms in addition to liberalizing trade.

As Daniel Griswold notes in his chapter, free trade alone does not guarantee growth. In addition to trade, developing nations must implement other market reforms found on the road map such as property rights, low regulation, openness to foreign investment, and a low cost of government. The road to prosperity, just like marriage, requires serious commitment and perseverance. One step on the road will not reap prosperity. Countries that choose to implement partial measures to avoid short-term pain will sacrifice long-term prosperity.

Partial measures will leave countries dependent on the generosity of others. To become self-sufficient, countries must implement reforms across the board. Taking steps on the road to prosperity will help developing countries to achieve a degree of success that will benefit generations to come. Implementing these steps guarantees prosperity that foreign aid has not and cannot produce.

Edwin J. Feulner
*President*
*The Heritage Foundation*

# Introduction

## A New Way of Thinking About Economic Development: The Origins of *The Road to Prosperity*

*Marc A. Miles*

THE ROAD TO PROSPERITY: *The 21st Century Approach to Economic Development* highlights and defines a new solution to an old problem. It is the first book to bring together in one place ideas that have been percolating and expanding for at least a quarter-century. These are the ideas that form the foundation for many of the innovative policies now flourishing in the emerging countries of Eastern Europe.

The new perspective no longer artificially divides the world into developed and developing countries. Just as people around the world put their pants on one leg at a time, each country's economy can be explained by the same set of economic rules. Activities that are subsidized tend to expand, and those that are taxed find the going tougher and contract. In the same way, all countries are "developing" in the sense that they are constantly reacting and changing to the evolving world economy.

Similarly, the old economic development poverty solution of transferring income from one government to another is discarded. The new approach captured in these pages is more concerned with the welfare of people and less focused on government actions. Its goal is to make economies hum along by letting people—rather than the government, the World Bank, or any other institution—figure out how best to improve their lives. In other words, let individuals use their wits and abilities to determine how best to put a roof over their families, food on their tables, and shoes on their children's feet.

Within this framework, government's role is to cultivate an environment in which people can achieve their potential and thus make the most of their abilities and other resources in the economy. Only in such an environment can we safely assume that the desired shelter, the desired food, the desired clothing, and other essentials will be available to families.

A healthy economic environment may be created and maintained in part by ensuring that contracts are enforced, that individuals retain clear title to the houses and businesses they have acquired or created, that there is a stable currency so that prices can be anticipated and future decisions easily assessed, and that there is a close relationship between effort and reward.

Today, however, governments and international organizations all too often throw up roadblocks that inhibit individuals from reaching their potential. These barriers force individuals from the road to prosperity onto byways full of potholes and obstacles that distract attention from goals, drain energy needed for a sustained journey, and leave them well short of reaching their full economic potential. As a result, far too many people are consigned to making do with less to eat, use, or keep for a rainy day.

Specifically, these roadblocks appear in the form of:

- Tariffs that raise prices and deprive individuals from getting the most for their incomes;
- High tax rates that discourage work and production, thereby taking food from the family table;
- Regulations that prevent individuals from pursuing their natural abilities; and
- A lack of property rights, which leaves people stuck with unequal treatment before the law, unenforceable contracts, and the inability to convert one form of wealth to new, more promising opportunities, such as starting a new business.

Instructively, The Heritage Foundation's *Index of Economic Freedom* documents that the countries perennially ranked among the world's poorest also tend to have the most and highest roadblocks. This fact should come as no surprise, for poverty merely manifests the impact of government barriers on people's incentives and actions. Where roadblocks deny individual opportunity, workers arise each morning to face the reality that they will be spending their time and efforts in activities that bear little fruit. The same problems appear over and over in a vicious circle, with no apparent end to the misery and poverty. The nation's people become frustrated.

Unleashing a country's potential requires removing the economic road-blocks that inhibit its people. As the barriers tumble one by one, a country can begin to move down the long, previously elusive road to prosperity.

This seems simple enough, so why don't countries adopt the Nike slogan and "just do it"? In some countries, historical traditions must be adapted or overcome before barriers fall. In others, the rulers' desire for power and money may trump the needs of their people. In most cases, however, those in authority are simply misguided by prevailing perspectives on how to jump-start their countries' economies.

These prevailing beliefs may be what the leaders' teachers taught them—just as *their* teachers were taught by their teachers, and so on for several generations. These beliefs—repeated constantly by reporters, pundits, professors, policymakers, and other movers and shakers—may seem to be facts, to have always been true. Yet chances are that these truisms are only myopic readings of history. The root of the continued failure to progress economically may lie in economic ideas that originated in—and are unique to—the 20th century.

In other words, much of what is taken today as time-tested economic truths or facts is only ideas—and recent and unreliable ideas at that.

## A Brief Overview of the Origin of Unreliable Ideas

Three hundred years from now, when economists look back on economic theory, they are likely to observe that the 20th century was a sidetrack on the main line of economic thought. The late 19th century through the mid-20th century was a time of tremendous social experimentation, born of the new and rapidly evolving view that governments could solve most human problems.

This concept may be traced to Bismarck's unification of 22 German states as the German Empire in 1870. It first appeared in the United States with the 1880s emergence of the "Trustbusters," intent on corralling what they saw as the growing power of industrial companies. The origin of this movement paralleled the emergence of what we now call an economy.

The experiment was further advanced by the socialists of the early 1900s, who envisioned a utopian state in which the fruits of a nation's production would be shared equally among its inhabitants and preached government policies that they felt would move countries in that direction. The global Great Depression of the 1930s provoked a response that centered on enhancing the role of government in providing solutions.

In short, it was a period in which the role of the state grew in most areas of daily life. Emerging thought identified the state as the vehicle or catalyst for solving most problems—including the set of problems that found individuals around the world trapped in poverty.

But concern in this area presented a problem in itself: Mainline classical economics did not support these experimental ideas. A new view of economics was necessary. And, so, Keynesian economics was born.

What are the main differences between the classical and Keynesian perspectives? Classical economics analyzed how changes in tax rates and other relative prices made some people richer and others poorer (the income effect) and how price changes alter incentives and behavior (the substitution effect). The Keynesians threw out the impact on behavior (the incentive or substitution effect) and focused exclusively on how some were made richer and others poorer. This change in analysis fit neatly into—and justified—the growing obsession with the distribution of income.

The single-minded focus on income winners and losers is characteristic of both fiscal Keynesians (who emphasize manipulation of tax revenue, spending levels, and deficits) and monetarist Keynesians (who emphasize money supply). Both zero in on how income changes might affect total economic demand, hoping for increased total production.

The fiscal Keynesians' framework is exemplified in their embrace of increased domestic income transfers; that is, paying Paul today by taxing Peter either directly today or in the future as government bonds are retired. Think of Social Security. Part of the Social Security taxes you (Peter) pay today are immediately transferred to recipients (Paul). The excess—yes, more is temporarily being put into Social Security than is being taken out—is sent to the general revenue fund, in exchange for some intergovernmental bonds, to pay for farm subsidies, highways, or the Rock and Roll Hall of Fame and Museum in Cleveland. Thus, the overall government budget deficit is even worse than reported by the amount of Social Security surplus siphoned off. In a few years, when the demographic tables are turned and more is being taken out of Social Security than put in, those left paying taxes not only will have to pay for the spending excesses of today, but in addition will have to pay back the money borrowed from the Social Security fund.

Taxing "the rich" to provide transfers to the poor was viewed not only as alleviating poverty, but also as stimulating growth in the economy. The fundamental assertion was that the poor simply spent more of their income, and hence that total demand must increase. (That is how we end up with higher tax rates for the rich and welfare for the poor: Take more income away from the "idle rich," who would let it gather dust, and hand it to the "idle poor," who at least would run out and spend it on something.)

Any accompanying disincentives and distortions on work, investment, and production were deemed unimportant. So what if the higher-taxed rich could retain a smaller proportion of every dollar they earned? So what if the idle recipients had an incentive to remain idle in order to continue qualifying for payments? The transfers were considered a win–win activist policy because they simultaneously tackled the twin concerns of growth and income inequality.

Monetarist Keynesians also focused exclusively on income effects. Milton Friedman's famous example of a "pure monetary" policy, with the helicopter flying over the country and dropping dollar bills, relied on the income effect for the eventual income or inflation increase. As people scampered to collect the falling dollars, they felt richer and demand rose, resulting in increased production and/or rising prices.

As the activist role of the state grew, proposed solutions to economic problems increasingly fell into two categories: regulation and transfers. Regulation was used in the hope of addressing perceived problems of economic behavior ranging from monopoly to pollution. Transfers were perceived as the mechanism that could alleviate apparent inequalities in society. Thus, income was transferred from the taxpayer to the state and from the state to the victims of inequality—the poor, the aged, the unemployed, and the otherwise disadvantaged.

Because of the apparent impact of government actions, the emphasis and discussion of economics shifted from the impact on people to the successes of government. As these discussions continued in academic journals and the popular press, the "emerging" ideas became the "prevailing wisdom."

Economic development theory created in the last century largely confined its analysis to the same perspective. The prevailing policies of improving the plight of poor *people* could be adapted to improve the plight of poor *countries*. Just as the rich provided funds for transfers to the poor, rich nations could be the source of transfers to poor nations. Again, the income infusions to poor countries could tackle the twin concerns of income inequality among nations and slow growth in the less developed world. That these transfers might also produce counterproductive behavior within both rich and poor countries was simply not considered.

Thus, foreign aid became the centerpiece of development theory. Persistent poverty was to be addressed either by rich governments directly transferring resources to governments of poor nations or by funneling aid through international financial institutions such as the International Monetary Fund or the World Bank. In either case, the aid amounted to government-to-government transfers. The recipient government would know best how to alleviate social concerns.

The recipient government's solution often consisted of infrastructure or other massive government projects. Improved water, sewer, or roads would provide immediate jobs and close the gap between living standards in developed and developing nations. Combined with internal Keynesian policies of taxing the rich to give to the poor, inequalities in income distribution could be alleviated as well.

This political and economic framework is the rhetorical and legal legacy that still motivates the majority of today's government policies. However, in the last half of the 20th century, some economists began to question the underlying assumptions. In *The Road to Serfdom*, Fredrick von Hayek warned of the consequences of placing too much power and resources in the hands of government bureaucrats. Peter Bauer pointed out fallacies in prevailing economic development perspectives in such books as *Reality and Rhetoric: Studies in the Economics of Development*. Certainly, when two tribes begin to trade, they do not start by paving a road between their villages.

But more questions followed. Many were stimulated by the failure of Keynesian theory to explain the problems of the 1970s. In that decade, countries found themselves experiencing simultaneously high unemployment and high inflation. Such a plight was inconsistent with Keynesian theory, for if unemployment was high, demand should have been low and inflation impossible. The improbability of the situation necessitated the creation of a new word: "stagflation."

Some economists responded to this dilemma by returning to microeconomic theory for answers. They began to reconsider the substitution or incentive effects on people and businesses—concerns discarded by the Keynesians. Considering this full impact of taxes, regulation, and transfers cast prevailing policies in an entirely new light. For example, the win–win combination of taxing the idle rich at higher rates to transfer income to the idle poor now became a lose–lose policy. One drawback is that taking an extra dollar of taxes might provide only, say, 60 cents of services. A second is that the higher tax rate on the rich leaves them with less from each extra dollar earned, discouraging them from trying to earn another dollar and diverting more of their savings to investments with the highest after-tax return rather than the best overall (pre-tax) return. A third is that punishing the poor who work by taking away benefits discourages them from pursuing productive jobs.

This new perspective shifted the focus of analysis from the role of government to the impact on people. Taxes were no longer viewed merely as a positive means of redistribution. There was also recognition that taxes change behavior, often causing workers and investors to allocate their efforts and money inefficiently. This can cause total production to decline, leaving less available for individuals and families to consume.

The new perspective revealed that transfers have a negative side. Need-based transfers such as welfare and unemployment require people to remain in the needy state to receive benefits. The transfers rationally cause people to focus on how to continue to qualify, not on how their efforts might be most productive for the economy. The resulting disincentives discourage people from following their natural desires to improve the lot of their families and themselves.

Much of this analysis was conducted under the supply-side rubric—but not all, for supply-side economics was simply trying to demonstrate an appreciation of earlier classical economics. The ideas of lowering tax rates, reducing regulation, privatizing public businesses, and deregulating industries emanated from the classical recognition that reducing the distortions (the negative substitution effects) and other incentives for corruption would lower barriers that keep people from achieving their potential. This new appreciation for classical economics underlies what is emerging as 21st century economics.

## The 21st Century Approach to Development

What we have called the 21st century approach to development incorporates this shift back to the mainline classical framework. Hence, it also entails a shift in focus back to people rather than governments. The way people react to policy changes (incentive effects) is reincorporated. The full impact of high taxes, tariffs, quotas, regulations, and other barriers that inhibit the accomplishment of one's dreams is an integral part of the analysis.

This new paradigm departs from today's prevailing wisdom in at least two ways:

- It ends the distinction between "developing" and "developed" countries.
- It makes "level of poverty" a less important criterion for development assistance, concentrating instead on the availability of opportunities to escape impoverishment.

As Arthur Laffer points out in Chapter 7, "In effect all economies are developing economies. No country should ever stop developing. There is not one set of rules for one class of countries and another set of rules for others." Even the United States is a developing country, reacting and evolving to cope with changing world conditions. This revelation arises from a more general point: that there is only one set of economic principles. What is true for the individual is true for the country and for the world as a whole.

With a renewed appreciation for people rather than governments, the goal of economic development is to free *people* to use their abilities to the fullest in pursuit of *their* goals of housing, feeding, and clothing their family. The problem in much of the world is that people are not allowed to do that.

Thus, where 20th century development economics looked at poor countries and saw persistent poverty, the 21st century approach looks at poor countries and sees what perpetuates poverty: people's lack of opportunity. In technical terms, it is not the level of poverty that is most vicious, but rather the absence of change or opportunity to escape that poverty. Where the 20th century approach produced a vicious cycle of aid, default, and dependency on foreign governments, the IMF, or the World Bank, the 21st century approach holds out the prospect that countries can generate growth and prosperity themselves, without foreign interference.

In the 21st century view, the "goodness" of a government is not measured by the extent of its intervention. Rather, it is rated by the extent to which a government creates the *environment*, the "rules of the game," that allows individuals' abilities and desires to flourish. Only such an environment offers the opportunity to escape poverty. If we care about the people of a country, we will measure *their* interests, not the interests of bureaucrats.

The existence or nonexistence of this enabling environment is what the *Index of Economic Freedom* captures. Economic freedom is about people and their opportunities: their freedom to work, to produce, to consume, and to invest in the ways they feel are most productive and beneficial. Perhaps most important, economic freedom may be created without aid from—or dependence on—outside countries or organizations. With the proper commitment, countries can achieve prosperity on their own. In other words, by adopting policies that promote economic freedom, a country can say goodbye to the IMF and its vicious cycle of aid and dependency.

To achieve economic freedom, countries need a road map. They need to know what steps must be taken to create the opportunities now missing in their economies. The *Index of Economic Freedom* presents such mileposts. As Ana Eiras points out in Chapter 2, the 10 factors of the *Index* outline the 10 steps that lead to self-generated development and economic stability. These 10 mileposts are the road to prosperity.

But keep in mind that one milepost is no more important than the others. Empirical tests have shown that the 10 factors are equally important, much like the 10 most essential parts of a car. What is the most important part of a car? The motor? The tires? The transmission? The steering wheel? The brakes? Clearly, without any one of these components, a car cannot go very fast or very far.

Think of a country that has passed only half the mileposts on the road to prosperity as a car with only half of its most essential parts—not a good candidate to reach its goal any time soon. Moreover, unless those other parts are added, breakdowns and trouble surely lie ahead. Alternatively, countries like Chile that have worked for years to make it all the way down the road now have a car with all the essential parts. They can go faster and farther and reach goals about which other nations can only dream.

The goal of this book is to elaborate the journey down this road, to provide an understanding of the new framework by which a country can escape poverty. To this end, the book describes the failed approaches of the past, presents the alternative framework, and illustrates empirically the relationship between the road to prosperity and the escape from poverty.

Adam Lerrick highlights how the track record of World Bank aid has been spectacularly unsuccessful. He presents an innovative plan for turning that international financial institution into a self-funding foundation that rewards results, not promises.

Ana Eiras describes the 10 steps to prosperity. She shows how countries that have followed the road have achieved accelerated growth, while countries that have ignored the road have not.

Richard Roll answers the question "Why are some countries rich while others are poor?" He finds property rights, regulation, informal market activity, stable monetary policy, trade barriers, and government expenditure to be among the most important determinants of a country's wealth. His findings reinforce the concept that the 10 mileposts of the *Index* can help to guide a country from poverty.

The next five chapters focus on specific mileposts:

- Dan Griswold describes the benefits that workers, producers, and consumers derive when domestic markets open to global trading.
- Hernando de Soto explains the essential role of property rights in progressing toward prosperity. He argues that the poor outside the West are not so poor. They just lack the ownership rights for turning their wealth into more productive uses.
- I describe why a stable currency with price stability simplifies choices and allows individuals to follow their natural incentives toward the best allocation of resources.
- Arthur Laffer explains the impact of changing tax rates on output and tax revenue, first in terms of the "Laffer Curve" and subsequently in terms of the two-factor (workers and capital) "Laffer Ellipse." In the process, he differentiates between the incidence and burden of taxes and also considers the impact of expenditure.
- Sebastian Edwards's empirical analysis demonstrates that neither controls on capital inflows nor controls on capital outflows have been very effective. He concludes that, while capital account liberalization should not be one of the first reforms instituted, lifting these restrictions is very important for a country's development.

Also in these pages, Robert Barro investigates what policies and conditions are most conducive to economic growth. He finds that the rule of law, investment, and the openness of the economy have a positive effect on growth, while higher levels of government consumption and inflation affect growth negatively. Again, these empirical results reinforce the lesson that the road to prosperity produces positive results for a country.

Finally, Sara Fitzgerald Cooper discusses some of the problems encountered in trying to obtain a free trade agreement through the World Trade

Organization and considers an alternative should the Doha Round fail: a Global Free Trade Association in which willing countries could unilaterally eliminate trade restrictions with each other.

This book is not meant to be used in isolation. As stated previously, *The Road to Prosperity* focuses on the 10 factors measured in the *Index of Economic Freedom*. While *The Road to Prosperity* explains the paradigm or framework of self-generated growth and prosperity, the *Index* provides case studies of more than 160 countries and assesses the extent to which they have progressed down this road. Together these two books provide unparalleled insights into the state of the world's economies.

Critics will suggest that *The Road to Prosperity* does not explain the source of all problems in all countries. We are not claiming that it does. Such a goal is probably more than we can hope to achieve. But we are confident that the book satisfies the 80/20 rule of thumb: 80 percent of the problem can be explained with 20 percent of the effort or factors. If countries can solve 80 percent of their perpetual poverty problem, the world will indeed be a better place.

# Chapter 1

# The World Bank as Foundation: Development Without Debt

**Editor's Summary**

Those who view economic freedom with a skeptical eye commonly criticize poor developing nations for their inability to tap the vast benefits of international markets because of poverty, a history of poor governance, and general lack of creditworthiness. Such reasoning has led many policymakers in developed nations to oppose fundamental reform of international financial institutions, like the World Bank, that provide subsidized loans to developing nations.

Despite the World Bank's lack of positive loan results, its tradition of awarding aid based only on country promises persists. Adam Lerrick categorizes the failures:

- After 50 years and more than $1 trillion in aid, global efforts to close the gap between rich and poor countries have failed.
- The 10 largest recipients of World Bank aid have seen their standards of living rise a negligible 0.2 percent per annum

over the past 30 years despite injections of $40 billion.

- Forty-two recipient nations with a per capita income of $1 a day, concentrated in sub-Saharan Africa, are headed in the wrong direction. They are growing poorer, suffering a 25 percent decline in per capita income since 1980.

Lerrick proposes an ingenious transformation of the World Bank. Specifically, if its current resources were used more effectively, the Bank could be converted from an outdated, ineffective development bureaucracy into a grant-making agency. Lerrick proposes that the Bank invest its existing portfolio resources in international capital markets and use the profits to finance development grants that would be disbursed only after positive results on competitively bid projects are confirmed by independent audits.

Multiple benefits accrue from the grant format. Results-based grants would sidestep that corruption, waste, and incompetence that all too often cripple aid's efficacy. More important for the long run, Lerrick's proposal encourages recipient responsibility by requiring countries to pay immediately for a portion of the project. No longer would they be able to palm off debt incurred on ineffective projects to future generations. To finance their share of the projects, recipient nations would have to utilize international financial markets, which ultimately hold the key to their long-term prosperity.

# The World Bank as Foundation: Development Without Debt

*Adam Lerrick*

THE NEED TO REDUCE global poverty and underwrite the fundamentals for economic growth in the developing world has become a moral imperative for industrialized nations. Not to give is no longer an option, but *how* to give wisely, cost-effectively, and directly for the benefit of the poor remains an elusive goal.

After 50 years and an outpouring of more than $1 trillion in aid, global efforts to close the gap between rich and poor countries have clearly failed. For the World Bank, steward of $500 billion of these funds, the problem is that not enough money has been donated. The solution therefore lies in more and more money for more and more lending. If only miserly donors will double aid flows to $1 billion each year, poverty—together with its root causes—will be halved by 2015.

In contrast, many members of the international community funding the Bank are taking a critical look at the effectiveness of its traditional ways of doing business. There is little to show from past lending to the poor except for a heavy debt burden. The record is a sad one.

- Standards of living are flat or declining.
- For two-thirds of World Bank projects in the poorest countries, by the Bank's own optimistic evaluation of its efforts, benefits have long fallen short of costs.
- After $40 billion of resource transfer, the 10 largest recipients of pure World Bank aid have seen their per capita income rise a negligible 0.2 percent per annum over the past 30 years.

- At the lowest end of the economic spectrum, 42 nations concentrated in sub-Saharan Africa are desperately poor and growing poorer. Their 700 million citizens who subsist on less than $1 per day have suffered a 25 percent decline in per capita income since 1980. This will worsen as populations double within the decade.

- Project failure is the norm, and indebtedness is accumulating to unsustainable levels. In 1996, when collective debt mounted to $200 billion (equal to 255 percent of exports), a Heavily Indebted Poor Country (HIPC) initiative recognized that the loaned money was long gone and that these economies could never hope to repay. Bilateral and multilateral donors united in a promise to forgive debt down to manageable levels.

This sad history aside, the demographics of World Bank aid do not add up: 800 million people in 17 rich countries are being asked to do the heavy financial lifting for the 2.5 billion people in countries where the per capita income is less than $2 per day and populations are growing five times as fast. The seven pennies out of every $10 of national income that aid proponents say will transform the world is just the first installment. At current levels of theft, waste, and diversion from productive ends in poor countries, there will never be enough disposable funds in industrialized budgets to elevate the world's poorest masses.

Reliance on official lending is an anachronism in an age when financial power has been transferred to a private sector whose resources dwarf what the multilateral agencies can muster. Before dusting off the checkbooks of Group of Seven (G–7) taxpayers, the relevance of an outdated lending paradigm must be challenged. The private sector must be enlisted to leverage resources already on World Bank balance sheets in a sustainable new formula for the delivery of aid to the poorest.

## Before the Capital Markets

The origins of the World Bank reach back into what now seems to be economic prehistory. In July 1944, when the Bank was founded at a conference in Bretton Woods, New Hampshire, the international financial system was strictly delineated. The gold standard fixed exchange rates between currencies; trade barriers and capital controls limited the flow of goods and funds; developing countries were not a priority for private investment; financial markets were small and segmented.

The Bank was to be an institutional meeting ground where rich industrialized members would supply resources and AAA credit backing to enable the Bank to gather money in the capital markets with one hand and lend the funds to creditworthy but impoverished developing members with the other. The Bank's original goals are found in its official title: The International Bank for Reconstruction and Development (IBRD).

For the first 40 years, the Bank was the dominant source of international resources to emerging economies. Knowledge and financing were tied in an effort to establish the conditions for growth. During the Cold War, lending was often a strategic gesture that demanded large blocks of capital for containment of perceived threats.

However, political, social, and economic parameters were transformed in the last decade of the 20th century. Communism no longer threatened democracies. Economies opened their doors; international trade burgeoned; human, technological, and financial capital moved freely across borders. And in developing nations, a new generation of public-sector and private-sector leaders, educated in the graduate schools of the West, grew into skilled borrowers and capable decision-makers able to determine their own policy directions.

The explosion of the private financial markets was central to this change. The small, segmented, and cautious capital markets that were the rationale for the World Bank's founding grew exponentially in size, sophistication, and willingness to tolerate the risk that once deterred projects in the developing world. The Bank's comparative advantage in development lending had vanished.

Today, the World Bank is no longer a significant source of funding for the emerging world and cannot match a fraction of what the private sector routinely offers. Although the Bank pretends to focus on the global stepnations that are denied access to the capital markets and on projects that the private sector would ignore, traditional lending to creditworthy borrowers dominates. An overwhelming 70 percent of IBRD resources flows to a dozen countries that simultaneously enjoy easy access to the capital markets that channel $99 in resources for every $1 the Bank provides.

## The IDA: Debt the Real Poor Can Never Repay

Lending continues as the mantra at the International Development Association (IDA), the aid arm of the World Bank that focuses on its 81 poorest members with a per capita income of less than $875. The record shows, however, that a stream of $142 billion in loans since the IDA's inception in 1960 has failed to provide an exit from poverty. In 2003 alone, $7.3 billion in 141 operations was channeled to 55 countries. (See TABLE I, "Recipients of IDA Loans.")

The IDA extends 40-year loans, with a 10-year grace period, that carry an interest rate of 0.75 percent. This near zero charge reduces the present value of these repayment promises to 30 cents on the dollar and translates into a gift component equal to 70 percent of their value. In reality, these are loans in perpetuity that the poorest borrowers seldom repay. Technical defaults are rare, for the Bank routinely rolls over obligations with enough funding added to cover interest. Replenishments of $14 billion–$15 billion from rich countries are needed every three years to continue these lending programs.

It was for these stepchildren of the system that in March 2000, the International Financial Institution Advisory Commission (Meltzer Commission) proposed a major three-stage change in the format of development aid:

1. End traditional loans to impoverished nations that cannot repay the money.
2. Instead, provide outright grants for the basic improvements in living standards and infrastructure that are the foundation for the climb from poverty to productivity.
3. Finally, measure output and pay only for performance instead of disbursing funds without regard to whether or not results are achieved.

In speeches to the World Bank and the G–7 governments in 2002, President George W. Bush proposed a plan to transform half of IDA assistance to these exacting standards.

## Double the Effectiveness to Double the Aid

For the world's truly poor nations, the provision of rudimentary levels of health care, primary education, and physical infrastructure remains the starting point toward a better living standard and the precondition for economic growth. Yet these are the very countries in which corrupt and inefficient environments undermine the ability to benefit from aid.

# Table 1
# Recipients of IDA Loans 2003 ($ Millions)

| Africa | | Africa | |
|---|---|---|---|
| Angola | 50 | Benin | 10 |
| Burkina Faso | 160 | Burundi | 78 |
| Cameroon | 81 | Cape Verde | 16 |
| Chad | 137 | Congo Dem. Rep. | 454 |
| Congo Rep. | 41 | Eritrea | 60 |
| Ethiopia | 404 | Ghana | 220 |
| Guinea | 25 | Kenya | 111 |
| Madagascar | 162 | Malawi | 137 |
| Mozambique | 201 | Niger | 60 |
| Nigeria | 230 | Rwanda | 116 |
| Senegal | 46 | Sierra Leone | 105 |
| Tanzania | 251 | Uganda | 407 |
| Zambia | 150 | | |
| | | **Total Africa** | **$3,722** |

| Middle East & N. Africa | | Latin America | |
|---|---|---|---|
| Djibouti | 23 | Bolivia | 80 |
| Yemen | 177 | Grenada | 7 |
| Total Middle East | | Guyana | 17 |
| & N. Africa | **$200** | Honduras | 22 |
| | | Nicaragua | 27 |
| | | **Total Latin America** | **$153** |

| East Asia | | Europe & Central Asia | |
|---|---|---|---|
| Cambodia | 69 | Albania | 43 |
| Indonesia | 145 | Armenia | 40 |
| Lao People's Dem. Rep. | 25 | Azerbaijan | 66 |
| Mongolia | 8 | Bosnia-Herzegovina | 23 |
| Samoa | 5 | Georgia | 75 |
| Vietnam | 293 | Kosovo | 11 |
| **Total East Asia** | **$544** | Kyrgyz Rep. | 28 |
| | | Moldova | 25 |
| | | Serbia-Montenegro | 225 |
| South Asia | | Tajikistan | 20 |
| Afghanistan | 215 | Uzbekistan | 25 |
| Bangladesh | 554 | **Total Europe & Central Asia** | **$581** |
| India | 687 | | |
| Nepal | 97 | | |
| Pakistan | 297 | | |
| Sri Lanka | 233 | | |
| **Total South Asia** | **$2,083** | **Total All Countries** | **$7,283** |

**Source:** World Bank 2003 Annual Report

It is easy to quantify primary education skills, vaccination rates, miles of passable roads, provision of electricity, and delivery of water and sanitation, and to specify contracts for competitive bid. Skilled international suppliers in the service sectors and non-governmental organizations are increasingly mobile and would welcome a grant structure in which concessions and delivery contracts were paid in large part by a AAA-rated agency.

In contrast to loans, grants would be released after audited delivery of service under a system of user fees: No results, no funds expended. Payments would be based on numbers of children vaccinated, kilowatts delivered, cubic meters of water treated, students passing literacy tests, and miles of functioning roads. This would eliminate the distortional effects of financing cost subsidies (traditional development bank loans and guarantees) by maintaining the relative prices of inputs. Because the World Bank is obligated to pay directly for delivered services, the revenue guarantee for agents that provide execution is dependable and substantially free of the political risk that a specific country will default.

Since payment is ensured directly to the concessionaire, the private sector will generate the necessary funding. From the concessionaires' standpoint, the proposed system has the distinct advantages of allowing them clear responsibility to deliver a product they understand while eliminating the need to negotiate financing with a myriad of official lenders.

The poorer the country, the greater the need for grants. Under the IDA, all recipients benefit from the same subsidy, though some are clearly less poor and others are able to generate resources domestically and from capital markets abroad. If, instead, all IDA loans were converted to grants and the aid element varied according to need (from 90 percent of the service cost for the poorest without capital market access to 50 percent for those nearing graduation), the result would be an average subsidy of 70 percent. This is identical to the current aggregate level of subsidy in IDA loans—but with an important difference: The distribution of aid would be more equitable.

Assume, for example, that a country with a per capita income of $250, qualifying for 90 percent grant resources, determines that vaccination of its children against measles is a desired goal. If the development agency confirms the need, the government then solicits competitive bids from private-sector agents; non-governmental organizations (such as charitable institutions); and public-sector entities (such as the Ministry of Health). If the lowest qualifying bid is $5 per vaccination, the World Bank then agrees to pay $4.50 (90 percent) directly to the provider for each child vaccinated. The government would be responsible for the remaining $0.50 (10 percent) fee. Payments would be made only upon certification by an auditor independent of all participants—the government, the World Bank, and the provider of vaccinations.

Some might argue that the proposed grant system's reliance on international contractors and non-governmental organizations for its execution would obstruct the growth of local institutions, which is the long-range goal of development effort. In reality, however, as basic needs are satisfied at lowest cost, local labor skills and entrepreneurs will be fostered and will compete for future contracts, and countries will eventually become self-sustaining.

A multiplicity of benefits accrues from the grant format. Specifically:

- Because they are an outright gift, the populations of needy nations will no longer accumulate debt and will no longer be forced to service and repay often ill-considered borrowing agendas.
- Because funding will not be distributed without results, grants will sidestep the classic pitfalls of corruption, wanton waste, and incompetence.
- Loans may default, but with grants, there can be no losses for donor taxpayers.
- The pool of resources for future aid remains intact, independent of the recipients' ability to repay.
- Grants increase discipline by demanding a current co-payment, no matter how small, rather than a repayment obligation 20–40 years in the future.

## Development Equivalency: New Grants and Traditional Loans

It would seem logical that, if money is given freely instead of being lent, the stockpile of funds will eventually vanish. Not so. Grants can deliver the same amount of aid without diminishing the funding pool and without increasing the current financial demand of the industrialized world's taxpayers.

Nor will grants cost more than loans. The funding requirement is the same when the monetary level of aid is the same. Donors will not have to hand out more aid unless they wish to do so.

An IDA loan that has a 70 percent subsidy cannot cost more than an outright grant that pays 70 percent of program outlays. In both cases, recipient countries pay the remaining 30 percent. How can lending $100 and asking for a repayment of only $30 be any different from giving $70? If the same level of assistance is maintained, grants cannot cost more than loans.

With traditional loan aid, $100 of loans supports $100 of development programs. With grants, if the level of aid is less than the 70 percent subsidy equivalency, a smaller grant can support the same $100 of programs. A larger volume of programs can then be supported with the same grant resources. If the level of aid rises above the 70 percent benchmark, more funding is required and fewer programs can be financed on the same budget. (See section on "The Mathematics of Grants" and FIGURE 1.)

The benefits from the circulating pool of aid funds generated from the cash flow of repayments of old loans are always advanced as a reason to block the shift from loans to grants. The argument is that, with outright grants, the pool will shrink. But real-life practices disprove this reflow claim. As noted, most debts are simply recycled to the same borrowers with added funds to cover interest payments. Ultimately, many debts must be forgiven

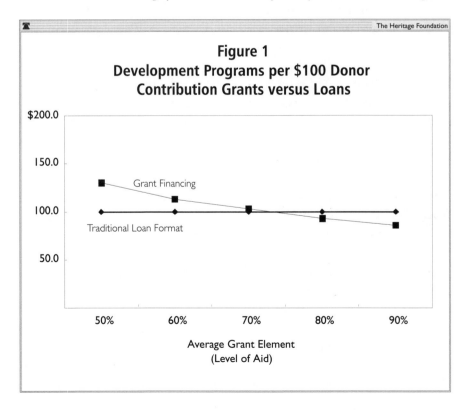

The Heritage Foundation

**Figure 1**
**Development Programs per $100 Donor**
**Contribution Grants versus Loans**

Grant Financing

Traditional Loan Format

Average Grant Element
(Level of Aid)

as in the current relief initiative. Whether recycled or forgiven, traditional loans are simply grants in disguise.

Grants will maintain the Bank's capital intact. The pool of donor-country funds now used for lending, plus future contributions, would be transformed into an endowment that invests in the capital markets and produces the income to supply a stream of payments for services. Only the income earned on the endowment would be disbursed as grants.

## Capital Markets: Core Contribution

Leverage makes possible the transformation from loans to performance-based grants by drawing on the technical skills and financial capacity of the private sector. The low creditworthiness of most truly poor countries and the lack of immediate profit potential in social-value projects have long been advanced as obstacles to development's private-sector funding. A direct World Bank contract removes these impediments.

For very poor countries with no access to the capital markets, the World Bank's direct payment obligation would equal 90 percent of total cost, eliminating 90 percent of the political–credit risk for the provider and, hence, its banker. The major risk for the capital markets is therefore that of the fulfillment of obligations by contractors—major international firms and non-governmental organizations—rather than host countries. Investors would bear the recipient's credit risk only on its 10 percent share. As the income level or capital market access of the beneficiary country increases and the ability of the economy to attract private lenders and to generate domestic resources rises, the share of the World Bank payment in total cost would decline to as little as 50 percent.

## The Mathematics of Grants

Lump-sum grants of $100 million are not required to accomplish the same ends as $100 million of IDA loans. Annual grants of $7.8 million over 25 years will, on average, suffice if the level of aid is maintained at the current 70 percent benchmark. Every dollar of annual grants replaces thirteen dollars of loans for the nations that need it most.

The only true aid component of development assistance, and the only cash requirement of the grant format in a world of sophisticated financial markets, is the subsidy that fills the gap between the amount that impoverished recipients can afford to pay and the real cost of supplying the service.

This should range from 90 percent to 50 percent, depending upon the recipient nation's per capita income and ability to attract private capital.

Poor countries will not be compelled to borrow in order to finance the implementation of projects. Instead, the annual grant stream will be leveraged by the private sector. The private sector will provide financing for projects based on service contracts—contracts in which the Bank's direct responsibility for the lion's share of every payment greatly reduces risk.

Under the traditional loan system, a $100 million 25-year-average-life project, when financed through a 40-year amortizing IDA-subsidized credit, requires $100 million of aid resources. But if the income level and capital market access of the recipient qualify for 70 percent grant aid, the identical project would be provisioned through 25 annual payments of $11.2 million upon certified delivery of results. The World Bank would enter into a direct contract to pay the service provider $7.8 million per annum (70 percent of the $11.2 million), and the recipient government would enter into a similar contract to pay

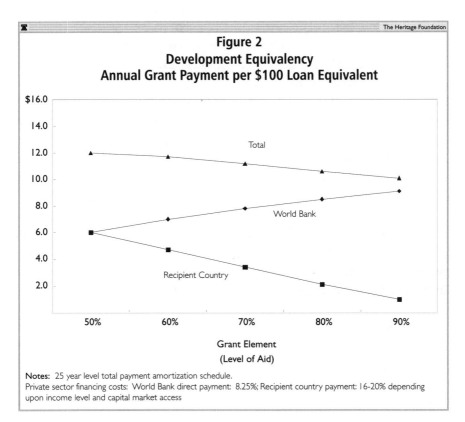

**Figure 2**
**Development Equivalency**
**Annual Grant Payment per $100 Loan Equivalent**

The Heritage Foundation

Grant Element
(Level of Aid)

**Notes:** 25 year level total payment amortization schedule.
Private sector financing costs: World Bank direct payment: 8.25%; Recipient country payment: 16-20% depending upon income level and capital market access

the remaining $3.4 million each year. Together, the two contracts would constitute the security needed by the service provider to obtain private-sector funding.

The capital markets will lend $81.5 million against the direct World Bank revenue stream. This is the present value of the annual $7.8 million payment over 25 years discounted at an 8.25 percent yield. Similarly, the financeable value of the recipient country's annual $3.4 million obligation at an 18 percent yield is $18.5 million. The sum of the two present values is $100 million. Thus, a World Bank commitment of $7.8 million per annum would be leveraged by private-sector lenders to supply the requisite $100 million in funding.

The annual World Bank grant payment, equivalent to $100 of traditional IDA credits, varies from $6.00 to $9.10 as the grant rises from 50 percent to 90 percent of the total payment. Additional resources, mobilized from donor and host governments, would be equally forthcoming under the grant format. (See FIGURE 2.)

## A Seamless Transition from Loans to Grants

The grant program endowment would start by using the $44 billion that is now available in IBRD paid-in equity capital and IDA undistributed, uncommitted funds. As borrowers repay past IDA credits, these resources would be added to the endowment. At a conservative 8 percent investment return, each $100 increment would produce $8 in additional income for grants. At every moment during the 40-year transition period, a larger volume of development programs, gross annual flows, and net annual flows would be supported under the grant structure than is the case under the traditional loan delivery system.

Similarly, tri-annual donor country replenishments and other contributions would not be lent. They would be invested in market instruments to generate income for grants. The relationship is linear. Each increase of $100, regardless of origin, would produce $8 in additional annual investment income each year in perpetuity.

## The World Bank as Foundation

Merging the balance sheets of the IBRD and its concessional arm, the IDA, is a logical course of action. The merger would modernize the World Bank's segmented structure, which was devised and implemented in what is now financial prehistory. The strength of the combined entity would be greater than the sum of its parts, with a heightened AAA debt capacity to benefit existing IBRD bondholders. Total assets would reach $273 billion, and total Bank borrowing of $116 billion would be secured by $157 billion of investment securities, $103 billion of industrialized-member callable capital, and $116 billion of developing country loans. (See TABLE 2.)

This begins the transformation of the Bank into the World Development Agency. It creates a foundation that focuses on the poorest nations without access to alternative resources; it adapts the World Bank's methods of intervention and structure to a global economy that is dominated by private capital; and it improves dramatically the efficacy of its programs. The World Development Agency is the institution that is now needed in the matrix of development aid finance.

Existing resources in the Bank can generate an annual stream of $12.6 billion in perpetuity while maintaining the Bank's capital intact. The World Bank has $157 billion in paid-in equity resources. Paid-in capital and retained earnings on the IBRD balance sheet amount to $38 billion. The IDA holds $119 billion. If this $157 billion endowment is invested in market

## Table 2
## World Bank as Foundation:
## A Pro Forma Balance Sheet ($ billions)

| Assets | | Liabilities | |
|---|---|---|---|
| IBRD traditional loans | $116 | Borrowing for IBRD loans | $116 |
| Investment securities | $157 | | |
| | | Total liabilities | $116 |
| | | Equity | $157 |
| | | Additional callable capital of industrialized members | $103 |
| Total assets | $273 | Total liabilities and equity | $273 |

Source: World Bank 2003 Annual Report.

## Table 3
## Grants versus Loans: Aid per Dollar of World Bank Resources
### ($ amounts in billions)

| | Existing IBRD & IDA System of Loans | Proposed Grant System |
|---|---|---|
| Total World Bank equity | $157 | $157 |
| IBRD traditional loans | $116 | $116 |
| Return on capital endowment | n.a. | 8% |
| Annual income | n.a. | $12.6 |
| One-half of IBRD/IDA administrative expense | n.a. | $0.8 |
| Net income for grants | n.a. | $11.8 |
| Capital at risk in poor countries | $119 | $0 |
| Total aid resources for poor countries | $119 | $154 |

Notes: 1) Private sector financing costs: World Bank direct payment: 8.25%
Recipient payment: 18%

2) Internal World Bank amortization schedule of grants: 25 year level total payment

3) Average grant element: 70%

instruments at a conservative return of 8 percent, it earns gross annual income of $12.6 billion. Net income will reach $11.8 billion after deducting $750 million, or one-half of the combined IBRD/IDA $1.5 billion annual administrative expense. The remainder is assigned to IBRD classic lending activities.

Grants to the neediest countries would not affect IBRD non-aid lending. Lending can be maintained at current levels and financed by conventional capital market borrowing if donor governments deem the benefits of these programs worthy of their taxpayers' costs and risks.

## Conclusion

There is money for a significant increase in aid *right now* on the World Bank's balance sheet. The effective use of existing resources would support $154 billion in aid programs for the world's poorest countries in perpetuity, or 30 percent more than the current $119 billion maximum under the IDA's prevailing system of concessional lending. (See Table 3.)

The risk to World Bank capital would be dramatically reduced. A $119 billion exposure to the poorest countries would be eliminated because, under grants, the endowment and income stream are unaffected by the financial fortunes of the recipients.

More important, for the poor part of the world whose welfare is the Bank's mission, one burden would be permanently lifted: There would be no more debt.

# Chapter 2

# Why Economic Freedom, Not Aid, Is the Answer to Poverty

**Editor's Summary**

Foreign aid's track record shows that sending money to poor countries for more than 40 years has done almost nothing to lift them out of poverty. In most recipient countries, income per capita is as low today as it was before those countries became recipients of aid.

Despite this evidence, many still claim that more foreign aid is the way to lead poor nations from poverty to prosperity; but as Ana Isabel Eiras writes in her chapter, the experience of Chile, Australia, and other countries demonstrates that economic freedom provides the only path by which the poor can finally escape poverty. Unlike foreign aid, economic freedom built on a strong rule of law permits people to have real opportunities to increase their wealth and achieve lasting prosperity.

Economic freedom succeeds because it creates the "rules of the game" by which competition, not coercion, coordinates the economic activity of millions of people. The annual Heritage Foundation/Wall Street Journal *Index of Economic Freedom* provides a useful framework for understanding the degree to which the world's countries permit competition, refrain from intervening in the economy, protect property rights, and, therefore, are truly on the path to prosperity.

The *Index of Economic Freedom* is not just a record of economic freedom around the world. The 10 factors of the *Index* provide a clear road map to prosperity, and only by following the highlighted route can a country achieve economic freedom, prosperity, and self-sufficiency.

# Why Economic Freedom, Not Aid, Is the Answer to Poverty

*Ana Isabel Eiras*

Most people would like a world without poverty. For years, experts from many fields—sociology, economics, politics, world affairs, and international relations—have debated the most effective way to lift the 70 percent of the world's people who live in poverty and extreme poverty out of their misery.

The debate is now centered on two main positions: sending money (foreign aid) to the poorest and opening markets so that the poor can create their own wealth. The first position is targeted at using government to raise levels of income; the second, at creating opportunities for individuals to escape from poverty by increasing their own incomes. The overwhelming majority of empirical work in development economics indicates that opening markets, not sending money, is the key to permanently lifting people out of poverty.

Despite this evidence, however, leaders of poor and not-so-poor countries vocally support the "sending money" theory while refusing to support the opening of markets. Rather than give markets a chance to succeed, they simply claim that opening markets "does not work" or "works for the rich and not for the poor." And they make these claims with an outstretched hand despite the evidence of more than 40 years that handouts have done absolutely nothing to lift the poor out of poverty. In fact, in most recipient countries, income per capita today is as low as or lower than it was before those countries became recipients of aid.

## Economic Freedom: The Only Real Chance for the Poor

The literature on economic growth, development, and prosperity largely agrees that the key to prosperity is economic freedom built on a strong rule of law.[1] Economically free countries are characterized by sound monetary policy, minimal and transparent regulation, minimal state participation in economic activity, and a strong rule of law that permits the enforcement of property rights and regulations and the adjudication of contracts.

The annual Heritage Foundation/Wall Street Journal *Index of Economic Freedom*[2] provides a framework for understanding how free citizens of any given country engage in economic activity; the degree of state intervention in the economy (whether through taxation, spending, or regulation); and the strength and independence of a country's judiciary to enforce rules and protect private property.

*Economic Freedom* is defined as the "absence of coercion or constraint on the production, distribution, or consumption of goods and services beyond the extent necessary for citizens to protect and maintain liberty itself."[3] In other words, good governance requires defining the "rules of the game." All government action necessarily involves coercion, a minimal amount of which may be desirable to enforce people's rights and protection. The government exercises this coercive power primarily through legislation that limits people's freedom and alters their incentives to do certain things; therefore, the greater the legislative burden, the greater these effects because people are then less free to work, produce, consume, and invest in ways they find most productive.

To measure economic freedom, the *Index* takes into consideration approximately 50 variables that fall into 10 "categories" of freedom, including:

---

1. Examples of these studies include Richard Roll and John Talbott, "Why Developing Countries Just Aren't" at *www.worlddevelopmentnow.com/id21.htm*; Robert J. Barro, *Determinants of Economic Growth: A Cross-Country Empirical Study* (Cambridge, Mass.: MIT Press, 1997); Robert Cooter, "The Rule of State Law and the Rule-of-Law State: Economic Analysis of the Legal Foundations of Development," 1996, in Edgardo Buscaglia, William Ratliff, and Robert Cooter, eds., *Law and Economics of Development* (Greenwich, Conn.: JAI Press, 1997); and Hernando de Soto, *The Other Path* (New York: Harper and Row, 1989).

2. Marc A. Miles, Edwin J. Feulner, and Mary Anastasia O'Grady, *2004 Index of Economic Freedom* (Washington, D.C.: The Heritage Foundation and Dow Jones & Company, Inc., 2004).

3. *Ibid.*, p. 50.

**1. Trade Policy.** Free trade improves people's living standards because it allows them to consume better-quality goods at cheaper prices. Any nation that focuses on producing goods in which it has a comparative advantage will be able to sell those goods in exchange for other goods that are produced more efficiently in other countries. As a result, consumers have more to enjoy, and that nation's standard of living rises.

Trade between nations is the same as "trade" between people. Consider what your life would be like if you had to produce everything that you consume, such as food, clothing, cars, or home repairs. Compare that to what your life is like as you use your talents and skills to produce just one thing (for example, computer programming) to earn a salary with which you can purchase food, a car, a home, clothing, and anything else you need or wish to purchase. The freer the trade, the more people can enjoy the new technologies, products, and other things that add convenience to their lives.

In measuring trade policy, the *Index* takes into consideration the following variables: (1) weighted average tariff rates; (2) non-tariff barriers; and (3) corruption in the customs service. The more a country suffers from these barriers, the less it will be able to exchange freely with countries that have stronger abilities in other areas. Moreover, because they discourage local producers from exploiting the benefits available from focusing on products they are better suited to producing, these barriers also encourage the overproduction of goods that would be best produced somewhere else.

**2. Fiscal Burden.** The fiscal burden of government has two components: (1) top marginal tax rates, both individual and corporate, and (2) changes in government expenditures. Marginal tax rates are the price that people and corporations pay for supplying economic effort, and what is left over after taxes is the "rewards" of those same efforts.[4] The higher a country's taxes, the less the incentive for individuals and firms to engage in any economic activity.

The annual change in government expenditures also captures the extent to which higher taxes burden the economy. According to the *Index*, "No matter how a given level of government expenditure is financed—by current taxation, or future (debt issuance or money creation), or varying amounts of each—resources are going to be diverted from the private sector."[5] This is the

---

4. *Ibid.*, p. 54.
5. *Ibid.*

reason that Milton Friedman, for example, believes government expenditures are the most complete measure of the fiscal burden of government.

**3. Government Intervention.** This factor measures both the government's use of scarce resources for its own purposes and the level of state control or ownership of domestic enterprises. According to the U.S. Department of Commerce, "government consumption totals net purchases of goods, services, and structures (for example, bridges and buildings); wages paid to government employees; net purchases of fixed assets; and inventory changes in government enterprises."[6] Since the government, unlike the private sector, does not produce wealth, every dollar of resources the government uses to support itself is necessarily diverted from the productive private sector. The more resources are diverted, the less freedom the private sector has to enjoy the fruits of their labors.

To measure government consumption, the *Index* takes into consideration the following variables: (1) government consumption as a percentage of gross domestic product (GDP); (2) government ownership of business and industries; (3) the share of government revenues raised from state-owned enterprises and government ownership of property; and (4) economic output produced by the government. The more a country's economy bears these burdens, the less incentive and opportunities people have to engage in economic activity.

**4. Monetary Policy.** Inflation is a subtle way to confiscate individuals' wealth. As inflation increases, the real value of people's savings, income, and investments decreases. This fact was pointed out by John Maynard Keynes, who observed that, "by a continuing process of inflation, governments can confiscate, secretly and unobserved, an important part of the wealth of their citizens."[7] At the same time, inflation distorts prices and raises the cost of doing business. For these reasons, countries with high inflation tend also to have lower levels of investment and growth.

To measure this factor, the *Index* uses the weighted average inflation rate for the past 10 years, giving the greater weight to more recent inflation. The country's average inflation determines its factor score.

---

6. *Ibid.*, p. 57.

7. John Maynard Keynes, *The Economic Consequences of the Peace* (London: Macmillan and Co., Ltd., 1919), as quoted in Miles, Feulner, and O'Grady, 2004 *Index of Economic Freedom*, p. 59.

**5. Capital Flows and Foreign Investment.** Restrictions on capital flows and foreign investment thwart economic freedom by limiting the funds available to create opportunities for people to be more productive. Some countries welcome foreign investment and treat it much the same way that they treat domestic investment; others restrict foreign investment from seeking its highest return, granting foreign investors fewer benefits than local investors. As a result, local and foreign investments compete on a less than level playing field and individuals suffer from insufficient investment, lower growth, fewer job opportunities, and an overall reduction in economic freedom.

To assess this factor, the *Index* takes into consideration the following variables: (1) foreign investment code; (2) restrictions on foreign ownership of business; (3) restrictions on industries and companies open to foreign investors; (4) restrictions and performance requirements imposed on foreign companies; (5) foreign ownership of land; (6) equal treatment under the law for both foreign and domestic companies; (7) restrictions on repatriation of earnings; (8) restrictions on capital transactions; and (9) availability of local financing for foreign companies.

**6. Banking and Finance.** A country's banking and financial system is its lifeblood. Financial institutions make funds available to start businesses, purchase homes, and buy durable consumer goods, in addition to providing a place for the safe storage of individuals' savings and income. The government can severely restrict and divert this lifeblood in many ways. It can attempt to control banks through restrictions on the amount or allocation of credit, restrictions on the range of services provided, and restrictions on branches and ATMs. The government may also limit the number of private banks and foreign banks that are allowed to provide services to the public. The tighter these restrictions, the less free banks are to support opportunities with the greatest potential and to provide services to customers, and the less free individuals are to access bank services at low cost. The same is true for the securities market, which provides a large source of credit for companies, particularly in developed countries.

This is not to say that all bank supervision is damaging. According to the *Index*, "supervision serves two major purposes: ensuring the safety and soundness of the financial system and ensuring that financial services firms meet basic fiduciary responsibilities."[8] Such supervision, however, relates

---

8. Miles, Feulner, and O'Grady, *2004 Index of Economic Freedom*, p. 62.

more to the government's duty of enforcing property rights and protecting people from fraud.

For this factor, the *Index* takes into account the following variables: (1) government ownership of financial institutions; (2) restrictions on the ability of foreign banks to open branches and subsidiaries; (3) government influence over the allocation of credit; (4) government regulations; and (5) freedom to offer all types of financial services, securities, and insurance policies.

**7. Wages and Prices.** The price mechanism is the most important form of communication in a market economy. Prices help producers to assess the demand for their products and consumers to assess the availability of what they wish to consume. For example, a company that needs personnel signals this by offering jobs at a competitive wage; if it needs personnel desperately, it will offer higher wages. Likewise, an individual that wants to sell his home quickly will lower the price to attract more buyers; but if there are many buyers, the price will rise. The price mechanism also helps firms to determine the extent to which they should adjust their production. A high price for clothing, for example, signals to designers, manufacturers, and retail sales outlets that people want more clothing. Accordingly, the production and inventory of clothing will increase.

When the government distorts prices—through subsidies or a direct mandate—it also distorts this delicate information system, creating false or illusory signals. In this way, it erodes individuals' opportunities to produce what the market demands and to consume what they would consume if the intervention did not exist. The more the government controls prices, the lower the level of economic freedom.

For this factor, the *Index* takes into consideration the following variables: (1) minimum wage laws; (2) freedom to set prices privately without government influence; (3) government price controls; (4) the extent to which government price controls are used; and (5) government subsidies to businesses that affect prices.

**8. Property Rights.** Individuals' ability and desire to accumulate private property—that is, wealth—depends on the security of property rights. For that reason, a strong rule of law is a key determinant of a country's long-term prosperity. When property rights are secure, people feel confident to save and invest: They are free to plan and work for their future.

In this factor, the *Index* explores how well the legal system functions, whether court decisions are made independently, and whether rules and regulations are properly enforced. Specifically, the *Index* takes into consideration the following variables: (1) freedom from government influence over the judicial system; (2) the presence of a commercial code that defines contracts; (3) sanctioning of foreign arbitration of contract disputes; (4) government expropriation of property; (5) corruption within the judiciary; (6) delays in receiving judicial decisions; and (7) legally granted and protected private property. The stronger the protection of property rights, the greater the level of economic freedom.

**9. Regulation.** Regulations, like taxes, increase the cost of doing business. Some countries have little regulation, while others have extensive regulations that affect businesses of all sizes and shapes. According to Peruvian economist Hernando de Soto, in many countries, particularly in the developing world, it takes years and several trips to bureaucratic offices to obtain a license to start a business.[9] As a result, corruption in the bureaucracy tends to be high as a lot of people resort to bribery in order to open a business and begin operation faster. Then, once they are in business, people face labor, environmental, zoning, and all sorts of regulations that continue to add to the cost of doing business.

In Argentina, for example, an employer must grant, by law, several employee benefits, including holidays, vacations, sick leave, health insurance, paid overtime, an annual bonus, and some paid months before laying off an employee.[10] Similarly, in France, employers must grant, by law, at least 2.5 working days of paid vacations per month; pay over 30 percent of salary in contributions to social security; offer a complementary pension scheme, a 35-hour work week, and time off; and abide by a burdensome bureaucratic procedure to dismiss employees. Perhaps large businesses, like multinational factories, can afford to comply with these regulations because of their size and global diversification, but the burden of these regulations destroys small and medium-size entrepreneurs, who often have their entire savings at stake in their business investment.

Small and medium-size businesses therefore often choose to do business and create jobs in the informal sector, where these benefits are negotiable and tied to performance, and not forced by law. For that reason, in

---

9. Hernando de Soto, *The Mystery of Capital: Why Capitalism Triumphs in the West and Fails Everywhere Else* (New York: Basic Books, 2000).

10. *The Labor Market and Its Legal Context*, Executive Summary, Deloitte & Touche, July 2003.

most of the developing world, the amount of informal economic activity is so large that, in many cases, it overshadows the formal economy.

In assessing the evidence for this factor, the *Index* examines regulations affecting the establishment of a new business, bureaucratic steps involved in obtaining a license, environmental and labor regulations, and corruption in the bureaucracy.

**10. Informal Market.** Informality is a reflection of obstacles in the marketplace—such as a high tax, a burdensome regulation, corruption, or something that is simply outlawed. In this factor, the *Index* tries to capture "the effects of government interventions not always fully measured elsewhere."[11] High trade barriers protecting local products, for example, encourage smuggling and the informal sale of the protected good. Likewise, weak property rights and weak enforcement encourage the piracy of intellectual property.

For this factor, the *Index* specifically measures corruption, smuggling, piracy, and the extent to which agriculture, manufacturing, services, transportation, and labor are supplied informally.

For each of the above factors, the *Index* provides a score from 1 to 5, according to a methodology in which 1 is freest and 5 is repressed. That first qualification provides a sense of the state of a country's economic openness. After each factor is scored, the *Index* averages the 10 scores and comes up with the overall "country score." The country score indicates into which of the four possible "categories of freedom" the country falls: "free," "mostly free," "mostly unfree," and "repressed." At the same time, the *Index* uses the country score as the basis for a "ranking of economic freedom," which shows how open a country is relative to the rest of the world.

The 10 factors of the *Index* create a 10-step road map that, when followed closely, leads to self-generated development and economic stability. Some countries have a substantial degree of freedom in all factors; others have a degree of freedom in just a few. One of the most important findings of the *Index* is that economic freedom is required in all aspects of economic life—that is, in all of the 10 factors—for a country to achieve its economic potential, improve economic efficiency, sustain growth, and consequently improve the living standards of its people.

CHART 1 shows the relationship between economic freedom and income per capita (measured in purchasing power parity). In free

---

11. Miles, Feulner, and O'Grady, *2004 Index of Economic Freedom*, p. 66.

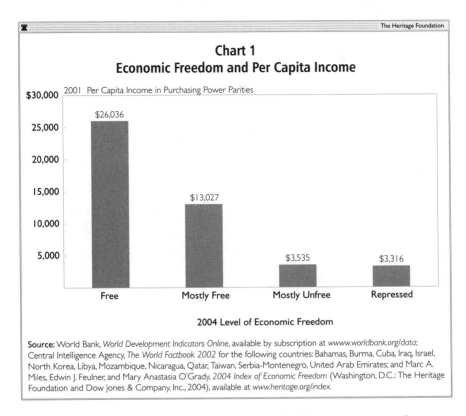

**Chart 1**
**Economic Freedom and Per Capita Income**

2001 Per Capita Income in Purchasing Power Parities

Free: $26,036
Mostly Free: $13,027
Mostly Unfree: $3,535
Repressed: $3,316

2004 Level of Economic Freedom

**Source:** World Bank, *World Development Indicators Online*, available by subscription at *www.worldbank.org/data*; Central Intelligence Agency, *The World Factbook 2002* for the following countries: Bahamas, Burma, Cuba, Iraq, Israel, North Korea, Libya, Mozambique, Nicaragua, Qatar, Taiwan, Serbia-Montenegro, United Arab Emirates; and Marc A. Miles, Edwin J. Feulner, and Mary Anastasia O'Grady, *2004 Index of Economic Freedom* (Washington, D.C.: The Heritage Foundation and Dow Jones & Company, Inc., 2004), available at *www.heritage.org/index*.

economies, the average income per capita is double the amount of average income per capita in mostly free economies and about 10 times higher than the average income per capita in mostly unfree and repressed economies. The reason is simple: Economic freedom fosters economic growth. As shown in CHART 2, during the past seven years of the *Index*, those countries that had the biggest improvements in economic freedom also had the fastest average growth rates. More economic freedom generates growth, employment, and a greater standard of living, thereby giving poorer nations an opportunity to catch up with richer nations.

## A Reality Check

The benefits that economic freedom brings to ordinary people have been well-documented for decades. As noted, to an overwhelming degree, studies in development economics agree that the key to prosperity is economic freedom built on a strong rule of law. Yet, despite those studies and real-time evidence from countries like Chile, Korea, Singapore, Ireland, and

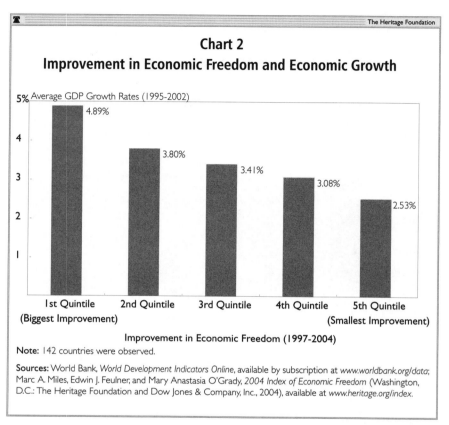

## Chart 2
## Improvement in Economic Freedom and Economic Growth

Average GDP Growth Rates (1995-2002)

5% — 4.89% (1st Quintile)
3.80% (2nd Quintile)
3.41% (3rd Quintile)
3.08% (4th Quintile)
2.53% (5th Quintile)

1st Quintile (Biggest Improvement)
2nd Quintile
3rd Quintile
4th Quintile
5th Quintile (Smallest Improvement)

Improvement in Economic Freedom (1997-2004)

**Note:** 142 countries were observed.

**Sources:** World Bank, *World Development Indicators Online*, available by subscription at *www.worldbank.org/data*; Marc A. Miles, Edwin J. Feulner, and Mary Anastasia O'Grady, *2004 Index of Economic Freedom* (Washington, D.C.: The Heritage Foundation and Dow Jones & Company, Inc., 2004), available at *www.heritage.org/index*.

many others that rose from poverty to development by opening markets, many still claim that "markets" and "liberalization" benefit only a few at the expense of the poor.

For example, at the extreme, some claim that globalization, which is in fact a phenomenon that has stemmed largely from the opening of markets, "is about the few who run global corporations crushing the aspirations of peoples in communities, regions and nations for self-governance."[12] There are also those who argue that:

> [G]lobalisation, the march of international capitalism, is a force for oppression, exploitation and injustice…. Governments, meanwhile, are accused of bowing down to busi-

---

12. Richard Grossman, *What Is Globalization?* Organic Consumers Association, May 29, 2001, at *www.organicconsumers.org/corp/richardgrossman.cfm*.

ness; globalisation leaves them no choice. Private capital moves across the planet unchecked.... [I]t puts profits before people.[13]

What these arguments fail to recognize is that globalization simply means "access" and that ordinary people need access to as many markets as possible in order to increase their economic opportunity. Particularly during the past three decades, the increase in trade, capital, and migration has helped to spread benefits to millions of people throughout the world. Thanks to globalization, many of the poorest have seen improvements in health care, longevity, education, and other social indicators.[14]

Nevertheless, many people in both the developing and developed worlds actually "blame" globalization and the opening of markets for their failure to foster development in their own countries. Consider one argument from Michael Weinstein, Director of Programs at the Robin Hood Foundation, in an article entitled "The Economic Paradox of Ghana's Poverty":

> Ghana cannot grow out of poverty—at least not on its own.... Countries in sub-Saharan Africa that make every smart economic move will almost certainly remain crushingly poor unless there is much more help from the rest of the world.... Ghana is...a fully fledged, multi-party democracy.... President John Agyekum Kufor oversees a relatively corruption-free, hard working administration.... Civil peace, democracy, waterfront, exports: these are tickets for economic success. But in Ghana, these tickets go unpunched.... Ghana and other poor sub-Saharan countries do not, and cannot, make it on their own....[15]

If Weinstein's argument were true and opening markets were not enough, we would expect to see Ghana ranked as a free country in the *Index of Economic Freedom*—that is, with a 1 or 2 in each factor of the *Index*—yet

---

13. "Globalisation and Its Critics," *The Economist*, September 27, 2001, at *www.economist.com*.

14. Allan Meltzer, "The International Financial Institution Advisory Commission Report," March 2000, available in English at *http://www.house.gov/jec/imf/meltzer.htm* and in Spanish from The Heritage Foundation.

## Table 1
## Ghana's Economic Freedom Score

| Economic Freedom Factor | Score |
|---|---|
| Trade Policy | 4 |
| Fiscal Burden | 4 |
| Government Intervention | 3.5 |
| Monetary Policy | 4 |
| Capital Flows and Foreign Investment | 3 |
| Banking and Finance | 3 |
| Wages and Prices | 3 |
| Property Rights | 3 |
| Regulation | 3 |
| Informal Market | 3.5 |
| Country Score | **3.40** |
| Country Economy | Mostly Unfree |

still poor. Put another way, Ghana's markets would be open but still would have failed to relieve the country's poverty. According to the *Index*, however, Ghana's experience with the markets has been completely different from Weinstein's account.

TABLE 1 illustrates that Ghana falls short in all 10 measures of market openness. Ghana has high tariffs that hurt ordinary Ghanaian consumers and producers; very high taxes on people's income and on businesses; high rates of inflation; and markets that, at best, are only moderately open and in just a few areas. Doing business in Ghana is very difficult, especially for the poorest, who lack the money to grease bureaucratic obstacles to doing busi-

---

15. Michael Weinstein, "The Economic Paradox of Ghana's Poverty," *Financial Times*, November 10, 2003.

ness. The lack of economic freedom explains, for example, why Ghana also has a very large informal market.

The problem with Weinstein's argument is that it is built on the wrong assumptions: that Ghana is a largely free state with low levels of corruption. As shown in TABLE 1, Ghana is not a "free state" (in fact, it is mostly unfree). In addition, according to Transparency International's *Corruption Perceptions Index*, Ghana suffers from a high level of corruption, which undermines any economic activity.[16] It would therefore be wrong to conclude that free-market policies have not worked for Ghana, because the country's markets have never been free. The inability of Ghana's leaders to allow people the freedom to undertake any commercial activity explains why Ghana's income per capita, according to the World Bank, is $15 lower today than it was in the 1960s.[17] Ghana is poor precisely because its leaders have failed to create an environment that is conducive to growth and development.

Ghana's alleged "free market experiment" not only illustrates the story of the entire developing world's failure to develop, but also contrasts sharply with the story of Chile, which has been opening its markets for more than three decades, allowing more and more competition and fostering a strong rule of law. These efforts have paid off in many ways. Chile now has one of the highest per capita GDPs in Latin America, has experienced high levels of economic growth, and conveys an institutional trust that has attracted local and foreign investment. Most important, it has severed itself from reliance on the international aid on which most other Latin American countries still depend. By following the 10 steps to economic freedom, Chile has become more prosperous.

Chile's reforms began in the mid-1970s under the government of General Augusto Pinochet and have continued ever since. The Chilean reform process over the past nine years has been remarkable, particularly compared to the rest of Latin America (see CHART 3) as chronicled by the *Index*. While the rest of Latin America has remained, on average, "mostly unfree," Chile has moved across the "mostly free" category of economic freedom and in 2002 and 2004 crossed the threshold into the "free" category.

What is most remarkable in CHART 3 is that, to move from "mostly free"

---

16. Transparency International, *Corruption Perceptions Index*, 2003, at *www.transparency. org/cpi/index.html#cpi*.

17. World Bank, *World Development Indicators*, 2003, on CD–ROM.

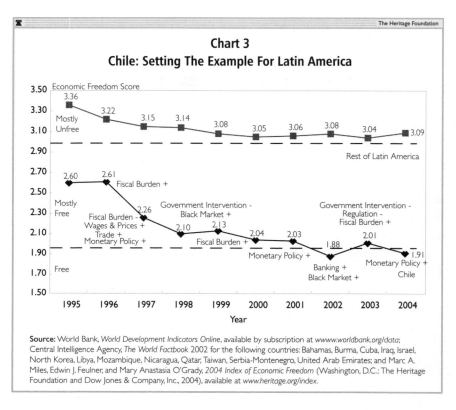

**Chart 3**
**Chile: Setting The Example For Latin America**

Source: World Bank, *World Development Indicators Online*, available by subscription at *wwww.worldbank.org/data*; Central Intelligence Agency, *The World Factbook* 2002 for the following countries: Bahamas, Burma, Cuba, Iraq, Israel, North Korea, Libya, Mozambique, Nicaragua, Qatar, Taiwan, Serbia-Montenegro, United Arab Emirates; and Marc A. Miles, Edwin J. Feulner, and Mary Anastasia O'Grady, *2004 Index of Economic Freedom* (Washington, D.C.: The Heritage Foundation and Dow Jones & Company, Inc., 2004), available at *www.heritage.org/index.*

to "free," a country must undertake extensive reforms in all 10 of the factor categories analyzed in the *Index*. In achieving the status of a "free" economy, Chile has undertaken reforms in the fiscal, trade, monetary policy, wages and prices, banking, and informal market areas in just the past nine years, in addition to the comprehensive reform efforts carried out on all 10 fronts since 1974. Today, as TABLE 2 shows, the Chilean economy is considered free in almost all accounts—that is, it has earned a 1 or 2 in each factor score—and Chile's country score corresponds to that of a country with a "free economy."

Chile is proof that free markets deliver. Specifically, Chile's free-market reforms have delivered more investment, more consumption, more economic efficiency, and sustained economic growth. Since 1995, its compounded growth rate has been 12 percent, while the average for the rest of Latin America has been only 1 percent.[18] Chile's sustained growth has increased the country's standard of living, particularly for the poor. The poverty rate

---

18. World Bank, *World Development Indicators*, 2002, on CD–ROM.

The Heritage Foundation

## Table 2
## Chile's Economic Freedom Score

| Economic Freedom Factor | Score |
|---|---|
| Trade Policy | 2 |
| Fiscal Burden | 2.6 |
| Government Intervention | 2 |
| Monetary Policy | 1 |
| Capital Flows and Foreign Investment | 2 |
| Banking and Finance | 2 |
| Wages and Prices | 2 |
| Property Rights | 1 |
| Regulation | 3 |
| Informal Market | 1.5 |
| Country Score | 1.91 |
| Country Economy | Free |

has fallen since the 1980s in incidence, depth, and severity. In 1998, the World Bank reported that 17 percent of Chileans were living in poverty (compared to 40 percent in 1987), while 4 percent were living in extreme poverty.[19] The number of pupils enrolled in primary education "jumped from 28 percent in 1991 to 82 percent in 1996 and the average time to graduate from primary school fell from 12.4 years to 9.7 years during the same period."[20] Today, 94 percent of the population has access to improved water, and 97 percent has access to improved sanitation.[21]

---

19. World Bank, *Chile: Poverty and Income Distribution in a High Growth Economy, The Case of Chile 1987–1998*, World Bank Report No. 22037-CH, August 30, 2001.

20. World Bank, Country Brief, at *lnweb18.worldbank.org/external/lac/lac.nsf/ Countries/Chile/71BC8229DD493B2A85256C5A005D9093?OpenDocument.*

The reform process in Chile provides important insight into what developing countries must do if they are actually to develop. The first lesson is that reform should proceed simultaneously across all 10 fronts of economic freedom. As Hernan Buchi, Chilean Minister of Finance from 1985 to 1989, has stated, "it is necessary to proceed with all reforms simultaneously and increase the pace in accordance with the perceived prospects for success.... [T]here is synergy among reforms: one reform helps another."[22]

Buchi has also pointed out that some reforms are necessary to reinforce the effects of other reforms:

> Progress is impossible in the absence of a properly functioning financial sector operating in accordance with the rules of the market. A private banking sector channeling credit to profitable projects is of primary importance for setting the economy on the proper path.... There is one additional reform that must be implemented at [the] initial stage.... I refer to the opening of trade. If the entire economy is moving toward an increase in efficient resource distribution, it is important that the changes in the competitiveness of the various sectors be stimulated by opening foreign trade. Belated reform in this area modifies the conditions facing economic agents and lessens the credibility of the entire reform process.[23]

While bold reforms do require some degree of political consensus, two things are critical to advancing reform and placing a country on the path to sustainable growth. The first is leadership. This means a leader "who is willing to absorb criticism and who, in addition to requirements in the area of technical competence, must also possess perseverance and an overriding faith in the market and free enterprise."[24] Leadership is essential to advancing reforms over long periods. The second critical element is respect for the

21. World Bank, Millennium Development Goals, at *devdata.worldbank.org/idg/IDGProfile.asp?CCODE=CHL&CNAME=Chile&SelectedCountry=CHL*.

22. Hernan Buchi, "Economic Reform Today: Reflections on Economic Reform in Chile," 2001, at *www.cipe.org/publications/fs/ert/e01/7buchib.htm*.

23. *Ibid.*

24. *Ibid.*

law and private property as the means to ensure that the rules of society are not changed arbitrarily or outside due process.

## A Tale of Two Policies

Sometimes, people argue that development is a consequence of uncontrollable factors such as culture, weather, immigration, or natural resources. However, it is not so much how many or what kind of resources a country has, but how those resources are employed. Brazil, for example, has abundant natural resources while Singapore has few. Yet Brazilians are far poorer than Singaporeans. The same is true for the Democratic Republic of Congo (formerly Zaire), which is richly endowed with natural resources while its people remain among the poorest in the world. Ireland, on the other hand, with much less favored weather and land, is becoming increasingly wealthy.

In a paper titled "Property Rights: The Key to Economic Growth," published in the *2002 Index of Economic Freedom*, Lee Hoskins and I highlight the importance of implementing sound policies for growth and prosperity by comparing and contrasting the story of two countries, Australia and Argentina.[25] These two countries are very similar in terms of resources. They are both in the Southern Hemisphere, are well-endowed with natural resources, have similar economic structures, are multicultural, and have similar climates. For both countries, agriculture, fuel, and minerals account for important percentages of their exports. Yet today, Australia has more than twice the wealth of Argentina.

What makes Australia wealthy and Argentina poor is their different policies. Specifically, in the past 25 years, Australia has lowered its trade barriers to an average of 3 percent, helping the Australian economy to be more competitive. In addition, the government has cut expenditures in order to achieve budget surpluses, which in turn have lowered the country's debt. Australian authorities have fostered a competitive environment through extensive privatization and deregulation of the economy. Equally important, Australia has fostered, throughout the past century, a transparent, independent judiciary that effectively protects property rights, thereby securing investment and private contracts.

---

25. Lee Hoskins and Ana I. Eiras, "Property Rights: The Key to Economic Growth," in Gerald P. O'Driscoll, Kim R. Holmes, and Mary Anastasia O'Grady, *2002 Index of Economic Freedom* (Washington, D.C.: The Heritage Foundation and Dow Jones & Company, Inc., 2001).

Argentina took a different policy path. The government raised trade barriers that are now a weighted average of 9 percent to abide by the laws of the Southern Cone Common Market (MERCOSUR).[26] Argentine authorities have consistently spent more than they collected through taxes. In the absence of economic growth, and constrained by the currency board from printing currency until 2001, the only remaining course was to finance the deficit with government debt. The continued lack of economic growth and widening deficit eventually drove the country, in December 2001, to default on its obligations to private local and foreign investors.

During the 1990s, the authorities deregulated the economy only partially while continuing to impose high taxes. The markets responded to the increased burden with lower investment, lower consumption, a high level of informal market activity, and an unemployment rate of 14 percent.[27] That little opening of the 1990s came to an end in the aftermath of the 2001 financial crisis, when the government imposed price controls, limited people's access to their money in the banks, and changed banking legislation so that most banks were forced into bankruptcy. In addition, since the 1930s, Argentina's judiciary has failed to protect property rights, thereby undermining long-term investment and imposing greater costs on contractual agreements. The result of market closure was corruption, little growth, a financial crisis, and the impoverishment of most ordinary Argentines.

By contrast, the combination of sound policy, open markets, and competition has allowed Australia to grow steadily and increase productivity. Multifactor productivity (i.e., productivity of capital as well as labor), at least up until 2000, had grown more than 2 percent per year—well over twice the average for members of the Organisation for Economic Co-operation and Development and faster even than in the United States.[28] It is this high level of productivity that has helped Australia to sustain growth for the past 20 years.

CHART 4 is a compelling illustration of how policymaking has affected both Argentina and Australia. The chart depicts real GDP per capita for both countries since 1900.[29] Although Australia was wealthier than

---

26. Miles, Feulner, and O'Grady, 2004 *Index of Economic Freedom*, p. 81.
27. Economist Intelligence Unit, *EIU Country Report for Argentina*, March 2001, p. 11.
28. "Miracle Cure," *The Economist*, September 7, 2000.

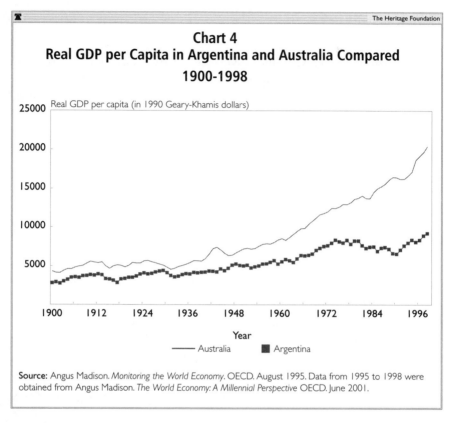

## Chart 4
## Real GDP per Capita in Argentina and Australia Compared
## 1900-1998

Real GDP per capita (in 1990 Geary-Khamis dollars)

Year

——— Australia    ■ Argentina

**Source:** Angus Madison. *Monitoring the World Economy.* OECD. August 1995. Data from 1995 to 1998 were obtained from Angus Madison. *The World Economy: A Millennial Perspective* OECD. June 2001.

Argentina throughout the 20th century, the gap between the two countries did not vary much until the late 1930s. After the 1930s, Australia's real GDP growth per capita increased much faster; and after the 1970s, the difference between the two countries accelerated.

As noted, the difference in wealth between the two countries is the result of different policies. Technological improvements to facilitate capital movements throughout the world have rewarded sound policy and punished poor ones. Australia, in this sense, has been rewarded for implementing sound economic policy. Argentina, by contrast, will continue to suffer until it decides to throw open its markets and strengthen the protection of property.

---

29. The Geary–Khamis approach is based on twin concepts of purchasing power parity of currencies and international average prices of commodities. The annual GDP per capita levels shown in Chart 4 were derived by merging GDP indices with benchmark values of 1990 GDP levels. In order to compare levels of output or output per capita in different countries, it is necessary to convert them into a common unit.

## Conclusion

Free markets and a strong rule of law allow people to increase their wealth and their standard of living. Foreign aid and loans do not. The overwhelming preponderance of research done in the field of development shows that opening markets and fostering a strong rule of law is the only way to allow people—both poor and not so poor—to build their own wealth.

Despite this evidence, however, many around the world still claim that opening markets is not enough: that markets need to be regulated to avoid their going "wild" and oppressing the poor. These same people claim that more redistribution of money from the rich to the poor is the key to development. They welcome aid money despite the fact that, for more than 40 years, the redistribution of wealth has done absolutely nothing to lift the poor out of poverty.

The *Index of Economic Freedom* is not just a record of economic freedom around the world. It is also a "test" that one can use to check whether countries that want aid money have ever given markets a chance. Ghana and Argentina, for example, have been dependent on foreign money for years. Ghana is poorer today than it was in the 1960s, when it started receiving aid, and all the money poured into Argentina could not prevent the financial catastrophe that reduced ordinary Argentines to poverty while dooming their recovery prospects. Neither Ghana nor Argentina has proved economic freedom wrong; they have, however, proved that the "sending money" theory does not work.

By contrast, Chile and Australia have chosen to open their markets, ending their dependency on foreign money. Today, Australia is a developed country with a high standard of living, and Chile is twice as wealthy as it was three decades ago and has the prospect of someday catching up to the developed world. Both of these countries survive the test of the *Index* and confirm that economic freedom is what really allows countries to grow and prosper.

Economic freedom leads to prosperity because free economies allow for competition, which is the only method by which the daily activity of millions of people can be coordinated without coercion. Competition, at the same time, requires the organization of institutions and respect for the "rules of the game," such as stable money, minimal and transparent regulation, minimal participation of the state in economic activity, and strong enforcement of property rights and regulations. The 10 factors of the *Index of Economic Freedom* provide an excellent framework for evaluating the degree to which different countries permit competition, limit government intervention in the economy, and protect property rights—and, therefore, the extent to which they are on a real path to a better life for their people.

# Chapter 3

# Economic and Political Freedom: The Keys to Development

**Editor's Summary**

The least understood question in economic development is: "Why are some countries rich while others are poor?" Nobel Prize–winning economist Amartya Sen has noted that no democracy has ever suffered a famine. Does a country have to be a democracy in order to achieve wealth? How important is economic freedom? Can a corrupt country prosper?

Richard Roll addresses these questions by empirically comparing gross national income (GNI) per capita with 14 factors: informal (black) market activity, property rights, political rights, civil liberties, freedom of the press, regulation, banking restrictions, trade barriers, monetary policy, foreign investment barriers, wages and prices, taxes, government expenditures, and government intervention. Among Roll's findings:

- Nine factors explain about 80 percent of the differences in income across countries.
- Basic indicators of economic freedom—property rights, regulation, and black

market activity—are important for explaining income differences.

- Political freedom—including voting rights, civil liberties, and freedom of the press—leads to greater wealth.
- Other economic variables that are important are monetary policy, trade barriers, and government expenditure.

Roll points out that these nine factors represent the rules of the game that allow individuals to work, produce, and invest with confidence. They also reflect institutions through which individuals can collectively eliminate corrupt officials and reverse repressive policies that hinder growth. These empirical findings strongly reinforce the concept of a road map to prosperity. It is economic freedom, along with political freedom, that paves this road.

# Economic and Political Freedom: The Keys to Development

*Richard Roll*[1]

ONE OF THE MOST studied and most fundamental questions in economics is also one of its least understood. Stated most simply: "Why are some countries rich while others are poor?" For the world's poor and suffering, there is not a more important question. With greater economic growth, a country's poor would have a chance to provide education for their children, care for their elderly and infirm, and apply their productive energy to improve their standard of living. Short of a repressive dictatorial regime, little deprives humans of freedom so much as living in poverty. The lives of the truly poor are devoted 24 hours a day just to providing the basic subsistence of life: water, food, shelter, and clothing.

Personal observation supported by DNA research suggests that humans around the globe are similar in nature and ability. If this is so, why are some countries so prosperous while others languish perpetually at extremely low levels of productivity? Hundreds of economics papers have

1. This article is an abridged version of a longer and more technical research paper—co-authored with John Talbott, a visiting scholar at the Anderson School at UCLA and former investment banker for Goldman, Sachs & Co.—that includes detailed descriptions and explanations of all empirical findings. The full paper is available at *www.anderson.ucla.edu/acad_unit/finance/wp/2001/19-01.pdf*. Some of this material also appeared in Richard Roll and John Talbott, "Political Freedom, Economic Liberty, and Prosperity," *The Journal of Democracy*, Vol. 14, No. 3 (July 2003), pp. 75–89. The author thanks The Heritage Foundation both for the data that make empirical work such as this possible and for its constant support throughout this endeavor.

been written on this subject, and hundreds of different explanations have been offered; yet the cross-country disparities in income persist and even worsen decade after decade. In *Eat the Rich*, author P. J. O'Rourke has argued that the explanation "is not a matter of brains. No part of the earth (with the possible exception of Brentwood) is dumber than Beverly Hills, and the residents are wading in gravy."[2]

It does not appear to be a lack of effort. Men, women, and children in poor countries work long hours, weekends included, and with few holidays, none of them paid, in order to eke out a meager existence. Entrepreneurial spirit exists everywhere, not just in wealthy countries. Consider the story of the peasant in Afghanistan during the recent conflict. He arranged brightly lit lanterns in his back yard at night in hopes the Americans would mistake it for an Osama bin Laden landing field, bomb it, and enable him to collect the scrap metal from the exploded bombs to sell in the marketplace.

Nobel Prize–winning economists seemingly have not come up with an answer either. According to Sir Arthur Lewis, the father of development economics, "Per capita growth depends on…natural resources and human behavior."[3] True, but hardly helpful as a guide to action. Paul Samuelson has stated that "England's economic 'Take-off' was in the 18th century, Japan's in the 19th century, the Congo's in the 1980's."[4] And Robert E. Lucas, Jr., has asked, "Is there some action a government of India could take that would make it grow like Egypt or Indonesia?"[5] Obviously, timing is critical when giving empirical examples.

What are Nobel non-winners saying? Steven Landsburg says, in *Armchair Economist*, that "People respond to incentives. Everything else is commentary."[6] William Easterly, in *The Elusive Quest for Growth*, succinctly summarizes his visits to developing countries on behalf of the World Bank by saying, "Wonderful people. Terrible governments."[7]

---

2. P. J. O'Rourke, *Eat the Rich* (New York: Atlantic Monthly Press, 1998), p. 1.

3. W. Arthur Lewis, *The Theory of Economic Growth*, quoted in Deepak Lal, *Unintended Consequences* (Cambridge, Mass.: MIT Press, 1998), p. 2.

4. Paul A. Samuelson, *Economics*, 7th edition (New York: McGraw–Hill, 1967), p. 743.

5. Robert E. Lucas, Jr., "On the Mechanics of Economic Development," *Journal of Monetary Economics*, Vol. 22 (1988), pp. 3–42, reprinted as Chapter 1 in Robert E. Lucas, Jr., *Lectures on Economic Growth* (Cambridge, Mass.: Harvard University Press, 2002), p. 21.

6. Steven E. Landsburg, *Armchair Economist: Economics and Everyday Experience* (New York: Free Press, 1993), p. 3.

In *Eat the Rich*, P. J. O'Rourke leaves the jokes behind when he points to "Property Rights, the Rule of Law, and Democratic Government."[8] O'Rourke, a non-economist, correctly concludes that these are indeed crucial factors for development. His insight is testimony that some humans have the capacity to make intelligent observations and form rational conclusions without the benefits of formal training or technical virtuosity.

## Earlier and New Research

In some of the earlier work, the researcher was interested in testing a single explanatory variable that he or she thought might explain the entire problem. The obvious danger is that statistical correlations arise between many variables, but that does not imply causation. For instance, causation could be in the opposite direction, from high income to the chosen explanatory variable, or the chosen variable could be correlated with some third, unknown true cause.

Some previous researchers were agnostic about possible explanatory factors and attempted to include as many as possible. There are, however, more candidate variables than data observations; thus, searching subsets is not an obligation. These results have been mixed. Ross Levine and David Renelt found no variables that passed their stiff test of statistical significance.[9] Gernot Doppelhofer, Ronald Miller, and Xavier Sala-i-Martin applied a novel approach. After running 10 million regressions covering combinations of variables, they concluded that four variables were strongly and robustly related to country growth: the initial level of gross domestic product (GDP), the amount of mining in the country, the number of years of trade openness, and whether the country's major religion was Confucianism.[10] Only one of these—trade openness—can be altered easily in an effort to improve economic conditions in a given country.

Although it might be interesting that Confucianism is correlated with growth, it is hard to imagine a government urging its citizens to change reli-

---

7. William Easterly, *The Elusive Quest for Growth* (Cambridge, Mass.: MIT Press, 2001), p. 285.

8. O'Rourke, *Eat the Rich*, p. 234.

9. Ross Levine and David Renelt, "A Sensitivity Analysis of Cross-Country Regressions," *American Economic Review*, Vol. 82, No. 4 (September 1992), pp. 942–963.

10. Gernot Doppelhofer, Ronald I. Miller, and Xavier Sala-i-Martin, "Determinants of Long-Term Growth: A Bayesian Averaging of Classical Estimates (BACE) Approach," National Bureau of Economic Research *Working Paper* 7750, June 2000.

gions. Instead, it seems natural to ask whether a country's government can uncover feasible policy tools that might be used to affect economic prosperity and what percentage improvement, if any, can be made by manipulating such tools.

Hence, our approach[11] was to examine conditions that are amenable to change, at least in principle. We decided to study The Heritage Foundation's economic freedom ratings and Freedom House's political ratings because they measure various government policies and institutions that (1) are mutable and (2) *might* have an influence on economic prosperity.

Heritage issues its *Index of Economic Freedom* each year and provides detailed backup information, by country, explaining why a particular rating was assigned. This is important because ratings could perhaps be considered more subjective than traditional hard economic statistics, such as foreign direct investment or capital flows. We verified that Heritage does not consider a country's economic performance in deriving its ratings, as this would have induced a spurious correlation unrelated to any true causation. We were assured of this at every level of the organization, from the associates collecting the data to the head of the *Index of Economic Freedom* project.

As for Freedom House, they do not deal with economic statistics at all, but only with political freedoms of various kinds. Consequently, we can be assured that their rankings are not influenced by historical economic growth.

The goal here is to derive quantitative relations between country per capita income and various policies, institutions, and conditions. Furthermore, we hope to ascertain their importance relative to each other. Heritage staff members had wondered about this because they knew the overall *Index of Economic Freedom* correlated well with country income, but they did not know the relative importance of each of its components. Academic literature, led by Robert Hall and Charles Jones, had shown that a country's aggregate "social infrastructure" is related to country income, but they did not measure the relative importance of the components of their aggregate measure, which were law and order, corruption, bureaucratic efficiency, risk of appropriation, trade tariffs, state monopolies, and currency convertibility.[12]

---

11. See note 1, *supra.*

12. Robert E. Hall and Charles I. Jones, "Why Do Some Countries Produce So Much More Output Per Worker Than Others?" *Quarterly Journal of Economics*, February 1999.

The Heritage and Freedom House data are more akin to "deep determinants" of country incomes, in contrast to such tertiary variables as the initial level of income, educational attainment (a proxy for human capital), physical capital, and population. These latter "predictors" do correlate strongly with country wealth, but what does this really prove? Wealthy countries have more capital, their populaces are better educated, and they utilize more advanced technology. Human capital is nothing more than another form of wealth, in this case the amount of personal investment a population has made in its education. In essence, such correlations merely relate different forms of wealth to aggregate wealth itself.

Moreover, such correlations provide no guide to action. Imagine advising a suffering country that it needs only more human and physical capital and better technology to rise out of poverty. Good advice would seem to depend instead on uncovering the "deep determinants" of country wealth (i.e., conditions and policies that actually *can* be altered to ease the creation of capital and technology).

The growth literature is naturally drawn to time series tests since growth rates themselves are time dependent, but most candidate explanatory factors vary much more across countries than over time. For example, in determining how important property rights are to country prosperity, the United States might have a property rights index of 4.1 in 1960 and 4.2 in 1995, while Cuba, for example, has a rating of 1.0 in both years. Clearly, the dramatic variation in economic and political institutions across countries gives the researcher more chance of explaining wealth differences than the relatively minor temporal variations within any one country. For this reason, we first conduct cross-country tests in several calendar years.

## A Cross-Country Analysis

Our data are described in TABLE I. The variable to be explained is gross national income (GNI) per capita. There are 14 candidate explanatory variables ranging from black (or informal) market activity through government expenditures.

The Heritage Foundation's fiscal burden rating is broken into its two constituents—taxes and government expenditures—in order to check their separate influences. Heritage's fiscal burden index is the simple average of two of its own sub-indices, the first measuring levels of personal and corporate tax rates and the second reflecting levels of government expenditures as

## Table 1: Description and Sources of Data

| Variable | Number of Countries (1999) | Range of Data | Meaning of Low Figure | Source |
|---|---|---|---|---|
| GNI per Capita | 164 | $440 to $41,230 | Low GNI per Capita | World Bank (PPP Adjusted) CIA World Factbook and Maddison [2001]* |
| Black Market Activity | 160 | 1 to 5 | Little Black Market Activity | Heritage Foundation (a) |
| Property Rights | 160 | 1 to 5 | Few Property Rights | Heritage Foundation (reversed scale)(a)(b) |
| Political Rights | 162 | 1 to 7 | Few Political Rights | Freedom House (reversed scale)(b) |
| Civil Liberties | 162 | 1 to 7 | Few Civil Liberties | Freedom House (reversed scale)(b) |
| Freedom of the Press | 163 | 1 to 147 | Weak Freedom of the Press | Freedom House (reversed scale)(b) |
| Regulation | 160 | 1 to 5 | Little Burdensome Regulation | Heritage Foundation (a) |
| Banking Restrictions | 160 | 1 to 5 | Few Banking Restrictions | Heritage Foundation (a) |
| Trade Barriers | 160 | 1 to 5 | Little to No Trade Barriers | Heritage Foundation (a) |
| Monetary Policy | 160 | 1 to 5 | Low Inflation | Heritage Foundation (a) |
| Foreign Inv. Barriers | 160 | 1 to 5 | Few Foreign Inv. Barriers | Heritage Foundation (a) |
| Wages and Prices | 160 | 1 to 5 | Few Price Restrictions | Heritage Foundation (a) |
| Taxes | 159 | 1 to 5 | Low Personal and Corp. Taxes | Heritage Foundation (a) |
| Government Expenditures | 151 | 9% to 74.3% | Low Government Spending/GDP | Heritage Foundation (a) |
| Government Intervention | 160 | 1 to 5 | Little Government Intervention | Heritage Foundation (a) |

Note: (a) 2001 Index of Economic Freedom. This publication provides a narrative description of each variable for every country. It is also available on the Internet.
(b) Original scale reversed so that a larger value now means more.

*Angus Maddison, The World Economy: A Millennial Perspective (Paris, France: Development Centre of the Organisation for Economic Co-operation and Development, 2001).

# Table 1 (continued)
## Components of Variables as Described in Original Sources

### Trade Barriers

- Average tariff rate.
- Non-tariff barriers.
- Corruption in the customs service.

### Taxes

- Top income tax rate.
- Tax rate that the average taxpayer faces.
- Top corporate tax rate.

### Government Expenditures

- Government Expenditures as a % of total GDP.
- Government Expenditures include transfer payments.

### Monetary Policy

- Weighted average inflation rate from 1990 to 1999 with more recent data more heavily weighted.

### Foreign Investment Restrictions

- Foreign investment code.
- Restrictions on foreign ownership of business.
- Restrictions on the industries and companies open to foreign investors.
- Restrictions and performance requirements on foreign companies.
- Foreign ownership of land.
- Equal treatment under the law for both foreign and domestic companies.
- Restrictions on the repatriation of earnings.
- Availability of local financing for foreign companies.

### Government Intervention in the Economy

- Government consumption as a percentage of the economy.
- Government ownership of businesses and industries.
- Share of government revenues from state-owned enterprises and government ownership of property.
- Economic output produced by the government.

### Banking Restrictions

- Government ownership of banks.
- Restrictions on the ability of foreign banks to open branches and subsidiaries.
- Government influence over the allocation of credit.
- Government regulations.
- Freedom to offer all types of financial services, securities, and insurance policies.

### Political Rights

- Free elections.
- Right to vote.
- Self-determination.
- Freedom from military and totalitarianism

### Civil Liberties

- Equality of opportunity.
- Rule of law, with people treated fairly under the law, without fear of unjust imprisonment or torture.
- Freedom of press, association, religion, assembly, demonstration, discussion and organization.

# Table 1 (continued)

## Wages and Prices

- Minimum wage laws.
- Freedom to set prices privately without government influence.
- Government price controls.
- The extent to which government price controls are used.
- Government subsidies to businesses that affect prices.

## Property Rights

- Freedom from government influence over the judicial system.
- Commercial code defining contracts.
- Sanctioning of foreign arbitration of contract disputes.
- Government expropriation of property.
- Corruption within the judiciary.
- Delays in receiving judicial decisions.
- Legally granted and protected private property.

## Regulation

- Licensing requirements to operate a business.
- Ease of obtaining a business license.
- Corruption within the bureaucracy.
- Labor regulations, such as established work weeks, paid vacations, and parental leave, as well as selected labor regulations.
- Environmental, consumer safety, and worker health regulations.
- Regulations that impose a burden on business.

## Black Market Activity

- Smuggling.
- Piracy of intellectual property in the black market.
- Agricultural production supplied on the black market.
- Manufacturing supplied on the black market.
- Services supplied on the black market.
- Transportation supplied on the black market.
- Labor supplied on the black market.

## Freedom of the Press

- System of mass communication and its ability to permit free flow of communication.
- Government laws and decisions that influence content of the media.
- Political or financial influence over the media.
- Oppression of the media.
- Censure of the media.

## GNI/capita

- 1995 to 1999 GNI per capita
- Compiled by World Bank
- GNI adjusted for Purchasing Power Parity (PPP)

a percentage of GDP. Heritage's summary tax rating is our taxes variable, and their raw government expenditures as a percentage of GDP is our government expenditures variable. We selected raw percentages for government expenditures because Heritage's summary rating score is based on different scales for developed versus developing countries.[13]

The 14 conditions measured by the variables in TABLE 1 are all, in principle, changeable by governments. There is, however, an annoying econometric problem: The conditions are quite correlated with each other. Countries with strong property rights are also likely to have smaller informal markets and are more likely to be democratic and even have lower rates of inflation.

Fortunately, there is a common statistical method that is designed to deal exactly with this "multicollinearity" problem. *Regression on principal components* involves forming several transformed variables, each of which is a weighted average of the original 14 variables. The transformed variables are constructed to be uncorrelated with each other. A regression is then computed with the transformed data, and the results are re-transformed back into the original 14 basic variables. This tool also allows us to check the functional form of the relation between income and the explanatory factors, which, as it turns out, is not linear.

The results are shown in TABLE 2. The same calculations were repeated in five separate years (1995–1999), and the results are relatively comparable across time. Over 80 percent of the observed cross-country differences in income are "explained" by the 14 variables in every year. The numbers reported in the table are the coefficients of the variables and their *t*-statistics. Each explanatory variable has both a linear and a non-linear term. A negative sign means that the variable relates negatively to country per capita income; i.e., as that variable increases, country income tends to decline. A *t*-statistic with an absolute value above approximately 2.0 indicates that the result is statistically significant, which means roughly that the measured effect is not simply due to chance. To aid in reading the table, significant variables are boxed.

---

13. In the 2004 edition of the *Index*, after thorough statistical analysis, The Heritage Foundation changed the government expenditure variable to the change in government expenditure as a fraction of GDP. Not only did this refinement improve the measurement of economic freedom, but it also eliminated the need for separate scales for developed and developing countries.

## Table 2

## Cross-Country Multiple Regressions
## of GNI/Capita on Country Policies, Institutions and Conditions.

In five separate years, country income (GNI) per capita is related to fourteen candidate explanatory variables using principal components cross-country regressions. There is both a linear and a non-linear term for each explanatory variable. The estimated regression coefficient is underlined and its t-statistic is italicized. Bordered entries indicate at least a 95% level of significance. The adjusted R-square gives the percentage of cross-country variation in income explained collectively by the fourteen variables.

| | Linear | Non-Linear | Linear | Non-Linear | Linear | Non-Linear | Linear | Non-Linear | Linear | Non-Linear |
|---|---|---|---|---|---|---|---|---|---|---|
| | 1999 | | 1998 | | 1997 | | 1996 | | 1995 | |
| Trade Barriers | -1235 | -857 | -155 | -570 | -1632 | -665 | -1234 | -337 | -1757 | -629 |
| | -6.26 | -2.61 | -6.46 | -1.73 | -8.73 | -1.93 | -4.79 | -0.88 | -7.24 | -2.15 |
| Taxes | 420 | 375 | -383 | 1004 | 292 | 437 | 319 | 1074 | 86 | 817 |
| | 0.74 | 0.50 | -0.74 | 2.77 | 0.43 | 0.59 | 0.68 | 1.81 | 0.19 | 1.49 |
| Government Expenditures | 2476 | -394 | 2111 | 468 | 1888 | -932 | 1102 | -659 | 980 | -1111 |
| | 5.49 | -1.01 | 5.32 | 0.73 | 5.36 | -2.48 | 2.98 | -1.54 | 1.13 | -1.92 |
| Government Intervention | 478.5 | -235 | 574 | -130.4 | 155 | -550 | 149 | -524 | 728 | -219 |
| | 1.17 | -0.41 | 1.32 | -0.26 | 0.34 | -1.16 | 0.51 | -0.93 | 1.63 | -0.48 |
| Monetary Policy | -1497 | 1423 | -1530 | 1217 | -1535 | 545 | -1490 | 600 | -1273 | 101 |
| | -7.89 | 4.37 | -8.00 | 3.30 | -7.84 | 1.58 | -8.49 | 1.86 | -7.04 | 0.30 |
| Foreign Inv. Barriers | -145 | -164 | -168 | 135 | -463 | 1152 | -476 | 1103 | -711 | 209 |
| | -0.48 | -0.23 | -0.49 | 0.17 | -1.29 | 1.31 | -1.29 | 1.54 | -1.80 | 0.39 |
| Banking Restrictions | -437 | -1120 | -361 | -397 | -293 | -1095 | -282 | 34 | -660 | -345 |
| | -1.66 | -1.92 | -1.10 | -0.70 | -1.02 | -1.79 | -1.07 | 0.05 | -2.77 | -0.62 |
| Wages and Prices | -294 | -716 | -222 | -948 | 210 | -1208 | 449 | -1282 | -344 | -131 |
| | -1.04 | -1.33 | -0.66 | -1.58 | 0.63 | -1.61 | 1.06 | -2.28 | -0.86 | -0.17 |
| Property Rights | 1778 | 2205 | 1849 | 1940 | 1958 | 2536 | 2102 | 2211 | 1665 | 1720 |
| | 12.61 | 8.92 | 12.34 | 7.31 | 9.75 | 9.80 | 10.00 | 10.10 | 9.46 | 6.86 |
| Regulation | -1495 | 783 | -1982 | -97 | -1507 | 904 | -2093 | -204 | -1905 | 581 |
| | -5.08 | 1.59 | -6.77 | -0.19 | -3.77 | 2.18 | -6.03 | -0.37 | -4.89 | 1.85 |
| Black Market Activity | -1607 | 1981 | -1465 | 1802 | -1667 | 1611 | -1511 | 1572 | -1264 | 2052 |
| | -11.08 | 5.99 | -7.34 | 5.74 | -7.90 | 5.12 | -9.42 | 3.85 | -9.51 | 5.21 |
| Political Rights | 533 | 427 | 506 | 487 | 629 | 490 | 792 | 431 | 877 | 775 |
| | 3.84 | 1.99 | 2.05 | 1.78 | 2.69 | 1.67 | 3.47 | 1.26 | 3.99 | 2.80 |
| Civil Liberties | 863 | 1343 | 909 | 836 | 1063 | 809 | 1160 | 778 | 1240 | 857 |
| | 5.28 | 6.66 | 2.96 | 2.48 | 3.77 | 2.72 | 4.65 | 3.14 | 5.29 | 4.08 |
| Freedom of the Press | 1074 | 1696 | 1125 | 1710 | 992 | 1581 | 1212 | 1719 | 1178 | 1514 |
| | 7.16 | 6.22 | 4.69 | 3.42 | 4.47 | 3.74 | 5.94 | 4.36 | 5.84 | 3.67 |
| Regression Intercept | 7878 | | 7916 | | 8378 | | 8105 | | 9220 | |
| | 16.50 | | 23.77 | | 22.29 | | 21.64 | | 11.33 | |
| Adjusted R-square | .846 | | .819 | | .818 | | .829 | | .819 | |
| Number of countries | 157 | | 156 | | 148 | | 142 | | 134 | |

The following variables are statistically significant in almost every year, with the direction of relation given by (+) or (–): property rights (+), regulation (–), and informal market activity (–), which could be considered basic indicators of economic freedom; political rights (or voting rights) (+), civil liberties (+), and freedom of the press (+), which seem more related to political freedom; and monetary policy (or inflation) (–), trade barriers (–), and government expenditures (+). While a *t*-statistic of 2 is the usual rule of thumb required to claim statistical significance, many of the aforementioned variables had much higher $t$-statistics, in the 5 to 12 range, indicating that their correlation with country incomes is very significant and robust.

The variables have all been adjusted to the same scale, so the absolute sizes of coefficients provide indications of relative importance. For example, per capita income is more strongly associated with freedom of the press than with voting rights. Although both voting rights and press freedom are features of open, democratic societies, it appears that the latter is more related to prosperity.

The strongest correlates with country wealth turn out to be property rights, which has a strong positive correlation, and informal market activity, which is strongly negative. Of the nine highly significant variables we have identified, political rights, or the popular vote, seems to have the least strong relation with income, but with $t$-statistics ranging from 2 to 4 across years, it is still highly significant statistically.

## Interpreting the Evidence

To this point, we have been careful to speak only about correlations between these significant variables and country incomes. Nowhere have we mentioned the causal direction: for example, whether increased property rights tend to make country incomes increase or whether, as country incomes increase, citizens demand better legal protection of their substantial properties.

For property rights, regulation, informal market activity, trade barriers, monetary policy, and government expenditures, previous research provides some indication of the causal direction. The variables just mentioned could be elements of "social infrastructure," a construct devised by Robert Hall and Charles Jones,[14] who used an instrumental variables approach to demonstrate that it does indeed "cause" higher incomes. We might rely on their results to make the same claim here.

Unfortunately, no prior research has found an unambiguous causal relation between income and political freedom. No one has demonstrated convincingly that democratic reform brings more rapid economic growth. Indeed, there is a large body of opinion, not yet substantiated by meaningful statistical results, that richer countries become better educated and demand democratic reform; i.e., the causal direction is from prosperity to democracy, not the other way around. Cross-country regressions of incomes

---

14. See note 12, *supra*.

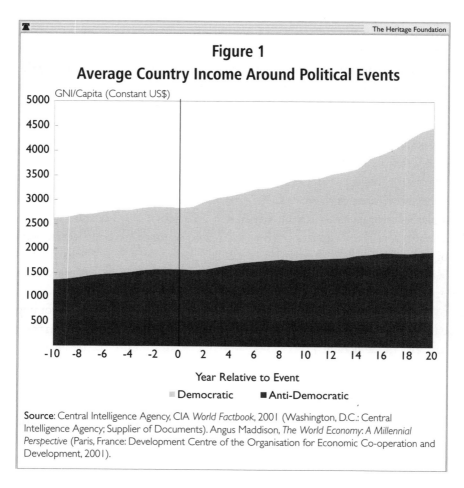

The Heritage Foundation

**Figure 1**
**Average Country Income Around Political Events**

GNI/Capita (Constant US$)

Year Relative to Event

■ Democratic   ■ Anti-Democratic

Source: Central Intelligence Agency, CIA *World Factbook*, 2001 (Washington, D.C.: Central Intelligence Agency; Supplier of Documents). Angus Maddison, *The World Economy: A Millennial Perspective* (Paris, France: Development Centre of the Organisation for Economic Co-operation and Development, 2001).

on democracy-related variables cannot determine causality, so an alternative statistical method is required to settle this issue. This method has come to be known as an *events study*, named after studies of the reaction of stock prices to corporate events, such as stock splits, that were pioneered by Eugene Fama, Lawrence Fisher, Michael Jensen, and Richard Roll.[15]

The events being studied in this case—either pro- or anti-democratic events—usually occur on different calendar dates for each country in the study. To measure the average impact of democratic change, all of the coun-

_____

15. Eugene Fama, Lawrence Fisher, Michael Jensen, and Richard Roll, "The Adjustment of Stock Prices to New Information," *International Economic Review*, Vol. 10, No. 1 (February 1969), pp. 1–21.

tries' time lines are shifted and are arranged so that their "event" occurs at what is called time zero. Then average growth in real per capita income can be tabulated before and after time zero for all the countries experiencing the same event. The method's empirical power is attributable to the fact that only the event under study is common across countries. Other possible influences on growth tend to be minimized because they are averaged across countries, having occurred at different calendar times.

To implement the events study, country background information was collected from the 2001 *CIA World Factbook*, and historical data on GNI per capita were taken from the Organisation for Economic Co-operation and Development's *The World Economy: A Millennial Perspective*.[16] Larry Diamond of the Hoover Institution kindly reviewed our characterizations of political events. His expertise provides comfort that events classified as "democratic" and "anti-democratic" conform to political scientists' consensus opinions about the exact nature of the events in our sample.

Data are available for two events studies involving countries becoming either more (44 events) or less (43 events) democratic at some moment in their history.[17] "Democratic" events include such political changes as the introduction of a second political party, the establishment of a legislature, or the initiation of popular voting. An "anti-democratic" event might be a military *coup d'e-tat*, suspension of a constitution, or the beginning of a dictatorial regime.

The results, reported in FIGURE 1, are rather striking. Anti-democratic events led to growth rates declining by almost half over the next 20 years. After their anti-democratic events, these countries were unable to sustain even a 1 percent real growth rate in per capita incomes.

In contrast, countries undergoing a "democratic" event saw growth increase dramatically, with real annual rates approaching 2.7 percent from years 10 to 20 after the event. This improvement, though seemingly modest, compounds sufficiently to double a country's per capita income every 26 years and would effectively enable every developing country on Earth to grow completely out of poverty within a century.

---

16. Central Intelligence Agency, *CIA World Factbook*, 2001 (Washington, D.C.: Central Intelligence Agency; Supplier of Documents). Angus Maddison, *The World Economy: A Millennial Perspective* (Paris, France: Development Centre of the Organisation for Economic Co-operation and Development, 2001).

17. For a list of events by country, see *www.anderson.ucla.edu/acad_unit/finance/wp/2001/19-01.pdf*.

Notice also in the figure that, prior to "democratic" events, these countries were not growing rapidly and had a rather meager real income per capita of $2,800 per person. This does not support the view that countries must be rich to accomplish democratic reforms or that they need to achieve some minimal level of education. Quite the contrary: The evidence suggests that, regardless of how poor a country may be, a democratic reform will, on average, be followed by immediate better growth at a rate that seems to improve over time.

This is our evidence that democratic reforms do indeed "cause" growth. The opposite direction of causation—from wealth to democratic reform—would require that the populace anticipated future prosperity, which led them to demand democratic reform now.

Based on these results and those of Hall and Jones, we therefore believe that nine mutable "deep determinants" (those that are significant in TABLE 2) likely cause countries to be rich or poor. As the R-squares indicate in TABLE 2, these mutable government policies and institutions explain a very large fraction—about 80 percent to 85 percent—of the differences in country incomes across the globe. This is good news: Not only are the major factors that are driving differences in income amenable to change by enlightened governments, at least in principle, but more than 80 percent of the current difference in country incomes could be eliminated over time by enacting appropriate policies.

Milton Friedman would not be surprised. In his seminal text, *Capitalism and Freedom*,[18] he argued for a direct relationship between strong property rights, democratic freedoms, and economic prosperity. While not trying to discern a causal direction, he did indeed point out that governments that allowed free markets to set prices were probably the same type of liberal governments that might entertain democratic reforms. Friedman argued that the same individual freedoms set loose with democratic reforms can be further unleashed through capitalist reforms. In a functioning free market, each participant makes his own individual decision about engaging in an economic transaction.

Recognizing that researchers should be careful in applying their own subjective interpretations to statistical evidence, we will now supply some plausible intuition about why the above variables might be important in positively or negatively affecting country incomes. Our personal biases have

---

18. Milton Friedman, *Capitalism and Freedom* (Chicago, Ill.: University of Chicago Press, 1962).

been confined to the narrative below and had no impact on the statistical work discussed above.

## Property Rights, Regulation, and Informal Market Activity

These three measures of economic freedom, or the lack thereof, appear to be among the most significant in their impact on country income. Each one relates to the conduct of economic transactions. Property rights represent the basis of private ownership in a capitalist system. Without strong property rights, it is hard to imagine what incentive individuals would have to make investments or improve their properties, and without investment, there can be no growth. We use the term "property" broadly to include businesses, homes, and even intellectual property.

As Lee Hoskins and Ana Eiras state in their chapter in the 2002 edition of Heritage's *Index of Economic Freedom:*

> The ability to accumulate private property, whether in the form of income, investment, or purchases, is the driving force behind a market economy. For individuals to work, save, invest, and for firms to begin operations or expand existing activities, they need to be secure in the knowledge that they will be the full owners of their property and that nobody will take it from them.[19]

It would be a mistake to think this influences only large inter-country investments. While government appropriation of private property or nationalization is a real concern for multinational corporations that are thinking of investing in a developing country, strong property rights are also the concern of the common man. As Hernando de Soto says in his recent text:

> The poor inhabitants of these (developing) nations—five-sixths of humanity—do have things, but they lack the

---

19. Lee Hoskins and Ana I. Eiras, "Property Rights: The Key to Economic Growth," Chapter 3 in Gerald P. O'Driscoll, Jr., Kim R. Holmes, and Mary Anastasia O'Grady, *2002 Index of Economic Freedom* (Washington, D.C.: The Heritage Foundation and Dow Jones & Company, Inc., 2002), pp. 37–38. See also Gerald P. O'Driscoll, Jr., Kim R. Holmes, and Melanie Kirkpatrick, *2001 Index of Economic Freedom* (Washington, D.C.: The Heritage Foundation and Dow Jones & Company, Inc., 2001).

process to represent their property and create capital. They have houses but not titles; crops but not deeds; businesses but not statutes of incorporation. It is the unavailability of these essential representations that explains why people who have adopted every other western invention, from the paper clip to the nuclear reactor, have not been able to produce sufficient capital to make their domestic capitalism work.[20]

As a concept, property rights is broader than just legal titling. De Soto would be the first to agree that it also includes a system of law and order, an independent judiciary, and a policing force that is fair and just.

It is also from de Soto's work that we derive examples that show the drag of overly burdensome regulations and informal market activity on a well-functioning economy.[21] With regard to excessive regulations, de Soto claims that in his native Peru, it takes 728 bureaucratic steps for someone to acquire legal title to his or her home and over 280 days to register a business—something that takes an afternoon in the United States. One would think such excessive regulation reflects an inefficient government, but there could be a darker explanation: Such burdensome regulation might be intended to exclude informal workers from competing for jobs and business.

Finally, informal market activity is highly negatively correlated with country wealth. Informal market activity describes not only illegal activities such as smuggling and illegal currency conversions, but also totally legal informal activities outside of the formal structure of the economy. Consequently, it is not counted in the official tallies of income, which implies that countries with high levels of informal market activity have downward biased reporting of per capita income.

Moreover, informal market activity is often the response either to weak property rights in a country or to overly burdensome regulation in the formal sector. It can also result from a high degree of corruption. The best way to avoid paying bribes to acquire and maintain official status for a business is never to seek formal status.

---

20. Hernando De Soto, *The Mystery of Capital: Why Capitalism Triumphs in the West and Fails Everywhere Else*, (New York: Basic Books–Perseus Books Group, 2000), pp. 6–7.

21. Hernando De Soto, *The Other Path: The Invisible Revolution in the Third World* (New York: Harper and Row, 1989), and *The Mystery of Capital*.

De Soto estimates the total value of untitled real estate at $9.3 trillion worldwide.[22] This is a mind-boggling number and includes not only many unregistered businesses, but also such activities as improvements on untitled personal property. Just as a business owner may not wish to invest without formal assurances of ownership, a property owner would be slow to make major improvements unless he or she were comfortable that the costs could be recouped in a future sale, which is unlikely for an informal owner. De Soto says that everybody in a poor village—even the dogs—knows where the homes' property lines are; they are just not recorded anywhere. He says the proof that the dogs know is that, as one walks across an unmarked but very real property line, the owner's dog begins his soulful barking.

## Political Rights, Civil Liberties, and Freedom of the Press

These three variables are measures of political freedom. They are highly correlated with each other across countries, but because each by itself turns out to be statistically significant, we are confident that each one has its own independent effect on country wealth.

Again, conventional wisdom is that a better-educated populace demands democratic reforms like voting rights. Our events study showed just the opposite. So how could greater political rights and freedoms lead to greater wealth?

Amartya Sen has pointed out that no democracy has ever suffered a famine in the history of the world. First, Sen argues effectively that droughts are natural disasters, but famines are genuine economic events.[23] Plenty of food is available during famines, but food is not distributed equitably. Sen proposes that horrific economic events like famines are avoided in democracies because political leaders receive effective and timely feedback information from the general populace about their economic situation. This efficient feedback mechanism is important in explaining how democracies are more prosperous.

Whereas feedback leads to prosperity in a democracy, the absence of feedback likely leads to vulnerability in a dictatorship. Mancur Olson predicted that some stable dictators would be motivated by the economic rent

---

22. De Soto, *The Mystery of Capital*, p. 35.

23. Amartya Kumar Sen, *Poverty and Famines: An Essay on Entitlement and Deprivation* (New York: Oxford University Press, 1981), and *Development as Freedom* (New York: Knopf Publishing/Random House, 1999).

they could extract from their population—not just in the first year, but over a long period.[24] Olson also predicted that some dictators might indeed invest some of their own capital to affect real growth. But where will a dictator get accurate feedback about the efficacy of his policies? His own people cannot vote when dissatisfied; they cannot outwardly protest. Surrounded by toadies, the dictator will have neither a free press nor informed op-ed pieces. In the recent war in Iraq, misinformation allegedly hurt the Iraqi leadership more than it confused the U.S. and British military. For example, when Iraq's Minister of Information insisted the Americans were definitely not at the Baghdad Airport, he may have been directing his comments as much to Iraqi leaders as to the public.

A subset of dictators seems to have benevolent intentions. Singapore is often mentioned as an example, and it has had incredible economic growth since World War II. Korea and Taiwan have shown strong economic growth with imperfect democracies. It seems that democracy is not an absolute prerequisite for growth. What is wrong with a benevolent dictator? Three things:

*First,* benevolent dictators are unlikely to maintain the effective feedback mechanisms that are inherent in democracies and that would help them to judge the results of their decisions.

*Second,* once the populace has surrendered its collective civil liberty, there is no assurance that a dictator or his successor will remain benevolent.

*Finally,* a well-meaning but inept and ineffective dictator cannot be voted out peacefully in the next election cycle.

In addition to the all-important feedback mechanism, democratic reforms act as a policing force for government. In the free market, every business is subject to the self-policing mechanisms of the market: Create profits or go bankrupt. Government has no such natural self-policing mechanism, and government operations are often bloated and inefficient. Political rights give citizens some control over government, but voting is an occasional and crude instrument. A negative campaign in the press or in the streets can be more immediately damaging to a politician's reputation or to an ineffective government program. Short of being violently deposed, a dictator faces no policing mechanism to prevent him from misappropriating

---

24. Mancur Olson, *Power and Prosperity: Outgrowing Communist and Capitalist Dictatorships* (New York: Basic Books, 2000).

funds, providing monopoly status to his choice businesses, or doling out overpaid government jobs to supporters.

Perhaps most important, economic stability is a major benefit provided by democracies. Democracies rarely change the rules that govern private property or expropriate investments without compensation. As a result, investors have more confidence in being able to reap the benefits of their activities, and investment proceeds at a more intense rate. The result: rapid growth.

## Monetary Policy, Trade Barriers, and Government Expenditures

The final three significant variables in explaining differences in country incomes are monetary policy, trade barriers, and government expenditures. The Heritage monetary policy variable is a weighted average of the country's inflation rate for the past 10 years. High and unpredictable inflation can be damaging to economic participants entering into longer-term purchase contracts for items such as housing and automobiles, but it can also be symptomatic of deeper government problems. Typically, high inflation is induced when a government prints money excessively because it cannot tax or borrow. Thus, inflation can be predictive of government ineptitude.

Hoskins and Eiras, in Heritage's *2002 Index of Economic Freedom*, state that:

> Even inflation can be evaluated in terms of property rights. As John Maynard Keynes observed, "by a continuing process of inflation, governments can confiscate, secretly and unobserved, an important part of the wealth of their citizens."… Holders of monetary assets and contracts suffer a loss of purchasing power with no offsetting compensation, and debtors arbitrarily gain rights to consume more than they otherwise would because they pay off with a currency that purchases less.[25]

Like many other researchers, we find that trade barriers—such as high tariffs, protectionism, and large informal market premiums—inhibit eco-

---

25. Hoskins and Eiras, "Property Rights: The Key to Economic Growth," p. 42

nomic development. Openness to new ideas is productive, but openness also acts as a natural deterrent to artificial pricing and monopolistic arrangements inside a country.

Pure trade levels, measured by exports as a percentage of GDP, were also included in one version of the regressions (not reported). Perhaps surprisingly, this variable is totally unrelated to country income. While many people intuitively remember the recent successful exporting strategies of Singapore, Taiwan, and Korea, they forget to realize that many economically successful countries, including Japan and the United States, have low levels of exports relative to their total economic size. It seems that the relevance of trade barriers for growth must be more attributable to other factors, such as corruption, than to their direct impact of discouraging trade.

The final significant variable is government expenditures, which is positively correlated with country wealth. This positive effect is smaller for more advanced countries. In essence, many poor countries fail to provide the basic infrastructure for development, such as roads and schools. While citizens of advanced countries may complain of large government presence, it appears that the developing world suffers from too much chaos and not enough cooperative effort.

## A Caveat

A battery of diagnostics checked the robustness of the empirical results. These revealed the probable omission of at least one important explanatory variable. We were not able to identify this missing element, but we did eliminate several possibilities.

One possibility was that the method used to convert country incomes into a common currency had various flaws, which made it appear as though there was a missing factor. Employing several alternative conversion methods did not change the results in any material respect, so we presume this is not the explanation.

Because of the delayed growth rate response, we also examined the time elapsed since political reforms were accomplished. Although this improved the explanatory power modestly, it was not a complete explanation.

Similarly, adding in non-mutable correlates of income—for example, language, religion, and historical factors (such as colonization)—did not have a material impact on the basic results, and, for the most part, these correlates were themselves insignificant.

Identification of the missing factor would be an interesting objective for further research.

## Conclusion

Nine variables, measuring nine different conditions within a country, explain a large fraction (more than 80 percent) of the observed cross-country variation in per capita income. What do these seemingly disparate nine variables share in common?

*First*, they represent the rules of the game. To create or maintain a vibrant economy—unless the rules of the game are clearly understood, fair, and stable—is extremely difficult. People will not invest if they have lost confidence in the system. They must be assured that corruption will be minimized and that miscreants will be punished. Inflation must be controlled and contracts honored. Property must not be expropriated by government or by others. Government cannot be properly policed without democratic rights and institutions.

*Second*, these variables all represent solutions to collective action problems, and this entails government participation. Individuals alone can do little to reduce trade barriers, enact titling procedures, reduce corruption, or sanction ineffective leaders. Only through effective government mechanisms can citizens collectively dismiss corrupt politicians, reduce inflation, provide security for property, create a system of law and order, and create the type of environment that will foster entrepreneurship and attract capital.

Good institutions represent the key to stimulating growth in a developing country. Rather than relying on donations from outsiders to support education, health care, or physical infrastructure, a much more successful strategy would be to encourage institutional change to create the proper environment for growth. Economic liberty and political freedoms appear to stimulate greater individual effort, productivity, and economic growth.

# Chapter 4

# Open Trade: An Important Milestone on the Road to Prosperity

**Editor's Summary**

"Trade not aid" has been an economic mantra for years. As Daniel Griswold notes in his chapter, countries that opened to global markets enjoyed growth that was significantly greater than those that attempted to avoid global competition.

Yet free trade alone does not guarantee growth. Free trade combined with other market reforms found on the road map—property rights, openness to foreign investment, and low regulation—makes growth more likely. Among Griswold's findings:

- Comparative advantage is a source of gains. By producing products at which they are more productive compared to other nations, countries can make more with the same resources. Their standards of living rise.
- Poor nations that engage in global trade can dramatically expand the size of markets for their producers and choices for their consumers.

- Poor countries that open to international trade and investment gain access to a much higher level of technology.
- Trade liberalization encourages more foreign investment, providing additional fuel for future growth.

As Griswold amply demonstrates, free trade is a significant step on the road to prosperity.

# Open Trade: An Important Milestone on the Road to Prosperity

*Daniel T. Griswold*

TRADE POLICY has always been at the center of development economics. A fundamental choice facing every sovereign nation is how free its citizens should be to trade, invest, and travel across international borders. How economic openness promotes and affects development has been the focus of intense debate for decades. The purpose of this chapter will be to explain the role of trade policy in development.

For more than two centuries, at least since the time of Adam Smith, economists have been studying how trade promotes economic growth and development. Smith noted in his classic 1776 work, *The Wealth of Nations*, that free trade promotes growth by allowing a greater division of labor among nations. International trade enables nations to produce more of what they make relatively efficiently, trading their surplus production for goods produced more efficiently in other nations. Smith argued that an individual family that insisted on producing all of its own clothing, shoes, furniture, and food would consign itself to poverty. The same applies to nations. As Smith famously observed:

> What is prudence in the conduct of every private family, can scarce be folly in that of a great kingdom. If a foreign country can supply us with a commodity cheaper than we ourselves can make it, better to buy it of them with part of the produce of our industry, employed in a way in which we have some advantage.[1]

Because of climate, the people of Cameroon can more easily grow bananas than the people of Finland. For other reasons, such as better education and machinery, Finland can more easily produce mobile telephones. Both nations are better off producing more of what they make best and trading the surplus. It would be senseless for the people of Cameroon to make their own mobile phones and the people of Finland to try to grow bananas in greenhouses. Additionally, as nations produce more of a product, their producers become more efficient. They become more skilled and can spread fixed costs over more customers, realizing economies of scale. Larger markets through globalization allow a finer division of labor and a greater degree of specialization, raising productivity and living standards.

## Comparative Advantage and the Gains from Trade

Free-trade theory was strengthened further in 1817 when British economist David Ricardo first explained comparative advantage. Ricardo noted that while a nation may produce all goods less efficiently in absolute terms, free trade would still boost the nation's well-being. *Comparative* advantage, in which a nation focuses on goods it makes *relatively* well, is more beneficial than *absolute* advantage.

The key to the theory is specialization. Even if people in a rich country are twice as efficient at making shirts as people in a poor country and simultaneously 10 times as efficient at making computers, it will still be advantageous for both if the rich country specializes in computers and imports shirts from the poor country.

To understand why this is true, consider the rich and poor countries in the example just given. (See TABLE 1.) Residents of Southland, the poor country, for instance, can produce either 1,000 shirts or two computers in 100 hours. Residents of Northland, the rich country, can produce either 2,000 shirts or 20 computers in 100 hours. It appears that Northland is more efficient at producing both products. Yet in Southland, producing one computer requires giving up 500 shirts, while in Northland, a computer will "cost" only 100 shirts. Northland thus has a comparative advantage in computers, and Southland has a comparative advantage in shirts.

---

1. Adam Smith, *An Inquiry into the Nature and Causes of the Wealth of Nations* (New York: Random House, 1937; first published in 1776), Book IV, Chapter II, p. 424.

| | Productivity (output per 100 hours) | | Autarky | | | | Free Trade | | | |
|---|---|---|---|---|---|---|---|---|---|---|
| | | | Output | | Consumption | | Output | | Consumption | |
| | Computers | Shirts | Computers | Shirts | Computers | Shirts | Computers | Shirts | Computers | Shirts |
| Northland | 20 | 2000 | 14 | 600 | 14 | 600 | 18 | 200 | 14 | 700 |
| Southland | 2 | 1000 | 1 | 500 | 1 | 500 | 0 | 1000 | 4 | 500 |
| Total | | | 15 | 1100 | 15 | 1100 | 18 | 1200 | 18 | 1200 |

**Table 1**

In the absence of trade (a condition known as autarky), let us assume that the people in Southland could meet domestic demand by dividing their labor equally between the shirt and computer industries, producing 500 shirts and one computer. The people of Northland, by similar assumption, could satisfy their demand for shirts with only 30 hours of labor, producing 600 shirts. With the other 70 hours, they could produce 14 computers. Combined production between the two nations under autarky would be 1,100 shirts and 15 computers.

If people in the two nations are allowed to trade with each other, computers will soon flow from Northland to Southland, where they can fetch a higher price in terms of shirts, and shirts will just as quickly begin to flow the other way. Barring import tariffs or high transportation costs, the two countries will trade until the internal price ratio of shirts to computers is roughly the same in both countries.

If Southland specializes exclusively in shirts, it can produce 1,000 shirts by devoting all of its labor to the industry in which it enjoys a comparative advantage. If Northland then specializes in computers, say by devoting only 10 hours to shirt production, it can produce 18 computers and 200 shirts. It can then trade its surplus of computers to Southland in exchange for the poor country's surplus of shirts. Combined production between the two nations would then be 1,200 shirts and 18 computers, compared to 1,100 shirts and 15 computers under autarky. Through trade, the world would be wealthier by 100 shirts and three computers, allowing people in both countries to consume more of both than they could under autarky.

Consider also an example from daily life. A star professional basketball player, because of his physical attributes, may be twice as efficient at mowing the expansive lawn surrounding his mansion than the teenager down the road. Yet because the basketball player is about 100 times more efficient at playing basketball, it will still make sense for him to hire the teenager to mow the lawn and spend the two hours he saves honing his professional skills. Everybody benefits: The teenager gets paid, and the athlete can realize additional income from those extra two hours that far surpasses the wage paid to the teenager.

Comparative advantage means that there is a place under the free-trade sun for every nation. No matter how poor, people of every nation can produce some products relatively more efficiently than they produce other products. For rich countries, comparative advantage means that the production they give up in a relatively less efficient domestic industry will be replaced by more production in more efficient industries. Trade with low-wage countries will pinch some domestic industries in the rich countries, but it will also spur the expansion of others. Thus, according to standard economic analysis, trade is a win–win arrangement for rich and poor countries alike.

Of course, this simplified model does not include all the complexities of the real world (economic models are, by definition, simplifications), but it does capture an essential truth that has successfully predicted how nations trade with each other in the real world. Less-developed countries (LDCs), because of their relative abundance of labor, tend to export goods that require more labor relative to other inputs. Advanced countries, because of their relative abundance of physical and human capital, tend to export goods that require more sophisticated machinery and skilled labor relative to other inputs. Comparative advantage applies especially well to trade between rich and poor countries because factor endowments and internal price ratios can differ widely between rich and poor countries.

## The Rise and Fall of "Dependency Theory"

Until recently, free trade had not been a common policy among poor countries. Through most of the 19th and early 20th centuries, many of them were colonies whose trade policies were set by the ruling European powers. Those policies often discouraged poor countries from trading with other poor countries or with rival colonial powers. The lack of open markets and free trade was one of the reasons poor countries stayed poor and colonies did not develop economically.

After World War II, almost all the former colonies gained their independence. Yet instead of opening their markets, many of them turned inward, rejecting the global economy as exploitative and inherently unfair to developing countries. The theoretical basis for this rejection came to be known as "dependency theory." It rests on the assumption that a free-market international economic system exploits the weak to favor the strong. It asserts that the capitalist system of the rich core countries either systematically ignores or impoverishes the poor nations, or keeps them mired in a state of "dependent development."

This theory first emerged in the context of Latin America and attempted to explain the chronic underdevelopment of the region in terms of a worldwide economic structure biased against poorer nations. A variant theory—the "structuralist" theory—first gained recognition through the U.N. Economic Commission for Latin America and then through the 1964 report, *Towards a New Trade Policy for Development*, published by the U.N. Conference on Trade and Development (UNCTAD), both under the leadership of Raul Prebisch.

Prebisch argued that the world was composed of a developed capitalist core and a chronically underdeveloped periphery, with nations on the periphery trapped in underdevelopment because of their reliance on the export of commodities. An alleged long-term decline of commodity prices relative to manufacturing prices caused a steady deterioration of the terms of trade, locking poor nations into a state of dependency. The way out, according to the UNCTAD analysis, was domestic industrialization through a policy of "import substitution"—closing the economy by raising tariff barriers and then substituting domestically produced goods for what had previously been imported.

Supporting the dependency theory was a theoretical exception to free trade known as the "infant industry" argument. Allegedly, under certain conditions, a nation can benefit in the early stages of development by protecting some industries that otherwise would not survive the rigors of competition from producers in more advanced economies. According to this theory, protective barriers can be lowered, and finally eliminated, as the protected industries mature and become more competitive in global markets.

The less-developed nations that adopted import-substitution policies based on infant-industry and dependency theories found the results disappointing. The protected "infant industries" failed to mature and proved to be inefficient and uncompetitive in global markets. In the end, the import-substitution strategy promoted by structuralist theory failed to promote sustained development in Third World nations. Protection of domestic industry has succeeded only in creating inefficient domestic producers; low-quality, high-cost goods for consumers; rent seeking; foreign-exchange shortages; and stop-and-go macroeconomic policies.

For example, India protected its domestic automobile industry for decades. The result was not the emergence of a globally competitive industry but the sheltering of an inefficient industry that offered low-quality, overpriced vehicles with few choices for consumers. As the Indian-born trade economist Jagdish Bhagwati recounted, "Sheltered from import competition, Indian car manufacturers produced such shoddy cars that, when they went up to India's Tariff Commission for renewal of their protection, the commissioners wryly remarked that in Indian cars, everything made noise except the horn!"[2]

In the past two decades, the development that has done the most to undermine dependency theory has been the rise of the newly industrialized countries (NICs) in the Far East. The spectacular development of South Korea, Hong Kong, Singapore, and Taiwan fits poorly into dependency theory. Why should these nations—all poor, dependent colonies before World War II—move swiftly from the periphery of the world economy to First World levels of development while other, similarly situated nations languish in underdevelopment?

The NICs show—in stark contrast to dependency theory—that poor nations can develop by integrating with the world economy. From typical Third World poverty in the 1950s, each has achieved an OECD (Organisation for Economic Co-operation and Development) standard of living today, with per capita incomes in Hong Kong and Singapore rivaling those of the wealthiest Western nations. Beginning with Chile in the mid-1970s and China later that decade, less-developed nations from Mexico and India to—more recently—Uganda and Vietnam have been opening their markets and welcoming foreign investment. The result has been impressive growth and sharply falling poverty rates.

The relative success of openness as a policy compared to protectionism has spurred a global movement toward unilateral trade liberalization. Since the mid-1980s, 60 less-developed countries have unilaterally lowered their trade barriers. Less-developed countries have flocked to join the World Trade Organization (WTO). Today, more than three-quarters of its members are LDCs, with others waiting in line to join.[3]

---

2. Jagdish Bhagwati, *In Defense of Globalization* (New York: Oxford University Press, 2004), p. 62.

## "Latecomer's Advantages"

The economic advantages of open trade and globalization apply all the more to poor nations, conferring on these countries what economists call a "latecomer's advantage."

*First,* poor nations that engage in globalization can dramatically expand the size of markets for both their producers and their consumers. Consumers gain access to a much wider range of goods and services at more competitive prices, raising the real standard of living for most workers. For people in poor countries especially, trade provides advanced goods—TVs, cell phones, medical equipment—and financial and other services that they otherwise would find it impossible or prohibitively expensive to produce on their own. Domestic producers gain access to a wider range and better quality of intermediate inputs at lower prices, and those that export enjoy a quantum leap in economies of scale by serving global markets rather than only a confined and underdeveloped domestic market.

*Second,* increased competition from trade spurs faster growth through "dynamic gains." As we have seen, comparative advantage yields important "static gains" from the one-time shifting of a nation's productive assets toward those industries where it is most productive. Yet the trade also yields dynamic gains year after year as domestic companies are forced to innovate and economize to meet ongoing foreign competition. Those gains result in higher growth rates and higher living standards over time. Dynamic gains can be especially important for developing countries that have been shackled by inefficient state-owned industries.

*Third,* poor countries that open themselves to international trade and investment gain access to a much higher level of technology. Rather than bearing the cost of expensive, up-front research and development, poor countries can import the technology off-the-shelf, embodied in such products as pharmaceuticals, electronic hardware, and new capital machinery that raises productivity. Hybrid seeds and new medicines are raising nutrition levels and extending lives in poor countries. Subsidiaries of multinational companies also bring with them new production techniques and employee training that add to the host nation's stock of human capital.

---

3. Organisation for Economic Co-operation and Development, *Policy Coherence Matters* (Paris: OECD, 1999), p. 45.

*Fourth*, trade liberalization encourages more foreign investment, providing additional capital to fuel future growth. Most less-developed countries are people-rich and capital-poor. Access to global capital markets allows poor countries to raise the level of domestic investment and to accelerate their pace of growth. Inward foreign investment can finance more traditional types of infrastructure, such as port facilities, power generation, and an internal transportation network, just as British capital helped to finance America's network of canals and railroads in the 19th century. Just as important, however, multinational companies can provide more efficient telecommunications, insurance, and banking services. Cellular telephone networks, for example, allow poor villagers in remote areas to bypass antiquated and unresponsive government landline monopolies. As many poor countries are discovering, an underdeveloped service sector retards growth in other sectors of the economy. A poor country that closes its door to foreign investment or fails to maintain sound domestic policies will forfeit the immense benefits this inflow of capital can bring.

*Finally*, engagement in the global economy encourages governments to follow the more sensible economic policies outlined elsewhere in this book. Sovereign nations remain free to follow whatever economic policies their governments choose, but free trade and globalization have raised the cost that must be paid for bad policies. With capital more mobile than ever, countries that insist on following anti-market policies will find themselves being dealt out of global competition for investment. As a consequence, nations have a greater incentive to choose policies that encourage foreign investment and domestic, market-led growth. By creating a more hospitable climate for foreign investment, governments in less-developed countries usually create a more friendly business climate for local producers and entrepreneurs.

A more open economy also reduces the opportunity for government officials to seek bribes for permission to import. As William Easterly, a former economist at the World Bank, has noted:

> Restrictions on trade create opportunities for corruption.
> If there is a high tariff on an imported good, there is an
> incentive to bribe customs officials to import the good at a
> lower tariff. And, if a license is needed to import the good
> and the good is in great demand, the license seeker will

have to pay a bribe. One study has found that countries that restrict the freedom of international trade are indeed more corrupt.[4]

For all those reasons, poor nations that open themselves to trade and investment typically grow faster than other poor nations that keep themselves closed. Of course, other factors also play a role in determining a nation's rate of growth, so the link between openness and growth is not perfect, but the empirical evidence strongly indicates that openness is good for growth. The annual *Index of Economic Freedom*, published by the Heritage Foundation and *The Wall Street Journal*, reveals that nations with the largest (top quintile) improvements in their trade policy scores between the 1997 *Index* and the 2004 *Index* enjoyed real per capita gross domestic products (GDPs) that were almost twice (1.6) those in the bottom quintile and annual growth rates that were one-and-one-half times faster.[5]

Another study, by World Bank economists David Dollar and Aart Kraay, grouped less-developed countries according to the growth of their trade sectors relative to national income during the past two decades. The top one-third of countries in terms of the growth of their trade sectors were classified as "globalizers," the bottom two-thirds as non-globalizers. The globalizers increased their trade relative to income by 104 percent during the two decades, compared to 71 percent growth among rich countries and an actual decline of relative trade among the non-globalizers. The globalizers cut their import tariffs by an average of 22 percentage points—twice the rate cut among the non-globalizers. Dollar and Kraay found that the globalizing poor countries saw their annual growth accelerate from an average of 1 percent in

---

4. William Easterly, *The Elusive Quest for Growth: Economists' Adventures and Misadventures in the Tropics* (Cambridge, Mass.: MIT Press, 2001), p. 249.

5. World Bank, *World Development Indicators Online*, and Marc A. Miles, Edwin J. Feulner, and Mary Anastasia O'Grady, *2004 Index of Economic Freedom* (Washington, D.C.: The Heritage Foundation and Dow Jones & Company, Inc., 2004), at *www.heritage.org/index*. This result is reinforced by other measures of economic freedom. For example, the annual *Economic Freedom of the World* report, published by the Fraser Institute in Canada, found that nations that were in the top quintile of trade openness from 1980 to 1998 enjoyed real per capita GDPs that were more than seven times greater than those in the bottom quintile and annual growth rates that were nearly five times faster. James Gwartney and Robert Lawson, *Economic Freedom of the World: 2001 Annual Report* (Vancouver, B.C.: Fraser Institute, 2001), p. 78.

the 1960s to 5 percent in the 1990s; in contrast, the non-globalizing poor countries saw their collective growth rates fall from 3 percent to 1 percent during this same time period. In other words, the globalizers enjoyed growth in the 1990s that was five times greater than the non-globalizers. Other studies confirm the link between trade and growth among developing nations.[6]

Trade liberalization alone will not guarantee more growth. Economic openness must be accompanied by internal reforms such as a non-inflationary monetary policy, secure property rights, economically rational regulation, a transparent and rule-based legal system, government spending restraint, and a tax system that allows workers to enjoy the fruits of their labors. Some nations that have opened themselves to the global economy have run into economic troubles, not because of globalization, but because of lagging domestic reforms. In East Asia in the late 1990s, South Korea, Thailand, and Indonesia experienced steep economic downturns because of growing doubts about politically dominated, opaque domestic financial systems. More recently, Argentina suffered recession and mounting foreign debt because of profligate government spending and a legal system that stifles entrepreneurial activity. While trade reforms do not guarantee growth, they make growth more likely when combined with other market reforms.

## Beneficial Effects of Trade Liberalization

Less-developed nations that open themselves to the global economy tend to grow faster than those that isolate themselves. The resulting growth lifts a rising share of their populations out of poverty; creates the domestic wealth necessary to raise environmental, labor, and general living standards; and creates conditions more conducive to political pluralism and respect for human rights. Those may seem to be tall claims, but they rest on two centuries of economic thought and experience.

**Lifting the Lot of the Poor.** The most dramatic progress against poverty has been in those poor countries that have moved most decisively to open themselves to the global economy. More open and competitive markets have

---

6. See Jeffrey Sachs and Andrew Warner, "Economic Reform and the Process of Global Integration," *Brookings Papers on Economic Activity*, Vol. 1 (1995), pp. 1–95; Sebastian Edwards, "Openness, Productivity and Growth: What Do We Really Know?" National Bureau of Economic Research, Working Paper No. 5978 (Cambridge, Mass: NBER, 1997); and Jeffrey A. Frankel and David Romer, "Does Trade Cause Growth?" *The American Economic Review*, June 1999, pp. 379-399.

# A Tale of Two Countries

Consider the tale of two African island nations—Madagascar and Mauritius. From the early 1970s through most of the 1990s, Madagascar followed an economic policy its government described as "Christian Marxism." That path led the government to nationalize industries, control domestic markets, and close its borders behind high tariffs. The result was stagnant growth and pervasive, persistent poverty, malnourishment, and illiteracy.

In contrast, nearby Mauritius engaged itself in the global economy by establishing an export-processing zone in 1972 to woo foreign textile producers from Hong Kong and other East Asian countries. Taking advantage of access to American and European markets, Mauritius rapidly expanded its trading sectors, becoming globally competitive in a labor-intensive industry that played to its comparative advantage.

As a result, Mauritius pulled away from Madagascar by virtually every measure of well-being: By 1998, its annual per-capita income had reached $3,690, compared to $250 in Madagascar; 22 percent of its residents owned phones, compared to 6 percent in Madagascar; and literacy had reached 100 percent compared to 45 percent in its poor neighbor.[i]

---

i. Helene Cooper, "Fruit of the Loom: Can African Nations Use Duty-Free Deal to Revamp Economy?" The Wall Street Journal, January 2, 2002, p. A1.

---

raised rates of growth, lifting incomes for poor families as well as the non-poor. Better-paying jobs have been created by foreign direct investment, especially in labor-intensive industries such as apparel and other light manufacturing. Such jobs typically pay wages that are much higher and offer benefits and working conditions that are much better than those offered by locally owned producers.[7] Lower trade barriers have brought the price of a wider range of consumer goods—cellular telephones, refrigerators, motorbikes, TVs, and VCRs—within reach of lower-income families. Better jobs and higher incomes have raised health standards and allowed more children to attend school.

Benefits to the poor are most visible in countries that have opened themselves to globalization. In China, two decades of economic reform and trade liberalization have raised growth rates, quadrupled real wages, and reduced the number of people living in absolute poverty by more than 150 million.[8] Chinese economic reform has been, quite simply, the greatest anti-poverty program the world has ever seen. Since 1991, poverty rates have also fallen sharply in Vietnam, India, and Uganda—all formerly closed economies that have liberalized their domestic and trade policies in the past decade. In each of these countries, lower poverty rates have been the result primarily of internal market reform and globalization, *not* foreign aid, internal income redistribution, or outside economic and political pressure.

A 2001 World Bank study found that "the only countries in which we have seen large-scale poverty reduction in the 1990s are ones that have become more open to foreign trade and investment."[9] In the two decades since 1980, the study could not find a single example of a poor country that had closed its markets and, at the same time, closed the income gap with the rich countries.[10] An April 2002 study on trade and poverty by Oxfam International, while critical of multinational companies and other aspects of globalization, nonetheless concluded: "History makes a mockery of the claim that trade cannot work for the poor. Participation in world trade has figured prominently in many of the most successful cases of poverty reduction—and, compared with aid, has far more potential to benefit the poor."[11]

**How Globalization Raises Standards.** Critics charge that globalization encourages a "race to the bottom" in environmental and labor standards. They argue that multinational companies, in a never-ending quest to cut

---

7. Edward M. Graham, "Trade and Investment at the WTO: Just Do It!" in Jeffrey Schott, *Launching Global Trade Talks* (Washington, D.C.: Institute for International Economics, 1999), p. 158.

8. The World Bank, *World Development Report 2000/2001: Attacking Poverty* (New York: Oxford University Press, 2001), p. 23.

9. David Dollar, "Globalization, Inequality, and Poverty Since 1980," World Bank, August 15, 2001, p. 17.

10. *Ibid.*, p. 13.

11. Oxfam International, *Rigged Rules and Double Standards: Trade, Globalisation, and the Fight Against Poverty*, 2002, p. 6, at *www.maketradefair.com/*.

costs and increase profits, roam the planet looking for countries with the least restrictive regulations and lowest wages. The governments of poor countries are thus encouraged to keep standards low so as not to frighten away footloose foreign investment. To prevent capital from fleeing to low-standard countries, so the theory goes, Western governments face relentless pressure to lower their own standards; thus, the supposed race to the bottom. The trouble with that scenario is that there is little theory and virtually no evidence to support it.

When Western multinational firms invest in less-developed countries, they typically bring higher, not lower, standards. For reasons of internal efficiency, as well as public perception, multinational companies expect similar standards from their affiliates, whether operating in less-developed or advanced economies. Thus, multinational companies tend to impose higher standards on their overseas production plants than those of domestically owned and operated companies, thereby raising average standards in the host country. Additionally, for most industries, the costs of complying with labor and environmental standards in host countries are so small as to make them relatively unimportant in choosing where to locate.

If low standards and low wages were the dominant factors driving investment flows, as the race-to-the-bottom thesis assumes, then we would expect poor countries to be capturing most foreign direct investment from developed countries. Yet the low social standards endemic to less-developed countries do not seem to confer any observable advantage in attracting foreign direct investment. The overwhelming majority of foreign direct investment comes from and flows to developed countries with similarly high wages and high labor and environmental standards. Those nations in the world today that have the highest labor and environmental standards are invariably those that also have the highest incomes and the most open economies. Globalization and the development it spurs lead not to a race to the bottom, but to a race toward the top.

Through the same dynamic of development, globalization is also enabling poor countries to raise their environmental standards. Openness to trade and investment allows less-developed nations to import the latest technology to help control pollution in the most cost-effective way. By encouraging competition, globalization helps to reduce wasteful consumption of resources. Multinational companies that set up operations abroad tend to follow higher standards of pollution control than those followed by the domestic companies in the host country. By promoting development, globalization makes it easier for less-developed countries to afford pollution-controlling technology. When incomes and education levels rise, citizens are more likely to demand more effective regulation of pollution. That explains why the most stringent environmental laws in the world today are maintained in developed countries that are relatively open to trade.[12]

Development by itself can have a mixed impact on the environment. All else being equal, an economy that produces more of exactly the same goods and services in exactly the same way will produce more pollution. Yet development changes not only the size of an economy, but also its composition and its level of technology. More sophisticated technology can mean cleaner production processes and more affordable and effective pollution abatement. With hybrid crops, for example, less fertilizer and land are needed for the same production.

As nations progress to a higher stage of development, they tend to move away from more resource-intensive activities such as mining, agriculture, and heavy industry and into light manufacturing, information technology, and services. An OECD study on globalization and the environment concluded:

> There is some evidence that, once a country begins to industrialize, trade liberalization helps to make the structure of its economy less pollution-intensive than in those countries whose economies remain relatively closed. In particular, freer trade seems to promote the transition from heavy resource-processing sectors to light manufacturing ones (at least at middle income levels).[13]

Of course, open trade and economic growth alone do not lead inevitably to higher environmental and labor standards. Absent clearly defined property rights, government regulation is usually necessary to protect common air and water resources from pollution that can endanger the

---

12. Daniel T. Griswold, "Trade, Labor, and the Environment: How Blue and Green Sanctions Threaten Higher Standards," Cato Institute *Trade Policy Analysis* No. 15, August 2, 2001.

13. Organisation for Economic Co-operation and Development, *Globalisation and the Environment: Perspectives from OECD and Dynamic Non-Member Economies* (Paris: OECD, 1998), p. 20.

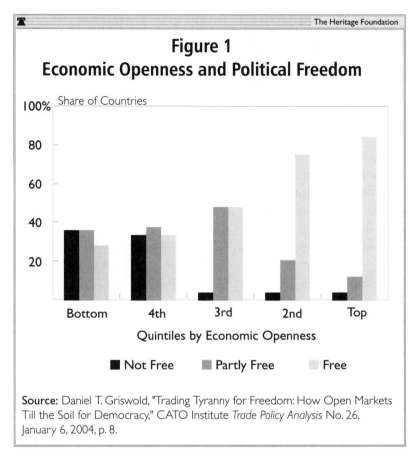

**Figure 1**
**Economic Openness and Political Freedom**

Source: Daniel T. Griswold, "Trading Tyranny for Freedom: How Open Markets Till the Soil for Democracy," CATO Institute *Trade Policy Analysis* No. 26, January 6, 2004, p. 8.

public's health. Government action may also be necessary to eliminate forced labor, the exploitation of children, and market distortions caused by anticompetitive practices, whether by industry or by labor unions. Yet the evidence is clear that economically sound regulations are perfectly compatible with an open economy.

**Tilling the Soil for Human Rights.** Economic openness and the commercial competition and contact it brings can promote civil and political freedoms within countries both directly and indirectly. Trade can influence the political system directly by increasing the contact a nation's citizens experience with the rest of the world through face-to-face meetings and electronic communications through telephone, fax, and the Internet.

Just as important, economic freedom and openness encourage democracy indirectly by raising living standards and expanding the middle class.

The faster growth and greater wealth that accompany trade promote democracy by creating an economically independent and politically aware middle class. A sizeable or dominant middle class means that more citizens can afford to be educated and take an interest in public affairs. As citizens acquire assets and establish businesses and careers in the private sector, they prefer the continuity and evolutionary reform of a democratic system to the sharp turns and occasional revolutions of more authoritarian systems. Simply put, people who are allowed to manage their daily economic lives successfully in a relatively free market come to expect and demand more freedom in the political and social realms.

Around the globe, the recent trend toward globalization has been accompanied by a trend toward greater political and civil liberty. In the past 30 years, cross-border flows of trade, investment, and currency have increased dramatically—far faster than output itself. Trade barriers have fallen unilaterally and through multilateral and regional trade agreements in Latin America, in the former Soviet bloc nations, in East Asia (including China), and in more developed nations as well. During that same period, political and civil liberties have been spreading around the world. Thirty years ago, democracies were the exception in Latin America; today, they are the rule. Many former communist states from the old Soviet Union and its empire have transformed themselves into functioning democracies that protect basic civil and political freedoms. In East Asia, democracy and respect for human rights have replaced authoritarian rule in South Korea, Taiwan, Thailand, the Philippines, and Indonesia.

Nations with open and free economies are far more likely to enjoy full political and civil liberties than are those with closed and state-dominated economies. Additionally, those that are closed are far more likely to suppress civil and political freedoms than are those that are open.[14] The accompanying chart (FIGURE 1) reflects the division of 123 nations into quintiles according to their economic openness, with the least open in the left quintile and the most open in the right quintile. Each of the 123 countries has been rated by the human-rights organization Freedom House according to the degree of political and civil freedom allowed by its government.

---

14. Daniel T. Griswold, "Trading Tyranny for Freedom: How Open Markets Till the Soil for Democracy," Cato Institute *Trade Policy Analysis* No. 26, January 6, 2004.

Freedom House groups countries into three categories: "Free" (where people enjoy full civil liberties to worship, assemble, and speak freely, and full political liberties to participate in free and open elections); "Partly Free" (where those rights are partly abridged); and "Not Free" (where those rights are widely or completely denied). As the chart shows, the share of nations in each quintile that are "Free" steadily rises along with economic openness, while the share of those that are "Not Free" steadily declines. The evidence indicates that open trade yields benefits for developing countries that go beyond faster economic growth alone.

## Current Controversies

Free trade remains controversial within rich and poor countries alike, but the terms and nature of the debate have shifted in significant ways in the past two decades. During the 1960s and into the 1970s, resistance to trade expansion was concentrated in poor countries, where dependency theory still held sway. Today, as we have seen, a large and growing number of developing countries have turned away from the closed economic model toward freer (if not yet truly free) trade.

The most vocal resistance to trade now seems to come from interest groups within the rich nations, often in the form of non-governmental organizations (NGOs) that are wary of free markets on principle and both industry and labor groups that believe trade with poor nations hurts their members' interests. For example, representatives of the domestic sugar and textile industries in the United States vigorously oppose opening the U.S. market to imports from less-developed countries because they believe lower-priced imports will hurt profitability and employment in their sectors.

The following are four broad areas of such ongoing controversy:

**1. Rich-Country Trade Barriers to Poor-Country Exports.** Countries tend to protect their least competitive industries, and the rich Western nations are no exception. The highest trade barriers in the West are typically against exports that are most important to people in poor countries: textiles; labor-intensive manufactured goods (such as clothing and shoes); and agricultural goods (such as sugar, fruits, and vegetables). On average, advanced countries impose tariffs on imports from poor countries that are four times higher than tariffs on imports from other advanced countries.[15]

By opening their markets to free trade from poor countries, Western nations would be doing themselves a favor by lowering the costs of goods for their own citizens and delivering substantial income to workers and farmers in poor countries. In fact, the annual cost imposed on poor countries by rich-country trade barriers is more than double the amount the rich countries donate in foreign aid.[16]

**2. Environmental and Labor Standards in Poor Countries.** Labor and environmental conditions in less-developed countries can strike Western observers as unacceptable, if not appalling. Yet two points need to be considered.

*First,* working conditions are likely to be even worse in non–trade-oriented sectors, such as services and subsistence agriculture—sectors that have been largely untouched by globalization.

*Second,* poor labor and environmental standards are not a new phenomenon, but have always been a chronic fact of life. "Sweatshop" conditions persist today not because of globalization—a relatively new phenomenon—but because of previous decades of protectionism, inflation, economic mismanagement, hostility to foreign investment, and a lack of legally defined property rights. Globalization is not the cause of lower standards in poor countries: It is the best hope for improving them.

Despite this evidence, however, the United States and other rich countries persist in attempting to condition trade with poor countries on their adherence to certain minimum environmental and labor standards. Poor-country governments have resisted those calls so far, arguing that imposing such sanctions would have the perverse effect of denying poor countries the necessary means to raise incomes so that they can afford higher standards.

**3. Globalization and Inequality.** Some critics charge that more open trade has bred rising inequality in the world, both within nations and among nations. They further argue that, even if globalization has made some people and nations richer, rising inequality has morally tainted the whole enterprise. Indeed, globalization has fostered faster growth in those poor countries that have expanded trade with the rest of the world, allowing them to close the gap with the richer countries. The study on trade and growth by Dollar and Kraay found that the globalizers not only grew faster than the non-globalizers, but also grew faster than the rich countries:

---

15. World Bank, *Global Economic Prospects 2002: Making Trade Work for the World's Poor,* November 2001.

16. *Ibid.*

"Thus, the globalizers are catching up with the rich countries while the non-globalizers fall further and further behind."[17]

Another major finding by Dollar and Kraay was the lack of any connection between a nation's growth rate and its level of domestic inequality. Less-developed nations were as likely to see inequality fall as they were to see it rise during periods of growth. In fact, the incomes of the poorest 20 percent of a nation's population rose, on average, at the same rate as the rest of the population. If globalization can spur faster growth, as the evidence indicates, then the poorest segments of society in the globalizing country will typically benefit to the same degree as everyone else. "The fact that increased trade generally goes hand-in-hand with more rapid growth and no systematic change in household income distribution means that increased trade generally goes hand-in-hand with improvement in well-being of the poor," Dollar and Kraay concluded.[18]

**4. Intellectual Property Enforcement.** Through the Agreement on Trade-related Aspects of Intellectual Property Rights (TRIPs), the World Trade Organization encourages poor nations to adhere to mutually agreed-upon standards of intellectual property protection. Advocates of TRIPs argue that exporters of intellectually protected property lose billions in sales every year because of illegal production of patented drugs, copyrighted music and movies, and other intellectual property in less-developed countries. If the legal producers of those goods cannot earn a profit, they will not have the incentive to make the necessary up-front investment in research and development. The end result would be less innovation and creativity. Without enforcement through the WTO, such violations will continue to distort and inhibit legitimate trade in intellectual property.

Critics of TRIPs argue that those rules, especially when applied to pharmaceuticals, deny important products to poor people simply because they cannot afford to pay the patent-protected price. They assert that the number of sales lost from the relaxation of patent rules in most poor countries would be so small that the economic loss to Western pharmaceutical companies would be minimal. Instead of promoting win-win trade liberalization, they argue that TRIPs makes the WTO a royalty collection agency

---

17. David Dollar and Aart Kraay, "Trade, Growth, and Poverty," World Bank, June 2001, p. 27.
18. *Ibid.*, p. 4.

for multinational companies headquartered in the advanced economies. TRIPs continues to be a point of controversy in ongoing negotiations for a new WTO agreement.

## Conclusion

Developed over the past two centuries, the economic arguments in favor of free trade apply equally to all countries, even so-called less-developed countries. Reducing barriers to trade is not a magic bullet for countries seeking to develop their economies, but expanding trade does, in practice, appear to be a necessary part of an effective policy for promoting development. Through trade, poor countries can dramatically expand their markets both for consumers and producers, enjoying efficiency gains from economies of scale and innovations spurred by competition. Through the hard lessons of the post-colonial era, a growing number of poor countries' governments have realized that there is no alternative.

# Further Reading

Cox, W. Michael, and Richard Alm, "The Fruits of Free Trade," Federal Reserve Bank of Dallas 2002 Annual Report, at *www.dallasfed.org/fed/annual/2002/ar02.pdf*.

Dollar, David, and Aart Kraay, "Spreading the Wealth," *Foreign Affairs*, Vol. 8, No. 1 (January/February 2002).

Gwartney, James, and Robert Lawson, *Economic Freedom of the World* (Vancouver, B.C.: Fraser Institute, various years). See especially Chapter 3, "Trade Openness, Income Levels, and Economic Growth, 1980–1998," in *Economic Freedom of the World: Annual Report 2001*.

Organisation for Economic Co-operation and Development, *Open Markets Matter: The Benefits of Trade and Investment Liberalization* (Paris: OECD, 1998).

World Bank, *The East Asian Miracle: Economic Growth and Public Policy* (New York: Oxford University Press, 1993).

# Chapter 5

## Law and Property Outside the West: A Few New Ideas About Fighting Poverty

**Editor's Summary**

Citizens in developing countries are not as poor as the numbers indicate; their wealth is simply not recorded because they lack property rights. Property rights are the foundation for wealth creation. Without property rights, owners cannot borrow against assets and turn them into other forms of productive capital like small businesses. How can you sell your property if you cannot prove that you own it?

Hernando de Soto explains the importance of property rights, their absence in the developing world, and the basics of how governments can create statutes and processes that will make assets fungible. In his chapter, the author notes that:

- In developing and former communist nations, 80 percent of the people do not have legal property rights over their assets.
- There is a connection between property systems and the creation of capital.
- Property rights would enable the poor to maximize their assets by allowing

them to exchange those assets "outside of [their] narrow local circles."

Property rights greatly expand the wealth of the poor. To establish property rights, governments must seek to replace bad laws with procedures that attach owners to assets. According to de Soto, "With titles, shares and property laws, people could suddenly go beyond looking at their assets as they are (houses used only for shelter) to thinking about what they could be (security for credit to start or expand a business)."

# Law and Property Outside the West: A Few New Ideas About Fighting Poverty

*Hernando de Soto*[1]

THE PROBLEM: Imagine a country where nobody can identify who owns what, addresses cannot be easily verified, people cannot be made to pay their debts, resources cannot conveniently be turned into money, ownership cannot be divided through documents, descriptions of assets are not standardized and cannot easily be compared, authors of fraud cannot easily be identified, and the rules that govern property vary from neighborhood to neighborhood or even from street to street.

You have just put yourself into the life of a developing country or former communist nation. More precisely, you have imagined life for 80 percent of its population, which is marked off as sharply from its Westernized elite as black and white South Africans were once separated by apartheid.

Over the past 10 years, with varying degrees of enthusiasm, Third World and former Soviet Union nations—where 5 billion of the world's 6 billion people live—have carried out the macroeconomic policies the West recommended: They have balanced their budgets, cut subsidies, welcomed foreign investment, and dropped their tariff barriers. Yet from Argentina to Russia, capitalist reformers are now intellectually on the defensive, increasingly derided as apologists for the miseries and injustices that still plague the poor.

---

1. This chapter is slightly adapted from an article by the author that appeared original-ly in *Axess Magazine*, published by the Stockholm, Sweden-based Axel and Margaret Ax:son Johnson Foundation, in August 2002.

As a result, we are now beginning to realize that you cannot carry out macroeconomic reforms on sand. Capitalism requires the bedrock of the rule of law, beginning with property. The property system is much more than ownership; it is the hidden architecture that organizes the market economy in every Western nation. What the property system accomplishes is so central to capitalism that developed nations have come to take its success for granted. Indeed, even most property experts are unsure about the connections between property systems and the creation of capital.

Yet these connections exist. Without them, buildings and land cannot be used to guarantee credit or contracts. Ownership of businesses cannot be divided and represented in shares for investors to buy. In fact, without property law, capital itself—the instrument that allows people to leverage their assets and their transactions—is impossible to create. The instruments that store and transfer value—such as shares of corporate stock, patent rights, promissory notes, bills of exchange, and bonds—are all determined by the architecture of legal relationships with which a property system is built. The problem is that 80 percent of the people in developing and former communist nations do not have legal property rights over their assets, whether those assets be homes, businesses, or intellectual creations.

When property law works, the capital value of assets rises in developing nations. In 1990, for example, the Compañía Peruana de Teléfonos (CPT) was valued on the Lima stock exchange at $53 million. The government of Peru, however, could not sell the CPT to foreign investors because they found that the company's property title—over its assets and Peruvian property law itself—was unclear.

Consequently, the Peruvians put together a hotshot legal team to create a legal title that would meet the standardized property norms required by the global economy. Documents were rewritten to secure the interests of other parties and create confidence that would allow for credit and investment. The legal team also created enforceable rules for settling property disputes that bypassed the dilatory and corruption-prone Peruvian courts. Three years later, CPT entered the world of liquid capital and was sold for $2 billion—37 times its previous market valuation. That is what a good property system can do.

The enterprises of the poor are very much like the Peruvian telephone company prior to its good title and ability to issue shares or bonds to obtain new investment and finance. Less than 20 percent of the people in

Third World and former Soviet nations have good property representations. As a result, most of them are undercapitalized, in the same way that a firm is undercapitalized when it issues fewer securities than its income and assets would justify. Without property records and representations, their assets remain financially and commercially invisible: They are dead capital.

In the West, by contrast, every parcel of land, every building, every piece of equipment or store of inventories is represented in a property document that is the visible sign of a vast hidden process that connects all of these assets to the rest of the economy. Thanks to this representational process, assets can lead an invisible, parallel life alongside their material existence.

They can be used as collateral for credit. The single most important source of funds for new businesses in the United States is a mortgage on the entrepreneur's house. These assets can also provide a link to the owner's credit history, an accountable address for the collection of debts and taxes, the basis for the creation of reliable and universal public utilities, and a foundation for the creation of securities (like mortgage-backed bonds) that can then be rediscounted and sold in secondary markets. By this process, the West injects life into assets and makes them generate capital.

Why have more reforms not been made outside of the West? One reason is that conventional macroeconomic reform programs have ignored the poor, assuming they have no wealth upon which to build.

That is a big mistake. My research team and I have recently completed several studies of the underground economy throughout the Third World. They prove that the poor are, in fact, not so poor. In Egypt, the poor's assets in real estate are worth an estimated $241 billion—30 times the value of equities on the Cairo Stock Exchange and 55 times the sum of all foreign investment in the country in the past 150 years, including the Suez Canal and the Aswan Dam. In Mexico, the estimate is $315 billion—seven times the worth of PEMEX, the national oil monopoly.

The problem is that most people outside the West hold their resources in defective forms: houses built on land whose ownership rights are not adequately recorded, unincorporated businesses with undefined liability, industries located where financiers and investors cannot see them. Because the rights to these possessions are not adequately documented, these assets cannot readily be turned into capital, cannot be traded outside of narrow local circles where people know and trust each other, cannot be used as collateral for a loan, and cannot be used as a share against an investment.

To some, this may seem hard to believe. After all, how is it that a piece of paper representing ownership can create value? One of the greatest challenges to the human mind is to comprehend and to gain access to those things we know exist but cannot see.

## Legal Property Is "Mind Friendly"

Not everything that is real and useful is tangible and visible. Time, for example, is real, but it can be efficiently managed only when represented by a clock or a calendar. Throughout history, human beings have invented representational systems—writing, musical notation, double-entry bookkeeping—to grasp with the mind what human hands could never touch. In the same way, the great practitioners of capitalism, from the creators of integrated title systems and corporate stock, were able to reveal and extract capital where others saw only junk by devising new ways to represent, through property systems, the invisible potential that is locked up in the assets we accumulate.

What distinguishes a good legal property system is that it is "mind friendly." It obtains and organizes knowledge about recorded assets in forms we can control. It collects, integrates, and coordinates not only data on assets and their potential, but also our thoughts about them. In brief, capital results from the ability of the West to use property systems to represent their resources in a virtual context. Only with such a system can minds meet to identify and realize the meaning of assets for humankind.

The revolutionary contribution of an integrated property system is that it solves a basic problem of cognition. Our five senses are not sufficient for us to process the complex reality of an expanded market, much less a globalized one. We need to have the economic facts about ourselves and our resources boiled down to essentials that our minds can easily grasp.

A good property system does that. It puts assets into a form that lets us distinguish their similarities, differences, and connecting points with other assets. It fixes them in representations that the system tracks as they travel through time and space. In addition, it allows assets to become fungible by representing them to our minds so that we can easily combine, divide, and mobilize them to produce higher-valued mixtures. This capacity of property to represent aspects of assets in forms that allow us to recombine them so as to make them even more useful is the mainspring of economic growth, since growth is all about obtaining high-valued outputs from low-valued inputs.

I do not believe that the absence of this process in the poorer regions of the world—where five-sixths of humanity lives—is the consequence of some Western monopolistic conspiracy. Rather, it is that Westerners take this mechanism so completely for granted that they have lost all awareness of its existence. The property mechanism is huge, yet even Americans, Europeans, and Japanese—who owe all of their wealth to their ability to use it—are blind to its overwhelming existence.

However, it is this system that has given the West an important tool for development. The moment Westerners were able to focus on the title of a house and not just the house itself, they achieved a huge advantage over the rest of humanity. With titles, shares, and property laws, people could suddenly go beyond looking at their assets as they are (houses used only for shelter) to thinking about what they could be (security for credit to start or expand a business). Through widespread, integrated property systems, Western nations inadvertently created a staircase that allowed their citizens to climb out of the grubby basement of the material world into the realm where capital is created.

This may sound too simple or too complex, but consider whether it is possible for assets to be used productively if they do not belong to something or someone. Where do we confirm the existence of these assets and the transactions that transform them and raise their productivity if not in the context of a formal property system? Where do we record the relevant economic features of assets if not in the records and titles that formal property systems provide? Where are the codes of conduct that govern the use and transfer of assets if not in the framework of formal property systems? Formal property provides the process, the forms, and the rules that fix assets in a condition that allows us to realize them as active capital.

In the West, this formal property system begins to process assets into capital by describing and organizing the most economically and socially useful asset characteristics, preserving this information in a recording system—as insertions in a written ledger or a blip on a computer disk—and then embodying them in a title. A set of detailed and precise legal rules governs this entire process.

Formal property records and titles thus represent our shared concept of what is economically meaningful about any asset. They capture and organize all the relevant information required to conceptualize the potential value of an asset and so allow us to control it. Property is the realm where we identify and explore assets, combine them, and link them to other assets. The formal property system is capital's hydroelectric plant. Property is the place where capital is born.

## Injecting Life into Dead Capital

Any asset whose economic and social aspects are not fixed in a formal property system is extremely hard to move in the market. How can the huge amounts of assets changing hands in a modern market economy be controlled if not through a formal property process? Without such a system, any trade of an asset, say a piece of real estate, requires an enormous effort just to determine the basics of the transaction: Does the seller own the real estate and have the right to transfer it? Can he pledge it? Will the new owner be accepted as such by those who enforce property rights? What are the effective means to exclude other claimants?

In developing countries and former communist nations, such questions are difficult to answer. For most goods, there is no place where the answers are reliably fixed. That is why the sale or lease of a house may involve lengthy and cumbersome procedures of approval involving all the neighbors. This is often the only way to verify that the owner actually owns the house and that there are no other claims on it. It is also why most asset exchange outside the West is restricted to local circles of trading partners.

As we are now discovering, the principal problem of developing countries and former communist nations is not the lack of entrepreneurship: According to studies done by the Institute for Liberty and Democracy in Peru, the poor of the developing world have accumulated nearly $10 trillion worth of real estate during the past 40 years. What the poor lack is easy access to the property mechanisms that could legally fix the economic potential of their assets so that they could be used to produce, secure, or guarantee greater value in the expanded market.

Centuries ago, scholars speculated that we use the word "capital" (from the Latin for "head") because the head is where we hold the tools with which we create capital. This suggests that the reason why capital has always been shrouded in mystery is that, like energy, it can be discovered and managed only with the mind. Capital cannot be touched unless the property system can record its economic aspects on paper and anchor them to a specific location and owner.

Property, then, is not mere paper but a mediating device that captures and stores most of the stuff required to make a market economy run. It is a means of controlling our environment to build prosperity. The capacity of property to reveal the capital that is latent in the assets we accumulate is born out of the best intellectual tradition of controlling our environment in order to prosper. For thousands of years, our wisest men have been telling us that life has different degrees of reality, many of them invisible, and that it is only by constructing representational devices that we will be able to access them. As Margaret Boden puts it:

> Some of the most important human creations have been new representational systems. These include formal notations, such as Arabic numerals (not forgetting zero), chemical formulae, or the staves, minims, and crotchets used by musicians. [Computer] programming languages are a more recent example.[2]

Representational systems such as mathematics and integrated property help us to manipulate and order the complexities of the world in a manner that we can all understand and that allows us to communicate regarding issues that we could not otherwise handle. They are what the philosopher Daniel Dennett has called "prosthetic extensions of the mind."[3] Through representations, we bring key aspects of the world into being so as to change the way we think about it.

The philosopher John Searle has noted that by human agreement, we can assign "a new status to some phenomenon, where that status has an accompanying function that cannot be performed solely in virtue of the intrinsic physical features of the phenomenon in question."[4] This seems to me very close to what legal property does: It assigns to assets, by social contract, in a conceptual universe, a status that allows them to perform functions that generate capital.

Therefore, formal property is more than a system for titling, recording, and mapping assets: It is an instrument of thought, representing assets in such

---

2. Margaret Boden, *The Creative Mind* (London: Abacus, 1992), p. 94.

3. Daniel C. Dennett, "Intentionality," in *The Oxford Companion to the Mind*, ed. Richard L. Gregory (Oxford: Oxford University Press, 1991), p. 384.

4. John R. Searle, *The Construction of Social Reality* (New York: Free Press, 1995), p. 46.

a way that people's minds can work on them to generate surplus value. That is why formal property must be universally accessible: to bring everyone into one social contract where they can cooperate to raise society's productivity.

How can modern property systems be established in non-Western countries?

As things stand, most arrangements that govern the holding and transaction of assets in non-Western nations are established outside the formal legal system. Extralegal property arrangements are dispersed among dozens, sometimes hundreds, of communities; rights and other information are known only to insiders or neighbors. To modernize any of these countries, all the separate, loose extralegal property arrangements characteristic of most Third World and former communist nations must be woven into a single system from which general principles of law can be drawn. In short, the many social contracts "out there" must be integrated into one all-encompassing social contract.

How can this be accomplished? How can governments find out what the extralegal property arrangements are?

That was precisely the question put to me by five members of the Indonesian cabinet. I was in Indonesia to launch the translation of my previous book into Bahasa Indonesian, and they took that opportunity to invite me to talk about how they could find out who owns what among the 90 percent of Indonesians who live in the extralegal sector.

Fearing that I would lose my audience if I went into a drawn-out technical explanation on how to structure a bridge between the extralegal and legal sectors, I came up with another way—an Indonesian way—to answer their question. During my book tour, I had taken a few days off to visit Bali, one of the most beautiful places on Earth. As I strolled through rice fields, I had no idea where the property boundaries were. But the dogs knew. Every time I crossed from one farm to another, a different dog barked. Those Indonesian dogs may have been ignorant of formal law, but they were positive about which assets their masters controlled.

I told the ministers that Indonesian dogs had the basic information they needed to set up a formal property system. By traveling their city streets and countryside and listening to the barking dogs, they could gradually work upward, through the vine of extralegal representations dispersed throughout their country, until they made contact with the ruling social contract. "Ah," responded one of the ministers, "Jukum Adat (the people's law)!"

Discovering "the people's law" is how Western nations built their formal property systems. Any government that is serious about re-engineering the ruling informal agreements into one national formal property social contract needs to listen to its barking dogs. To integrate all forms of property into a unified system, governments must find out how and why the local conventions work and how strong they actually are. This may sound oxymoronic or even subversive to Western readers who have come to believe there is only one law to obey, but my experience visiting and working in dozens of developing nations has made it clear to me that legal and extralegal laws coexist in all of them.

Over the past 15 years, what we have learned to do at the Institute for Liberty and Democracy—not only in South America, but also in the Middle East, Asia, the Caribbean, and North America—is to identify the written or unwritten extralegal norms and their representations; disembed them from their surroundings; and, on the basis of the common denominators we find, bring them together in one professionally crafted code that is acceptable to all. This process of moving norms and representations from informal and local contexts toward a formal and universal context we call the "representational ascent."

In each country where we work, once we have identified the main traits of the extralegal norms governing extralegal systems, we compare them to the official law—essentially an "elite law" because it is obviously rejected or not applicable to most of the nation. Then, through a process of consultations with both the extralegal and legal leaders, we blend the better parts of extralegal local laws with the acceptable parts of elite law so as to produce a unified formal code that is applicable throughout the land. The steps required to produce this representational ascent are sketched out in FIGURE 1 and FIGURE 2, which outline the process for formalizing real estate and businesses of the extralegal sector.

The reason we take extralegal law seriously is that it is stable and meaningful for those who work outside the legal system. The problem with extralegal law is that its application is limited to small, dispersed informal settlements and therefore gives economic agents a very small market in which to act and divide labor. Nowhere we have visited have we encountered working people who extralegally oppose integrating into the legal sector, provided that the law which is proposed to them is grounded in their customs and beliefs, explained to them in their vocabulary, and does not involve high transaction costs they cannot afford.

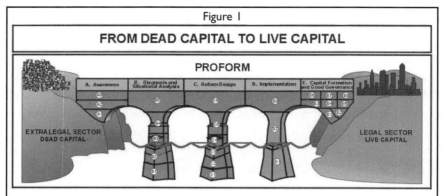

Figure 1

**FROM DEAD CAPITAL TO LIVE CAPITAL**

PROFORM

EXTRALEGAL SECTOR
DEAD CAPITAL

LEGAL SECTOR
LIVE CAPITAL

### A. Awareness
Raise awareness of:
A.1 Property law under capitalism.
A.2 The stake of the poor under capitalism.
A.3 The role of leadership in each country.

### B. Diagnosis and Situational Analysis
B.1 Identify, locate and classify extralegal assets (dead capital).
- Develop local recruitment specifications to penetrate extralegal sector.
- Locate the economic sectors and geographic areas where extralegal activities are most prevalent.
- Identify the ways in which property rights are held and exercised by the different informal settlements and areas.
- Determine causes for the accumulation of extralegal assets so as to develop workable typologies.
B.2 Quantify the actual and potential value of extralegal assets (dead capital).
- Develop appropriate methodologies to estimate the value of extralegal assets using existing information and data gathered in the field.

- Customize criteria to gather and process information and to confirm results.
- Establish the importance of the value of extralegal assets.
B.3 Analyze the extralegal sector s interaction with the rest of society.
- Research the relevant links between government and extralegal assets.
- Research the relevant links between legal business and extralegal assets.
- Identify processes where government has already dealt successfully with extralegal assets.
B.4 Identify the extralegal norms that govern extralegal property
- Detect and decode the extralegal norms that define the manner in which property rights are held and exercised by the different extralegal communities in the country.
- Identify points where extralegal norms, informal customs, and practice conflict with or coincide with the law.
B.5 Identify the principal institutional obstacles to transforming informally held assets into more productive formal property and determine the

We learned how to discover extralegal arrangements and how to integrate them into one legal system by studying how, over centuries, Western nations and Japan made the transition from dispersed, informal arrangements to an integrated legal property system on the basis of which the rule of law was established. This historical knowledge accounts for some of the inputs we obtained to make a transition process. Most of the knowledge, however, we obtained through our own empirical research in developing countries. In the field, we brailled our way through extralegal worlds and eventually learned how to get in touch with the social contracts that underlay property rights.

costs of extra-legality to the country, including:
- The costs to the extra legal sector.
- The cost to the legal business sector.
- The cost to government.

**C. Reform Design**

Design a comprehensive program of reforms containing alternative options to formalize informal assets in the urban sector on a massive and nationwide scale, including:

C.1 Ensure that the highest political level assumes responsibility for capitalization of the poor.

C.2 Put into operation agencies that will permit rapid change.
- Identify and connect with the capitalization process the different institutions that currently govern property rights or impinge upon their ability to generate surplus value.
- Design, obtain approval for, and put into operation agencies that will permit the rapid introduction of changes in the diverse processes required for capitalization. If possible, create a single organization with the sole mandate of capitalizing assets and decentralize offices to provide services throughout the country.
- Ensure that the capitalization process both incorporates the government's political priorities and reflects a consensus within society that makes the process easily enforceable.

C.3 Remove administrative and legal bottlenecks
- Calculate the costs of capitalizing extralegal assets, including requirements for permits at all levels of government, requirements for and the amount of payments for these permits, the number of forms and other documents required, requirements that cannot be met in practice, and all other transaction costs, including time delays, and remove administrative and legal bottlenecks by identifying and

modifying the institutions, statutes and practices that create unnecessary red tape.

C.4 Build consensus between the legal and extralegal sectors
- Determine the points where extralegal norms coincide with the law so that statutes can be drafted that recognize acceptable extralegal proofs of ownership with the support of extralegal communities.
- Ensure that the draft legal norms that incorporate extralegal property do so without compromising the level of security that the existing legal order now provides property that is duly recorded and effectively controlled so as to obtain acquiescence of the legal sector.

C.5 Draft statutes and procedures that lower the costs of holding assets legally below the costs of holding them extra-legally.
- Enact the statutes required for all property in a country to be governed by one consistent body of law and set procedures.
- Broaden the definition of proofs of ownership to suit the new process, and consolidate into administratively manageable packages the statutes and procedures that will govern the capitalization process.
- Consolidate currently separate but related laws into a single law.
- Develop institutions and procedures that permit economies of scale for all the activities that constitute the process of capitalization.
- Create an expedient and low-cost alternative to squatting and other forms of extralegal appropriation.
- Consolidate the legal process and respect for law by establishing incentives and disincentives aimed at encouraging legal and discouraging extralegal conveyance.
- Design and implement administrative or private processes, to substitute judicial

$\longrightarrow$

Discovering these arrangements is nothing like searching for proofs of ownership in a formal legal system, where you can rely on a record-keeping system that over the years has created a paper trail, a "chain of title," that allows you to search for its origin. In developing nations, the chain of title is at best blurry to the outsider. The extralegal sector does not have, among other things, the centralized recording and tracking bureaucracy that is at the center of formal society. What people in the extralegal sector *do* have are strong, clear, and detailed understandings among themselves on the rules that establish who owns what. Even the dogs obey them.

Consequently, the only way to find the extralegal social contract on processes, where suitable, so as to encourage settlement of disputes within the law.

C.6 Create mechanisms that will reduce risks associated with private investment, including credibility of titles and non-payment for public services.

**D. Implementation**

D.1 Design and implant field operation strategy, procedures, personnel, equipment, offices, training and manuals that enable governments to recognize and process individual property rights in the extralegal sector.

- Design mechanisms to obtain the massive participation of the members of extralegal settlements for the purpose of reducing the costs of capitalization.

- Carry out training courses for the organization of capitalization brigades that reflect the type of extra legality they will encounter.

- Develop manuals that explain to the leaders and the people of extralegal settlements the ways in which they can participate in the selection and collection of proofs of ownership.

- Prepare for capitalizing extralegal communities:

i) Identify and train local promoters with each community.

ii) Implement a local promotional campaign within each community.

iii) Educate each community about the proofs of ownership required.

iv) Train local leaders to record ownership information on registration forms.

v) Identify and train private verifiers to certify information collected by the community.

Gather and process information on physical assets:

i) Obtain or prepare maps showing the bound-aries of individual parcels (where necessary, prepare digital base maps to record boundary information).

ii) Verify that maps showing individual parcels correspond to what is on the ground.

iii) Enter the maps into the computer system.

Gather and process ownership information:

i) Gather ownership information and record on registration forms.

ii) Verify that ownership rights are valid under the new law.

iii) Enter the ownership information into the computer system.

iv) Officially register the ownership rights.

v) Hand out certificates to the beneficiaries at a public ceremony.

D.2 Implement communications strategies using appropriate media to encourage participation of the extralegal sector, support in the business community and the government sector, and acquiescence among those with a vested interest in the status quo.

- Conduct a campaign for each particular type of community in the extralegal sector to encourage their participation in the process.

- Devise mechanisms that show beneficiaries of the capitalization process that their assets are protected by the same institutional framework that protects the rights of private investors, both domestic and foreign. This will give these owners a reason to respect contracts governed by the formal legal order.

- Conduct a campaign for each legal community that many feel vulnerable.

- Design the means of communicating to the legal sector the benefits of capitalization, emphasizing the reduction in risks and making it clear that capitalization will neither affect existing property rights nor compromise the rights of third parties.

property in a particular area is by contacting those who live and work by it. If property is like a tree, the formal property system is diachronic in the sense that it allows you to trace the origins of each leaf back in time, from twig and branch to the trunk and finally to the roots. The approach to extralegal property has to be synchronic: The only way an outsider can determine which rights belong to whom is by slicing the treetop at right angles to the trunk so as to define the status of each branch and leaf in relation to its neighbors.

Obtaining synchronic information takes fieldwork: going directly to those areas where property is not officially recorded (or is poorly recorded)

- Conduct a campaign for professionals with vested interests in property definition, explaining their future role and increased involvement with an expanded legal sector after capitalization.

D.3 Re-engineer the record-keeping organization and registration processes so that they can pull together all the economically useful descriptions about a country's extralegal assets and integrate them into one data/knowledge-based computer system.

- Structure the organization of the registry and its internal work flows, simplify the registration processes, establish specifications for automating information, design and implement a quality-control system, select and train personnel, and establish procedures to ensure that the registry can handle a massive national program of capitalization.
- Construct GIS-based systems to provide spatial analytical capabilities.
- Establish control mechanisms to guarantee that enrollment and registration services are sufficiently efficient and cost-effective that users will not be motivated to slip back into extralegality
- Insert descriptions of features of extralegal property holdings into customized, computer-friendly registration forms where they can be differentiated, recorded and managed in one computer environment.
- Break down the information that is traditionally contained in deeds into simple categories that can be entered into computer software and systematized for easy access, after having effected a legally approved streamlining of existing information gathering procedures.
- Facilitate the update of computerized property information by placing data input centers close to the beneficiaries. The purpose is to cut down on transportation and transaction costs of legally registering property and property-related business and keeping their status legal.

**E. Capital Formation and Good Governance**

E.1 Coordinate joint operations between real estate and business formalization

E.2 Create facilitative law for assisting capitalization with: burdening of ownership documents against credit, issuing of shares to obtain equity, accessing risk-reducing mechanisms, like insurance, refinement of limited liability institutions, procedures to enter into and enforce contracts, accessing entrepreneurial information.

E.3 Identify and reduce new obstacles that affect the poor. This includes arranging mechanisms to get rid of additional obstacles in coordination with other government agencies.

E.4 Cut costs and increase benefits of entering the formal sector on an ongoing basis.

E.5 Provide legal access to assets by building alternatives to squatting, illegal subdivisions, and extralegal enterprises

E.6 Create a communications strategy tailored to each segment of society.

E.7 Relate formalization to capital formation; identification systems; national security; collection systems for credit, raters and taxes; housing and infrastructure; insurance and other value-added information services.

E.8 Assess the impact on credit and investment for extralegals by reviewing the availability of specific services such as: personal banking (checking and saving accounts), credit and mortgage applications, issuance and registration of bonds and shares and security interest, merger and change of legal status, personal or business insurance, bankruptcy and mortgage foreclosure.

and getting in touch with local legal and extralegal authorities to find out the property arrangements. This is not as hard as it sounds. Although oral traditions may predominate in the rural backwoods of some countries, most people in the extralegal urban sector in developing countries have found ways to represent their property in written form according to rules that they respect and that government, at some level, is forced to accept.

In Haiti, for instance, no one believed we would find documents fixing representations of property rights. Haiti is one of the world's poorest countries, and 55 percent of the population is illiterate. Nevertheless, after an intensive survey of Haiti's urban areas, we did not find a single extralegal

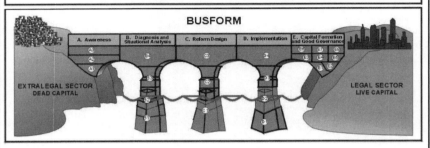

Figure 2

## FROM DEAD CAPITAL TO LIVE CAPITAL

**A. Awareness**

Raise awareness of:

A.1 Property law under capitalism.

A.2 The stake of the poor under capitalism.

A.3 The role of leadership in each country.

**B. Diagnosis and Situational Analysis**

B.1 Define and assess the impact of the extralegal business sector.

- Define the extralegal business sector and determine its magnitude.
- Identify the different kinds of extralegal business and their origins.
- Locate the geographic areas and sectors where extralegality is most active.
- Research the relevant links between government and extralegal businesses.
- Research the relevant links between legal and extralegal businesses.
- Identify processes where government has already dealt successfully with extralegal business.

B.2 Determine the costs of extralegality to the extralegal sector.

Examine the costs of extralegality by determining the degree to which extralegal businesses need to but cannot:

- Constitute a business organization capable of defining rules and responsibilities that are legally enforceable among associates and third parties; distributing risk, pooling capital and making otherwise impossible association viable through shares; bringing together the diverse resources required to address business opportunities; providing for succession; and defining the limits of financial risk and liability.
- Reduce risks by using legal institutions such as insurance, hedging and futures markets.
- Expand to achieve economies of scale, increase sales by using overt advertising, or

plot of land, shack, or building whose owner did not have at least one document to defend his right—even his "squatting rights." (For a selection of Haitian informal titles, see Figure 3.) Everywhere we have been in the world, most poor people living on the margins of the law have had some locally crafted or adapted physical artifact to represent and substantiate their claim to property. It is on the basis of these extralegal representations, as well as records and interviews, that we are everywhere able to build a concept of the social contract undergirding property.

Once we get our hands on extralegal representations, we have found the Ariadne's thread leading to the social contract on which one can build self-enforcing codes. Representations are the result of a specific group of people having reached a respected consensus as to who owns what property and what each owner may do with it.

invest significantly in capital goods (any of which would increase the risk of being detected by authorities).
- Access legal credit, which is much cheaper than extralegal credit.
- Protect against inflation and theft by reducing reliance on cash-based transactions.
- Use instruments of exchange such as bills of lading, warrants, letters of credit, etc.
- Export or import through legal ports of entry.
- Contract with public entities.
- Capture the value of reputation and other elements of goodwill.
- Be accountable and contract for infrastructure series (electricity, water, sewerage, telecommunications, etc.).

B.3 Determine the costs of extralegality to the state, society, and the business sector.
Examine the costs of extralegality by determining the degree to which government and society cannot:
- Increase the tax base and tax collection.
- Improve and expand access to publicly or privately supplied infrastructure services (electricity, water, sewerage, telecommunications, etc.).
- Increase opportunities for capital formation through securitization of assets.
- Improve access to information by the business community for investment decisions, marketing, etc.
-Increase the number of legal jobs (which enjoy social benefits).
- Increase the revenues of social programs (social security, pension funds, health care, housing funds, etc.) to improve or expand

their services and to contribute to the development of capital markets.
- Improve access to information required to set better economic and social policies.
- Protect third parties from extralegal liabilities by guaranteeing debentures with property.

B.4 Determine the costs of formalizing and staying in business.
Calculate the costs of formalizing different lines of business by establishing actual enterprises or analyzing case examples. This involves determining:
- Requirements for permits at all levels of government.
- Requirements for and the amount of payments for these permits.
- The number of forms and other documents required.
- Requirements that cannot be met in practice.
- All other transactions costs, including time delays.

**C. Reform Design**
C.1 Introduce institutional reform that enables massive business formalization and realizes the associated benefits.
- Prepare a draft law for business formalization so that: the costs of legality are obviously lower than those of extralegality, provisions are made to ensure that all of the benefits of legality are accessible, and all of the required government agencies and functions are in place to implement and administer formalization.
- Restructure the functions and procedures of government agencies to suit the needs of

→

Reading representations themselves and extracting meaning from them does not require a degree in archaeology. They contain no mysterious codes to be deciphered. People with very straightforward, businesslike intentions have written these documents to make absolutely clear to all concerned what rights they claim over the specific assets they control. They want to communicate the legitimacy of their rights and are prepared to provide as much supporting evidence as possible. Their representations have nothing to hide; they have been designed to be recognizable for what they are. This is regrettably not always so obvious because, when dealing with the poor, we tend to confuse the lack of a centralized record-keeping facility with ignorance.

When we obtain documentary evidence of representations, we can then "deconstruct" them to identify the principles and rules that constitute the social contract that sustains them. Once we have done that, we will have all formalization by: accepting applications at face value and introducing *ex-post* controls, reviewing all procedures to eliminate those that are unnecessary and to reduce the costs of those that are directly relevant, streamlining decision-making by delegating procedural authority to the front line while strengthening senior executive oversight and control, using public input and feedback to guide institutional reform and future adjustments.

- Introduce the laws and/or regulations that enable massive business formalization and allow benefits to government and society in general to be realized.
- Create an authority responsible for managing the entire formalization process.

C.2 Streamline public administration by adapting successful local and international practices.

- Eliminate regulatory requirements that are not directly relevant to creating a business.
- Eliminate requirements to comply with unnecessary, redundant, and costly red tape, which survives out of inertia because it generates additional fees and bribes.
- Simplify access to administrative services (avoid queues by using mail, phone, fax, etc.).
- Assign as much as possible of the administrative burden that is now borne by applicants to a streamlined public service.
- Perform legal certification *ex-post*.
- Where necessary, delegate responsibility for administrative work and legal authorizations, now generally assigned to an exceedingly small group of high-ranking executive officers, to a greater number of lower-ranking officers. In

this way, top managers are free to concentrate on planning, organizing, and facilitating the work of the offices under their administration, while more public servants will be authorized to attend to and resolve citizens' requests directly.

C.3 Modernize information systems and integrate exchange of information among relevant authorities

- Design computer systems adapted to the streamlined formalization process, and information networks linking the various public entities involved.
- Decentralize administrative procedure for formalization to the local level for more effective access, and integrate the resulting information into a national network.
- Achieve faster processing of documentation by optimizing public service standards.

**D. Implementation**

D.1 Implement systems to encourage public input and feedback, and integrate this information to improve the formalization process.

- Implement a system to obtain public input and feedback in person; through suggestion boxes; or by mail, phone, or fax.
- Involve the head of state or high-ranking political authorities in resolving complaints, either through public declarations or by directly calling attention to offenders.
- Define and implement a communications strategy for publicity and media involvement in explaining the advantages of business formalization and encouraging the public contribution of solutions.

the major relevant pieces of extralegal law. The next task is to codify them—organize them in temporary formal statutes so that they can be examined and compared with existing formal law. Encoding loose systems is also not a problem. In fact, it is not much different from government procedures to make legal texts uniform within countries (such as the U.S. Unified Commercial Code) or between countries at an international level (such as the many integrated mandatory codes produced by the European Union or the World Trade Organization).

By comparing the extralegal to the legal codes, government leaders can see how both have to be adjusted to fit each other and then build a regulatory framework for property—a common bedrock of law for all citizens—that is genuinely legitimate and self-enforceable because it reflects both legal and extralegal reality. That was basically how Western law was built: by

D.2 Implement more effective ex-*post* controls by government.
- Replace ex-*ante* controls that burden applicants with selective ex-*post* controls that reduce queues, time delays, paper work and corruption.
- Introduce legal sanctions for misrepresentation. Rigorously punish cases of fraud or false allegation, identified through sampling, with appropriate administrative, civil, and penal measures.
D.3 Accept applications from people seeking to formalize businesses at face value ex-*ante*.
- Issue immediate authorization to operate once applications are documented through affidavits containing all of the information necessary to exercise ex-*post* control.
D.4 Administer a program to ensure that the greatest benefits are achieved from formalization for both government and society.
- Administer ex-*post* controls.
- Implement an evolutionary program of product standards that encourages rather than discourages the transition from extralegality to legality.
- Enhance and accelerate the benefits of formalization to society by implementing services and programs that increase revenues, including those from taxation.
- Expand access to and the availability of infrastructure services.
- Increase access to credit and opportunities for capital formation through securitization.
- Reduce risks of doing business through insurance and other institutions.
- Provide business training and extension services to new legal entrepreneurs.

**E. Capital Formation and Good Governance**
E.1 Coordinate joint operations between real estate and business formalization.
E.2 Create facilitative law for assisting capitalization with burdening of ownership documents against credit, issuing of shares to obtain equity, accessing risk-reducing mechanisms like insurance, refinement of limited liability institutions, procedures to enter into and enforce contracts, accessing entrepreneurial information.
E.3 Identify and reduce new obstacles that affect the poor. This includes arranging mechanisms to get rid of additional obstacles in coordination with other government agencies.
E.4 Cut costs and increase benefits of entering the formal sector on an ongoing basis.
E.5 Provide legal access to assets by building alternatives to squatting, illegal subdivisions, and extralegal enterprises.
E.6 Create a communications strategy tailored to each segment of society.
E.7 Relate formalization to capital formation; identification systems; national security; collections systems for credit, raters, and taxes; housing and infrastructure; insurance and other value-added information services.
E.8 Assess the impact on credit and investment for extralegals by reviewing the availability of specific services such as personal banking (checking and saving accounts); credit and mortgage applications; issuance and registration of bonds and shares and security interests, merger and change of legal status; personal or business insurance; bankruptcy and mortgage foreclosure.

gradually discarding what was not useful and enforceable and absorbing what worked.

## Giving Governments the Tools for Reform

At the end of our work, we present the host government with a step-by-step program for reforming existing institutions that will allow it to integrate under one law all the economic stock and activities in the country. This will require replacing ineffective law and administrative practices with statutes and procedures that make assets fungible by attaching owners to assets, assets to addresses, ownership to legal accountability, and commitments to enforcement and by making all information and the history on assets and owners easily accessible. The goal is to create a formal property system that converts a previously anonymous and dispersed mass of owners

Figure 3

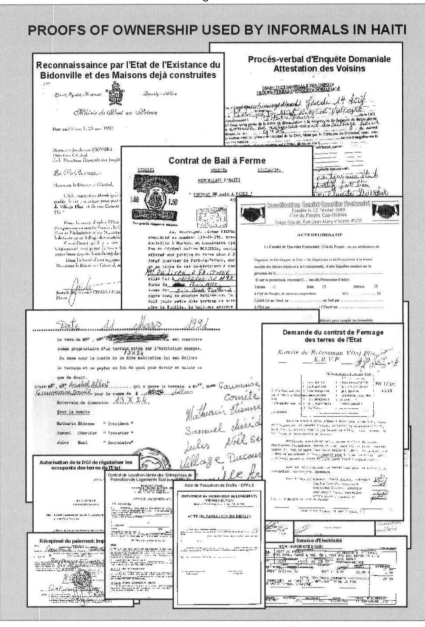

into an interconnected system of individually identifiable and accountable business interlocutors that are able to create capital.

This includes boiling down the reform program to a comprehensive vision and mission statement along with policy statements and publicity devices that allow politicians to motivate their constituencies toward reform. Such a communications program tailors the message to each constituency:

- The poor must be convinced that they will prosper more within a legal economy than outside it;
- Private businessmen and banks must see that integrating the extralegal economy means larger markets with goods and services;
- Politicians must be convinced that the government's tax base will be broadened so as to increase its revenues and reduce its reliance on foreign aid; and
- The whole nation must see that inclusion will decrease macroeconomic deficiencies and reduce the expansion of black markets, criminality, mafias, and drugs.

If all this sounds more like an anthropological adventure than the basis for legal reform and economic development, it is because knowledge about the poor has been monopolized by academics, journalists, and activists. These people are moved more by compassion or intellectual curiosity than by what it takes to create a suitable legal framework for economic reform.

If we push for reform, not in the name of an ideology, Western values, or the agendas of multinational firms and international financial institutions, but rather with the interests of the poor in mind, the transition to a market economy in whatever shape you want—"Third Way," "social market economics," or just plain "capitalist"—will become what it should always be: a truly humanistic cause and an important contribution to the war on poverty.

# Chapter 6

# Stable Money: A Critical Step on the Road to Economic Freedom and Prosperity

**Editor's Summary**

Purchasing power or value of money is extremely important to people. A stable currency, with low levels of inflation over long periods, simplifies choices and enables people to plan and anticipate outcomes regarding their investments and savings. Price stability provides an environment in which individuals can follow their natural incentives to generate the best resource allocation.

In contrast, inflation reflects lost economic freedom. It makes the world less certain, causes inefficiencies, and raises the cost of doing business. Higher costs slow growth. Inflation is a subtle way for governments to expropriate property and private resources. By generating inflation, the government erodes the value of income and property, thereby reducing the purchasing power of ordinary people.

Through inflation or a sudden devaluation of currency, governments can chisel away at the value of money. Either way, the purchasing power of assets denominated in money terms decreases significantly.

Price stability requires people to have confidence in a currency. Such confidence is often best achieved through a price rule, through which the value of money is maintained relative to the price of commodities continuously quoted in the marketplace. Only in this way can people know whether the government is maintaining its commitment and playing by the rules. A price rule, however, may have to wait for other government commitments such as eliminating excessive government spending.

# Stable Money: A Critical Step on the Road to Economic Freedom and Prosperity

*Marc A. Miles*

Iт is an empirical fact that countries with stable money (low rates of inflation) tend to grow faster than countries with high rates of inflation. For example, over the past half-century, growth in the United States has been lower when inflation has been higher. (See FIGURE 1.) Growth averaged 3.9 percent in years when inflation was less than 3 percent and only 2.7 percent when inflation exceeded 6 percent. A similar pattern is found in the European Union over the past decade. (See TABLE 1.) How is such stability achieved?

For at least 50 years, economists have debated whether the stable growth of money or the stable value of money is the most important target of government monetary policy. The answer for me was driven home from two questions I used to ask my university classes. The first was, "How many of you know how big the money supply of the United States is currently?" Invariably, there would be the wag at the back of the class who would respond, "Which definition?" I would offer to let them give me a number for any definition. Few, if any, hands were raised.

The second question was, "How many of you know how much gasoline (or milk, movie tickets, etc.) a dollar will buy today versus what it would have bought a year ago?" Nearly every hand in the class would be raised.

This small anecdote has a very powerful message. The same students probably had some idea of what the unemployment rate was because they would soon be looking for jobs, but they did not know what the money supply was because it essentially told them nothing. In contrast, the purchasing

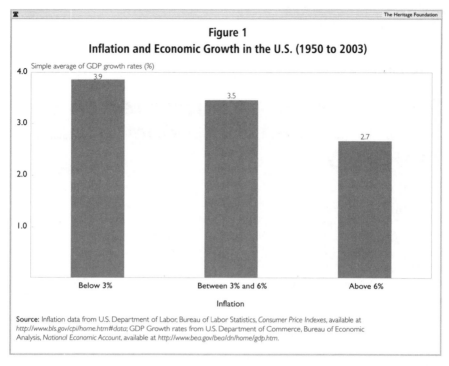

**Figure 1**
**Inflation and Economic Growth in the U.S. (1950 to 2003)**

The Heritage Foundation

Simple average of GDP growth rates (%)

Below 3%: 3.9
Between 3% and 6%: 3.5
Above 6%: 2.7

Inflation

**Source:** Inflation data from U.S. Department of Labor, Bureau of Labor Statistics, *Consumer Price Indexes*, available at http://www.bls.gov/cpi/home.htm#data; GDP Growth rates from U.S. Department of Commerce, Bureau of Economic Analysis, *National Economic Account*, available at http://www.bea.gov/bea/dn/home/gdp.htm.

power of money affected their daily lives. It affected their ability to make the right choices. The moral: It is the value of money, not the quantity, that people care about.

## Why Stable Money?

Stable money simplifies choices. Where prices are stable, the precise timing of purchasing or production decisions is not as important. Far less effort is diverted away from productive uses to trying merely to beat the next price rise. Since prices in the future will closely resemble those today, less effort is wasted exploring "what if" scenarios about possible losses of purchasing power. In other words, only price stability provides an environment in which individuals can follow their natural incentives to generate the best allocation of resources and products over time without distraction. Hence, only price stability allows economic freedom to act.

One of the main functions of money is as a unit of account, something to gauge the price of one thing relative to another. In other words, it is a source of information for deciding how to make the right choices. The more dependable that information, the better the chance we will make the right choice.

## Table 1
## Inflation and Economic Growth in the EU (1992 to 2002)

|  | Countries with a compound annual inflation rates below 3% | Countries with a Compound annual inflation rates above 3% |
|---|---|---|
| Average of Compound Annual Growth Rates (%) | 3.2 | 2.4 |

Source: International Monetary Fund, *World Economic Outlook Database*, September 2003

For example, when we walk into a shoe store, we ask for shoes in our individual size. How do we know what size that is? Presumably we have had our foot measured or have tried shoes of various sizes until we found the right fit. Once that is determined, we are confident that we can walk into most shoe stores and ask for the same size.

The reason is that shoe sizes are a unit of account. They provide us with information about the length and width of our feet relative to a standard. Since this unit of account does not vary from year to year, we spend very little time or energy thinking or worrying about what size to order. It is a reliable source of information for obtaining the most value and comfort for our money.

Suppose, however, that shoe sizes, instead of being stable, varied from year to year—or even worse, from month to month. Imagine the trauma for both shoe buyers and shoe sellers. Each month, a person wanting shoes would have to have his or her foot remeasured. Shoes marked as a certain size would also have to be dated. A shoe marked "10C" this month might be marked "11D" next month. How would we easily recognize the best value for our money? Suddenly, it takes more time and effort to find the right fit that we used to take for granted.

As bad as it would be for consumers, think of the poor shoe-store owners. With size indicators changing every month, imagine the difficulty store owners would encounter in trying to order shoes for the next season. Ordering would require forecasting what size system would be in effect on the day the order is shipped. The necessity of forecasting repeatedly (not to mention occasionally forecasting incorrectly) raises the cost of using the system.

Obviously, as reliability declines, the value of this unit of account starts to decline. At some point, people will stop using the unit entirely ("I'll just keep trying them on until one pair fits," or even "I'll go barefoot"), either developing their own systems or maybe using a more stable foreign system. As the shoe industry experienced a period of turmoil, uncertainty, and slow growth, it would quickly fall on hard times.

In the same way, money prices are a signal for deciding how to get the most value out of what purchasing power we have. Given prices, we compare how much apples, oranges, shoes, cars, and all other products cost us. Next, we compare the relative values of each of these products to us. Presumably, we purchase products until the next dollar (or whatever currency unit of account) spent on a product gives us the same satisfaction or pleasure as a dollar spent on any other one; and unless our needs or feelings about what is satisfying change, we will go on buying the same amount of everything each year.

That is where an unstable currency begins to tip over the horse cart. Unstable currency creates uncertainty, which causes spending patterns to change even where feelings about what satisfies do not. Now a new element enters the spending equation: i.e., when to buy. Some in the United States may remember the old Fram Oil Filter advertisement. An apparent auto mechanic has a Fram Oil Filter in one hand and an engine replacement part in the other. His message: "You can pay me now (for a good oil filter) or you can pay me later (rebuilding your engine)." The choice seems obvious: A series of cheap oil filters is less expensive than eventually rebuilding the engine.

However, with unstable money that choice is no longer obvious. Buying habits change, and resources become allocated in ways that may not be best for the economy as a whole. Fearing inflation, an individual may want to stock up on filters now rather than buying them over time. The result: Money that might go into savings, and thereby into investment through a financial intermediary like a bank or insurance company, is allocated to a shelf full of oil filters.

Conversely, fearing deflation, an individual may decide to forgo the better oil filters, thinking that by the time he has to replace his engine, the cost will have fallen significantly. The result in this case: Rather than maintaining his existing capital investment (his car), the individual lets it depreciate and deteriorate. Ill-performing cars are certainly not in the best interests of the country. Uncertainty has distorted spending habits, causing money to be allocated inefficiently from the economy's perspective.

Imagine, however, a world where money is truly unstable. What is a person to do? Truly unstable money may oscillate in either direction. In this case, the best expenditure decision is not clear even from the individual's perspective. Stock up on oil filters? What if the value of the currency were to appreciate, meaning that the same filters could be bought for less? Allow the engine to deteriorate as prices fall? What if prices take a U-turn into inflation and engine replacement becomes more expensive than ever imagined? Clearly, the more unstable or volatile the currency, the more expenditure decisions are distorted.

Prices are a source of information. Think of them as a "conductor" of an economic symphony, co-coordinating simultaneously the actions of many different parts of the economy. If the different musicians or parts of the economy have to guess what the next note will be, the result will be a mind-numbing cacophony of notes. However, if that conductor transmits to all exactly what note to expect next, the economy can make beautiful music.

## More Problems

The fact that prices may be significantly higher or lower in the future distorts expenditure decisions. If they anticipate higher future prices, individuals will buy faster or sooner before prices go up. If they expect lower prices, they will put off buying or maintaining.

However, the problems do not stop there. Unstable money produces further complications. The rate of price changes also affects interest rates and may affect the incentive to maintain capital due to other distortions in the economy such as poorly conceived tax provisions.

If you are willing to lend a friend money, you probably hope that in the end, you will get back the amount you lent plus some interest. How much interest? In the absence of inflation, you would want the equivalent of what you could earn on an alternative investment. After all, if you had not given your friend the money, you could have put it in the bank or invested in the stock market, bonds, or some other investment vehicle. For simplicity, assume that you could have earned a return $r$ in any of these alternatives.

With prices fluctuating, however, the computation changes. If inflation rules and prices are going up, the quantity of products a dollar can buy diminishes with time. Hence, the value or purchasing power of the dollars you eventually get back from your friend will be less than the value when the money was lent. There is a down-side risk that you will want to avoid. The way most avoid this risk is to demand that the borrower pay that expected loss of purchasing power in addition to the alternative return $r$.

Economist Irving Fisher first pointed out this fundamental relationship a century ago.[1] He summarized this relationship as:

$$i = r + \pi^e$$

where

$i$ is the nominal rate of interest,
$r$ is the return on alternative investments, and
$\pi^e$ is the expected rate of inflation.

Hence, the cost of borrowing goes up with inflation, but so does the cost of lending. Notice from the above equation that the interest rate charged will be based on the inflation rate that is expected to occur over the length of the loan. But predictions are not perfect. Underestimate inflation, and the interest rate will fail to cover the total drop in purchasing power due to the inflation. The borrower faces the same kind of problem, but just the reverse. He will benefit from underestimated inflation and lose if inflation has been overestimated.

Thus, at the very least, there is increased risk to both borrowers and lenders. Risk reflects an increased cost because the only way to eliminate the risk is to buy insurance in the form of a derivative like a futures contract. The details of such a contract are not important for the point being made. What is important is the added cost associated with the purchase of a futures or insurance contract, for anything that raises the cost of doing business reduces the amount of business conducted.

In other words, inflation drives a wedge between what borrowers pay and lenders receive. Because of the added risk, borrowers will pay a bit more than the expected inflation and lenders will receive a bit less. The higher cost of borrowing reduces the amount of borrowing that will occur.

---

1. Irving Fisher, *The Theory of Interest* (New York: Macmillan Co., 1930).

Likewise, the reduced rewards from lending reduce the amount of lending. Both supply and demand are reduced, which translates into less loan activity than if inflation had not occurred. If the swapping of resources in the economy had been efficient before, it is less than efficient now. In fact, the incentives are now to shift toward investing directly in real assets that are inflation-proof, which in turn would drive down the alternative return $r$.

## Inflation: The More Familiar Case

While unstable money can be associated with both rising and falling prices, the more common occurrence is inflation. Many a country has found its road to prosperity steepened or sidetracked by the effects of inflation.

Inflation reflects directly a loss of economic freedom, for it is a subtle, almost hidden expropriation of private resources by the public issuer of money. If a dollar issued one year buys four oranges, but then buys only three in the next year (the price of oranges and other products having risen by 25 percent), then the fourth orange is effectively a measure of the expropriation by government. People in the private sector find their choices associated with each dollar diminished. Moreover, they are simply worse off economically because their prosperity is diminished. Each dollar of income or wealth they have buys fewer and fewer oranges. This simple example illustrates precisely the link between a diminution of economic freedom and a diminution of prosperity.

But it gets worse. Inflation both distorts the cost of capital and shifts the employment of labor relative to capital away from optimal amounts. Rising interest rates certainly increase the cost of capital, but several other factors can shift incentives away from employing machines. Where corporate tax laws base depreciation of capital on purchase price instead of replacement cost, the impact of inflation is magnified. Owners of machines, buildings, vehicles, etc., are suddenly faced with a shrinking value of what they can subtract before taxes as the real value of what that capital cost them. The value of their investment declines.

For example, suppose you bought a delivery truck for your business and paid $30,000. Suppose further that the tax laws allow you to depreciate the truck by equal amounts over five years. If the tax laws do not take inflation into account, you may expense $6,000 per year, regardless of whether there is inflation.

With no inflation, no problem exists. The $6,000 per year remains one-fifth the cost of the truck. However, suppose inflation were 10 percent. In the second year, it would cost $33,000 to replace the truck. In the third year, it would be $36,300, and so forth. Therefore, to account fully for the depreciation in reduced purchasing power dollars, depreciation should be $6,600 in the second year, $7,260 in the third year, etc. By restricting the businessperson to subtracting only $6,000 per year, the tax law forces *underdepreciation* of the asset. The bottom line: Less than the real cost of buying the truck can be subtracted before taxes, and the cost of owning depreciable capital rises.

Inflation does not have the same effect on the services of workers.[2] Each year, the businessperson purchases these services at the prevailing price. That cost of labor can be subtracted directly from revenues before paying taxes. And since the yearly cost of labor services will rise with inflation (assuming no distortions like wage controls), labor costs, unlike the cost of capital, will be properly accounted for.

The reason for the discrepancy between accounting for capital costs and accounting for labor costs is that in economic terms, labor is a *flow* while capital is a *stock* of services. Labor services are purchased one year at a time, but the present and future annual services of capital are embodied in the price of a machine. Since the future services of the machine are capitalized in its price, a higher interest rate (the rate at which future services are discounted) has a negative effect on the value of those future services. To keep the value of future services of machines constant, more machines must be purchased. The cost of capital rises. Annual labor services are unaffected by higher rates.

Thus, with inflation, the price of capital relative to labor rises. Business owners, seeking to keep down costs, will therefore shift away from machines and toward labor. In other words, the ratio of capital to labor, or the capital intensity in the production process, will decline. Country-wide, payrolls will start ballooning and investment in capital will contract. Companies that are highly capital intensive, and those with the longest-lived capital, will feel the rise in the relative price of capital the most. Sales and output of those companies are likely to shrink the most.

As a result, businesspeople become more short-sighted. With higher interest rates and worsening underdepreciation of assets, there is pressure to

---

2. Not that inflation will not have an effect on the workers themselves. For example, where progressive tax rates are set in nominal dollars and not indexed to inflation, "bracket creep" sets in. As wages rise with inflation, break points for higher tax brackets occur at lower and lower real incomes. Hence, workers get pushed into higher marginal tax brackets and pay more of their pre-tax purchasing power in taxes.

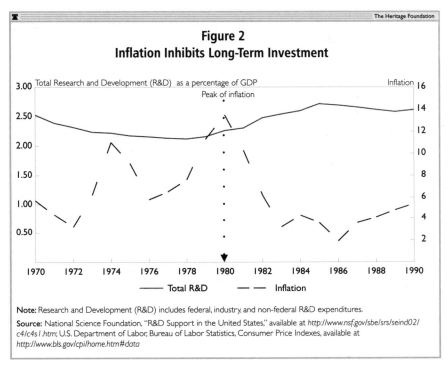

**Figure 2**
**Inflation Inhibits Long-Term Investment**

Total Research and Development (R&D) as a percentage of GDP — Inflation

Peak of inflation

Total R&D — — — Inflation

**Note:** Research and Development (R&D) includes federal, industry, and non-federal R&D expenditures.
**Source:** National Science Foundation, "R&D Support in the United States," available at *http://www.nsf.gov/sbe/srs/seind02/ c4/c4s1.htm*; U.S. Department of Labor, Bureau of Labor Statistics, Consumer Price Indexes, available at *http://www.bls.gov/cpi/home.htm#data*

turn a faster profit on an investment. Only those investments that promise a "fast buck" become attractive. Thus, one likely casualty of the higher infla-tion is research and development (R&D). Since there is often a long lead time between research and development and actual production and sales, companies become less inclined to head down that path. The rate of tech-nical innovation suffers along with the sale of machines. Again, gains in prosperity are retarded.

An excellent example of this phenomenon is the United States in the 1970s. As inflation began to accelerate in the United States (and much of the world for that matter) in the early 1970s, production in relatively capi-tal-intensive industries, particularly those with long-lived capital such as steel or automobiles, contracted. Investment was diverted from R&D, and overall investment contracted. (See FIGURE 2.) This pattern continued until inflation peaked in 1980–1981. Payrolls, on the other hand, ballooned. Not surprisingly, as incentives shifted toward less-efficient use of resources, this shock to the prevailing order disrupted the economy and growth rates trended downward. For example, the eight years of rising inflation during the 1970s were associated with low growth. (See FIGURE 3.)

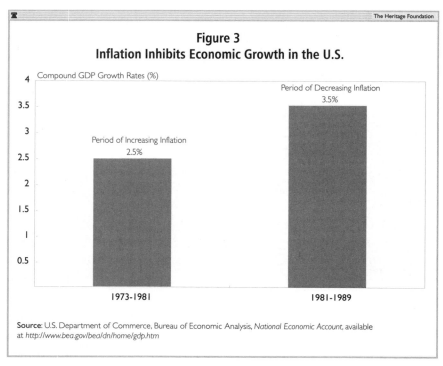

**Figure 3**
**Inflation Inhibits Economic Growth in the U.S.**

Compound GDP Growth Rates (%)

Period of Decreasing Inflation
3.5%

Period of Increasing Inflation
2.5%

1973-1981            1981-1989

Source: U.S. Department of Commerce, Bureau of Economic Analysis, *National Economic Account*, available at *http://www.bea.gov/bea/dn/home/gdp.htm*

In contrast, as inflation receded from the early 1980s, businesses could return to more efficient uses of machines and workers, and growth rates increased, payrolls declined, investment increased, research and development took off, and prosperity returned. FIGURE 3 shows that the average annual growth rate in the 1980s was a full percentage point higher than the earlier period. FIGURE 2 illustrates that during the same period, research and development as a percentage of GDP once again began to rise. It should come as no surprise, therefore, that this period coincided with the explosion of personal computers, the Internet, and technology in general.

## Devaluation: An Insidious Form of Unstable Money

There are a number of myths in economics. One of the most often repeated, and most harmful, is that destabilizing a currency through devaluation or depreciation can benefit a country. The potential downside from such a policy action should be obvious if one thinks about what exchange rates are. An exchange rate is simply the value of the yardstick or *numeraire* used for measuring prices in one country relative to the yardstick used for measuring prices in a second.

For example, when the euro is said to be worth 1.20 dollars, all that means is that trading a yardstick called the "euro" will result in being handed 1.20 yardsticks called the "dollar." While that might mean that four oranges that cost a euro yardstick might cost 1.20 dollar yardsticks, it does not tell us anything about the relative price of apples and oranges, or even bananas and oranges. Think of an exchange rate, therefore, as the relative length of yardsticks.

A devaluation or depreciation of the dollar means a shortening in the relative length of the U.S. yardstick. It is as though the government has "shaved off" part of the yardstick for its own purposes. Hence, the decline reflects not so much a policy tool as a reneging on a commitment. It implies that, rather than maintaining the stability (length) of money in terms of other *numeraires* or yardsticks, the central bank (or Treasury in the case of the United States) has chosen to undercut the value. In turn, the credibility of and faith in the central bank falls, as does the confidence in the currency. Risk rises. Those who can choose between how much of this currency versus other currencies they can hold in money portfolios react. Fearing that the word of the offending central bank will be less dependable in the future, these holders of diversified currency portfolios around the world shift their preferences away from the shortened currency to others, potentially exacerbating the decline in the currency's value.

This switching among currencies, known as currency substitution,[3] emphasizes the speed with which a money market can be disrupted. In this sense, we could describe devaluation as a currency-switching policy that reduces the role and usefulness of domestic currencies in portfolios throughout the world. Developing countries, where the tie to the domestic currency is probably most fragile because of readily available alternatives, are precisely those that are most susceptible to these effects and therefore should never devalue. The currency-switching effect magnifies the other evils of devaluation.

**What Devaluations Cannot Do.** Because the nature of devaluations or depreciations is misunderstood, so too are the effects. Devaluation is not a policy for achieving a more stable real sector of the economy. Devaluation is not a policy for correcting trade imbalances. Devaluation is not a growth-inducing

---

3. See, for example, Marc A. Miles, "Currency Substitution, Flexible Exchange Rates, and Monetary Independence," *American Economic Review*, Vol. 68, No. 3 (June 1978), pp. 428–436.

policy. Devaluation is therefore not a catalyst or stimulant for developing countries. The benefits are small, if any, and the costs are potentially enormous.

Often, the word "devaluation" is heard in the same breath as the phrase "trade balance." Radio, TV, and newspaper journalists repeatedly assert that there is a link. Experts make prognostications or policy based on it. Ph.D. candidates continue to write dissertations associating the two phenomena. This impression persists despite tenuous theoretical and empirical evidence.[4]

The problem stems from the fact that changes in exchange rates (a monetary phenomenon involving two *numeraires*) are often confused with changes in the terms of trade (the relative price of physical products). Yet shortening the yardstick or *numeraire* should affect only nominal variables like prices. If the value or length of the dollar is cut in half, prices of all products denominated in the dollar *numeraire* should double to maintain the purchasing power price.

For example, if you and two people are content to trade two apples for each orange, at this level they are unconcerned whether the orange costs fifty cents, a dollar, two dollars, or 20 dollars. They are concerned that, whatever the price, they get two apples for the orange; so if the dollar is shortened, they expect the price of both apples and oranges to rise by the same percentage in terms of that *numeraire*. As long as that price between the products (the terms of trade) remains true, the quantities they are willing to exchange remain stable. No change in the demand or supply of apples and oranges should occur.

The confusion of the nominal values with the terms of trade is just another relic of economics. The early Keynesian models of economies did not have formal discussions of monetary policy or price levels.[5] Monetary policy was assumed to be whatever was necessary to maintain a constant price level. In other words, monetary policy was passive and the nominal sector was irrelevant. The only parts of the economy that were considered were production and demand for products.

Another way of saying this is that these Keynesian constructs of the economy were essentially barter models. A barter model has no money

4. See, for example, Marc A. Miles, "The Effects of Devaluation on the Trade Balance and the Balance of Payments," *Journal of Political Economy*, Vol. 87, No. 3 (1979), pp. 600–620.

5. See, for example, Joan Robinson, "The Foreign Exchanges," *Essays on the Theory of Employment* (Oxford: Blackwell, 1947), reprinted in H. S. Ellis and L. Metzler, eds., *Readings in the Theory of International Trade* (Philadelphia: Blakiston, 1948).

(*numeraire*), and hence can have no explicit exchange rate (relative value of *numeraires*). The only "prices" are the relative price of products or the terms of trade. Therefore, when these models refer to an exchange rate change, they are really referring to a change in the terms of trade. As discussed above, changing the terms of trade is not the same as, and provides no insight into, the impact of an exchange rate adjustment, and vice versa. Hence, even if changing terms of trade provided information about changes in trade flows, devaluation or depreciation would not.

The misperception that declining currencies generate increased output or production in an economy is also a relic of the 20th century Keynesian barter models. If declining exchange rates really were the same as declining terms of trade, excess demands for the relatively cheaper good would appear, and this in turn would lead to more production of that good until relative prices readjusted. Again, this is quite different from a currency falling in value.[6]

**What Devaluation Can Do.** Not that devaluation is without direct effect. The primary impact is a higher relative rate of inflation. Shortening the value of the *numeraire* or yardstick means that more yardsticks are needed to purchase the same products. Hence, prices measured in the devalued *numeraire* should rise relative to those in the other *numeraire* by the percentage decline in exchange rates.

For a small country, which is unlikely to have much influence over price levels elsewhere in the world, this usually means that its inflation rate jumps by the rate of depreciation. The reason: Arbitrage will ensure that the price of oranges in one currency (assuming no barriers to trade) is the same as the equivalent cost of oranges in another currency. In simple math:

$$P_A = P_{B^*} (\$_A/\$_B)$$

where

$P_A$ is the price of oranges in country A,
$P_B$ is the price of oranges in country B, and
$\$_A /\$_B$ is the number of pieces of country A's currency that are received for one piece of country B's currency.

---

6. It also ignores the fact that there will be excess supplies and falling output of the good whose relative price has risen. Thus, even this argument that total production rises has serious shortcomings.

The above equation refers to price levels, but we want to know what happens when exchange rates *change*. In percentage change terms, this same equation would become:

$$\%\Delta P_A = \%\Delta P_B + \%\Delta(\$_A / \$_B)$$

With stable exchange rates ($\%\Delta\$_A/\$_B = 0$), the price of oranges should rise at the same rate in the two countries; but if the currency of Country A is devalued, rates of price change (inflation) diverge. If Country A is small, it will have little influence on the price of oranges in Country B, and orange prices in A will rise by an additional amount equal to the percentage of devaluation.

Evidence of this relative rise in prices appears immediately for items that are traded in well-established markets like commodities. For items whose prices appear only in government indices, it may take considerably longer. The delay, however, reflects less the stickiness of prices than the way prices are measured. While list prices might be unchanged, the market transaction price may fluctuate freely through arrangements like quantity discounts or the terms of payment. Alternatively, apparent price discrepancies can occur as a result of infrequent sampling or different methods of collecting or weighting government statistics.

However, the amount charged is only one aspect of the total price of a good. Non-price changes help clear markets as well. Changes in length of delivery schedule, quantity of product, or quality of product affect the total price but may not be captured in the measured index.[7]

The impact of this inflation is to destabilize and depress output. The role of inflation as a tax has already been discussed. In addition, where indexation is less than perfect, inflation raises tax rates through "bracket

---

7. Those interested in the economic debate about how closely prices move across countries are referred to Donald McCloskey and J. Richard Zecher, "The Success of Purchasing Power Parity," in Michael D. Bordo and Anna J. Schwartz, eds., *A Retrospective on the Classical Gold Standard 1821–1931* (Chicago: University of Chicago Press for the National Bureau of Economic Research, 1984). One of the authors' major points is that "success" does not necessarily mean perfect price parity across countries. In their opinion, the problem is the absence of intellectually sensible standards for measuring success. They propose such standards and conclude (p. 147) that "Purchasing power parity is not a failure. On the contrary, by the standards we have examined, it is a great success."

creep" (nominal wages rise with inflation, pushing people into higher "progressive" tax rates); by creating (and taxing) illusory profits on existing inventories whose value rises with inflation; and by undercounting the true depreciation costs. These higher tax rates create incentives to divert more resources out of the marketplace where it will be taxed and into the informal market beyond the eye of the tax man. In other words, devaluation is likely to shrink the country's tax base.

The shift into the informal market also illustrates how corruption increases the size of the informal market. By reneging on a promise to maintain the value of the currency and "shaving off" a piece of the yardstick, the government puts into motion forces that shift incentives toward getting out of the marketplace.

## How to Accomplish Price Stability

Price stability aligns the expectations of people in the economy and lets them work more efficiently toward their economic potential. Price instability disrupts the system by raising costs of doing business and (especially for inflation that expropriates resources) reduces economic freedom. Incentives are distorted and output is reduced. Policies that undermine the stability of money, such as devaluation and depreciation, serve only to enhance these insidious effects.

Pointing out the benefits of price stability is the easy part. Explaining precisely how to obtain stability is much more difficult. Economists have focused on this issue for at least the past 40 years and have presented an array of answers ranging from wage and price controls to reducing budget deficits, restraining the supply of money, and returning to a gold standard. This array of answers indicates that searching for the key to price stability is a bit like searching for the cure for the common cold. One sees a tremendous assortment of cold remedies on the drug store shelf. If any one of these remedies were *the* answer, working most of the time, it would soon dominate the market. That *caveat* in mind, let us now explore some tangible approaches to price stability.

**Price Stability as a "Confidence Game."** Price stability is a "confidence game," but in the good sense. Money is stable when people have confidence that the government that issues it will be able and willing to stand behind the value of the currency. The superficial answer about how to create and send this confidence signal is to be strong: strong in terms of the economy, strong in terms of property rights, strong in terms of allowing people to attain their potential. That is why economic freedom and price stability is a two-way street. Price stability is one part of the integrated car of economic freedom discussed in the introductory chapter of this book. Price stability adds to economic freedom, but an economically free country will tend to have a more stable currency.

How does a government transmit to residents and the rest of the world its intention—or, even better, its commitment—to have stable money? The most direct way is through a *price rule*. Going back to the example from the very beginning of this chapter, a price rule is essentially a way for the government to inform the students in class that the price of gasoline or clothing a year from now will be roughly the same as it is today. Such confidence in the stability of their stash of money makes it much easier to make plans and decide when best to work, purchase, invest, etc.

A price rule works because the country's government defines and maintains the country's basic monetary yardstick or unit of account in terms of something observable. In the case of the United States, the unit of account would be the dollar. The Treasury would tell the market that these dollar liability units would always be redeemable at a certain price in terms of the observable item. The promise gives the basic dollar unit a specific value. Even better, it also gives it to all the forms of money that are convertible into the basic unit. Bank accounts, Eurodollar accounts, and money market mutual funds, for example, may not be controlled directly by the Federal Reserve or the Treasury, but as long as the issuers of these monies define and redeem these accounts in dollars, the United States is stabilizing the *value* of these forms of monies too.

For example, under the Bretton Woods system that lasted from 1946 until the early 1970s, the U.S. Treasury fixed the value of the dollar to gold at $35 per ounce. Other currencies in turn were fixed in value to the dollar by the central banks throughout the world. The dollar's value was maintained because, at least in theory, if a foreign central bank presented a bundle of dollars to the Treasury, those dollars would be redeemed for the equivalent amount of gold. Alternatively, if a foreign central bank handed the Treasury gold, it would receive the equivalent amount of dollars in return.

The dollars that the foreign central bank had would be used in turn to peg its country's currency to the dollar. If a Frenchman presented francs to the Bank of France, he could receive the equivalent amount of dollars. Or if he presented dollars, he could receive a sum of francs corresponding to the pegged price of francs in terms of dollars. When the United States fixed the value of the dollar in terms of gold purchasing power, it was therefore simultaneously and indirectly stabilizing the purchasing power of bank accounts denominated in dollars, francs, pounds sterling, etc.

The Bretton Woods system disappeared over 30 years ago. Today, a dollar price rule would involve only pegging the price of the dollar to the value of gold or some other commodity. A direct benefit of such a price rule is that the Federal Reserve no longer has to worry about which monies it can or cannot control. Its only concerns would be the value of money it issues directly; standing ready to define it (redeem or supply it on demand in terms of the observable item); and consequently helping to bring stability even to the monies beyond its direct grasp.

The direct advantage to the private sector is that this price rule policy eliminates most of the guesswork. People throughout the country know whether the government is "playing by the rules." This information is transmitted directly through the marketplace, which reflects the stability of the financial quotations of the price of gold or whatever commodity was targeted.

Because both the government and the private sector can see these financial quotations, they have the same information and can react to each other's actions. The government knows precisely when to redeem or supply more money, and by how much. Simply put, any tendency for the target value of the commodity to move beyond its narrow price band requires the government to step into the market. The government must remain in the market as long as the price remains outside that band. No elaborate information gathering or ad hoc policy planning is required.

The private sector also knows what to expect. This side of the market is interested in the government's continuing to play by the rules. The private market has only to check the targeted value. If, say, spot silver prices are targeted, is the dollar price of silver stable? If the price does move beyond the target range, does it start moving back? If so, the government is doing its job. The public simply watches the commodity ticker tape (more likely their computers) for the latest quotes.

**Price Stability in a Large Country.** The ultimate goal of price stability is to stabilize a family's grocery bill from week to week, or to assure the family that is saving for a new washing machine or automobile that it can replace it at a price similar to what it paid for the last one. Most can agree easily on these goals, but how is one to accomplish them?

From the preceding discussion, we know the answer lies in a price rule: i.e., targeting market prices that are continuously quoted in the marketplace. Only by this means will the government know when and how much to intervene, and the public whether the government is playing by the rules. But, someone may say, there are many prices in an economy. Which one (or ones) should be targeted?

Should the exchange rate be pegged? Not for a large country. Such a peg simply ties the dollar yardstick either to one foreign yardstick or to a basket (weighted average) of foreign yardsticks. As the foreign yardstick lengthens, so must the dollar one. If the foreign yardstick shrinks (raising inflation), however, the dollar is again tied to the same fate. In other words, the fixed exchange rate is good for stabilizing *relative* purchasing power and inflation across countries. By itself, however, it does little—if anything—to stabilize the absolute domestic price level.

Historically, large countries have pegged their price levels to a commodity. Price rules have usually involved targeting the dollar or other large currencies directly or indirectly to a metallic standard such as gold or silver. By making the dollar continually worth, say, $35 per ounce of gold, the purchasing power is defined and the price level stabilized. This approach has produced stability in the grocery bills of the Smiths on Main Street for extended periods.[8] Because financial markets today provide more options, more modern approaches might be more complex, involving targeting a basket of commodities or an elaborate financial futures contract.

Pegging the price level to a commodity, however, is only a start. Elsewhere, I have suggested that one such price alone is not actually enough to produce complete price stability.[9] The problem is that a spot price rule stabilizes only prices today, while average families are also interested in prices in the future. Complete price stability therefore requires intervention in both the spot and futures markets of the targeted commodity. An alternative is to stabilize both prices in the spot market and interest rates in

---

8. Of course, if the value of gold changes relative to other commodities and goods, then inflation or deflation can occur.

9. Marc A. Miles, *Beyond Monetarism* (New York: Basic Books, 1984), particularly Chapters 9 and 10.

financial markets. Earlier, it was pointed out that interest rates reflect the return on alternative assets plus expected inflation. Stabilizing interest rates therefore stabilizes inflationary expectations. Stabilizing the rate at which prices will rise in the future, along with stabilizing the spot commodity market, implicitly stabilizes the future commodity market as well.

The important point here, however, is that regardless of which method of price stabilization a large country chooses, stable money in a large country serves as a potential price level anchor to the rest of the world.[10]

**Price Stability in Small Countries.** Development issues usually involve small countries, not large ones. The important difference between the two is that a small country has little or no influence over prices in the world market, so targeting commodities in global markets with the goal of stabilizing domestic prices is an exercise in futility. A small country must look elsewhere for stability; its best alternative is to hitch its currency to money from a large country that is likely to serve as a price anchor to the rest of the world.

One possibility is for the small country to enter into an "optimal currency area." Under this approach, the small country gives up its right to print its own unique currency in favor of making the large country's currency the coin of the realm. In this case, the currency of the large country *becomes* the currency of the small country, so inflation rates in the two countries are identical.[11]

In a sense, the 50 states or 12 Federal Reserve districts of the United States form an optimal currency area. Dollars issued by each Federal Reserve district are slightly different, but few check their dollar notes to see whether they contain the seal of the Federal Reserve Bank of Dallas, of Cleveland, or of Richmond, Virginia. Regardless of which bank issued them, these various dollar notes are just accepted at par. Panama and Ecuador are two other examples. Their currencies *are* the U.S. dollar.

---

10. This statement, of course, assumes that the country is simultaneously also following other steps along the road to prosperity such as reining in government deficits. The perils of failing to commit to all the steps are discussed below with respect to Argentina.

11. See Robert A. Mundell, "A Theory of Optimum Currency Areas," *American Economic Review*, Vol. 58 (September 1961), pp. 657–665. Differences in how data for the price indices in the large and small countries are collected or weighted may produce slight differences in the reported inflation rates. But the price of oranges in both countries should be moving almost identically.

Similarly, the Irish pound and the Scottish pound used to trade more or less on par with the British pound and were interchangeable most places in the United Kingdom.

In the 1970s and 1980s, the smaller countries of Europe tried to tackle inflation by implicitly tying their currency values to the deutschemark, which had been stable in purchasing power. More recently, this concept has been replaced in Europe by the euro, which is also an optimal currency area. Instead of attempting to achieve price stability on their own, the smaller countries of Europe have adopted a common currency that they hope will keep grocery bills from fluctuating significantly from week to week. This also has the positive effect of reducing transactions costs and currency uncertainty as people travel among European countries. The downside, of course, is that they have to give up economic freedom in terms of regulation, taxes, and government consumption in order to be part of this currency system. Such loss of economic freedom diverts them from the road to prosperity.

There are alternatives to optimal currency areas. One that has received attention in recent years is the concept of a "currency board." In this approach, a country still maintains its unique domestic currency, at least in terms of what circulates for money, but the issuance of this domestic money is strictly limited by the amount of foreign reserves held by the government. The reason for the limitation is that the government promises to freely convert domestic money into the foreign money on demand. That promise can be kept only if there are reserves to back each unit of domestic money printed.

The experience of Argentina at the end of the last century is held up as an example of why currency boards are prone to failure. Closer examination, however, reveals that the problem lay not uniquely in the currency board, but in Argentina's failure to follow simultaneously the other parts of the road to prosperity that are prerequisites for successfully maintaining this approach to price stability. Argentina is therefore both an example of the potential benefits of a price rule such as a currency board *and* an example of how horrible the consequences of imposing a price rule can be if a country does not simultaneously adhere to the "10-Step Road Map."

Argentina had a desperate reason for initially adopting the currency board. By March 1990, peso inflation had reached a year-to-year rate of over 20,000 percent, which, as expected from the earlier discussion, was wreaking havoc on the economy. The currency board was a bold attempt to put an end to the damaging inflation.

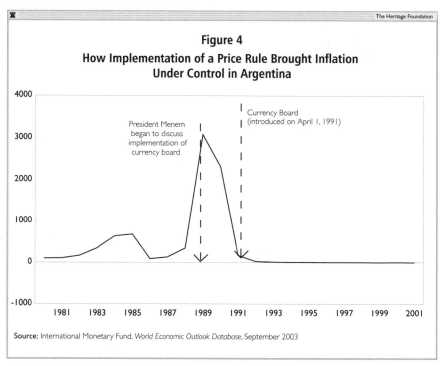

**Figure 4**
**How Implementation of a Price Rule Brought Inflation Under Control in Argentina**

Source: International Monetary Fund, *World Economic Outlook Database*, September 2003

As FIGURE 4 shows, the currency board approach initially met with extreme success. After taking office in mid-1989, President Carlos Menem began to discuss market-oriented policies, including currency convertibility. As those policy discussions turned more into actual policy, inflation expectations began to decline. Domestic inflation peaked in March 1990. The monthly rate of over 90 percent inflation in March plunged to 11 percent the next month. By the end of 1990, monthly inflation was below 5 percent. By the end of 1991, it was below 1 percent.

Simultaneously, the Argentine economy began to flourish. (See TABLE 2.) While Argentina had had negative growth during the high-inflation years, its growth rate turned decidedly positive under the currency board. For a time, it appeared that Argentina would be one of the showcases in economic development.

However, all was not well in the Argentine plan. Argentina was in effect picking only a few mileposts on the road to prosperity, hoping they alone would be enough. Certain mileposts were ignored completely. Among these were constraint in government consumption and the change in government expenditure. Specifically, the Argentine government found it politically

| | 1980-1990 (pre-currency board) | 1991-2001 (currency board) | 2002 (post currency board) |
|---|---|---|---|
| **Table 2** | | | |
| **Inflation and Economic Growth in Argentina (1980 to 2002)** | | | |
| Compound Annual Inflation (%) | 427.5 | 3.9 | 25.9 |
| Compound Annual Growth Rates (%) | -1.2 | 2.7 | -10.9 |

The Heritage Foundation

**Source:** International Monetary Fund, *World Economic Outlook Database*, September 2003.

impossible to refrain from continuing the Peronist tradition of running huge government deficits that were created by handing out political favors.

These continuing deficits, coupled with no political will to end them, sent a clear message to those in global money markets: The deficits were absorbing huge percentages of the Argentine economy, the supplies of foreign reserves would inevitably diminish, and the government could not sustain the promise to convert pesos to dollars indefinitely at the currency board price.

Hence, the currency board failed abruptly, and Argentina was plunged into financial panic. Dollar accounts of Argentines were frozen, and withdrawals were not permitted until these accounts were converted to pesos at huge discounts from the fixed conversion promise the government had made. By unilaterally diminishing the value of private accounts, the government effectively expropriated significant parts of the wealth of private account holders. Savings, businesses, and other assets of the Argentine middle class were simply wiped out. The living standards and hopes of families throughout the country were dashed. Inflation returned with a vengeance in 2002 (see TABLE 2), and the economy again contracted.

Argentina stands as one of the tragic cases of economic experiments gone awry, but at least two things should be remembered about this example.

*First*, while monetary stability existed in Argentina, the economy flourished.

*Second*, because the leaders of government did not understand that all 10 factors of the road to prosperity are equally important, they eventually imposed an even greater hardship on the country's people.

A possible third point is that progress in some factors on the road to prosperity may have to come before progress in others. The Argentine experiment was doomed because of a lack of effort to corral huge government deficits. Imagine if Argentina had attacked the deficits first. Such an historic change in policy would have increased the confidence of world money markets in the Argentine government, and this increased confidence would have worked in tandem with an eventual currency board experiment instead of being at odds with it as happened with the unfortunate path that was chosen.

## Conclusion

Price stability encourages economic growth and prosperity. With price stability, incentives are not distorted, resources are not wasted trying to anticipate the next up or down in inflation, and inefficient utilization of machines relative to workers is avoided. In short, stable money makes life easier for all and allows individuals to focus on attaining their goals and fullest potential. Economic freedom is increased.

The burning question, of course, is how a small country can attain price stability. The literature points toward either pegging the small country's currency to that of a larger, more stable one or forgoing a separate currency altogether and joining an optimum currency area based on the larger country's currency. Neither policy, however, can be adopted in isolation. Significant movement down the other mileposts of the road to prosperity must accompany the monetary innovation.

Devaluation or depreciation is not a desirable policy for a developing country. The allegedly positive effects have been overblown, and the downside is very large. Countries that devalue find that inflation quickly follows with all of its negative impacts on incentives, output, prosperity, and growth.

# Further Reading

Laffer, Arthur B., and Marc A. Miles, *International Economics in an Integrated World* (Glenview, Ill.: Scott, Foresman & Co., 1982).

# Chapter 7

# Taxation and Economic Development

**Editor's Summary**

Arthur Laffer, creator of the "Laffer Curve" and father of supply-side economics, compares two competing theories of economic policy and their impact on development. The first is the 20th century demand-side approach, which has dominated policy discussions for decades. The second is the 21st century supply-side approach that focuses on the "incentive" or "substitution" effects of government actions on individuals and firms. Reviewing the economic policies of the Kennedy and Nixon administrations, he compares the relative effectiveness of policies that reflected the two competing approaches.

Initially, the "Laffer Curve" is used to describe how government policy affects workers, machines, and production within a classical economic framework. However, the "Laffer Curve" must be expanded into the "Laffer Ellipse" to illustrate the simultaneous impact on two factors of production: workers and machines. This expanded framework is able to show how financing a government's desired level of expenditure can be achieved most efficiently, and in turn how the corresponding levels of taxes on workers and investors affect their incomes and total production. Issues considered include:

- The difference between the incidence and burden of a tax. A tax on trucks may lead to fewer trucks but, in turn, also leads to fewer opportunities and lower wages for truck drivers.
- How, in the short run, more of the burden will be borne by the factor with the more inelastic supply or more elastic demand.
- How the form of government expenditure benefits flowing to workers or investors (just like taxes taken from these people) can affect their incentives and behavior.

In the process, Laffer describes the classical economic model that considers the effects on all factors and the effects of both expenditure and taxation policies. Such an all-encompassing framework provides warnings of hills and valleys that government fiscal policy can create, as well as clear insights into how to create instead a level, more manageable road to prosperity.

# Taxation and Economic Development

*Arthur B. Laffer*

As a result of prevailing economic ideologies in the developed world during most of the past century, the degree of government involvement in the economy is considered the key to growth. The consensus view is that in developing economies, an active government is necessary to bridge the gap to developed status. Government is seen as the *sine qua non* to stimulate demand. Supply-side incentives, however, provide an alternative perspective on the impact of government involvement.

Government involvement requires revenues, or taxes. From the 20th century perspective of development, fiscal policy is one of the most important functions of government; but simply spending is no panacea. Taxation can alter entire incentive structures, often in perverse and unexpected ways. Some government revenues are obviously necessary, but the best way to raise the revenues for public-sector needs is by no means obvious to government officials—or, for that matter, to most economists.

In effect, all economies are developing economies. No country should ever stop developing. There is not one set of rules for one class of countries and another set of rules for others. To analyze taxation, policy, and economic development, therefore, it is best to focus on countries that historically were relatively more successful in developing.

The United States is still developing and, in the past century, served as a petri dish for preferable policy. Therefore, the United States provides a good starting place to compare two very different policy environments—one the 20th century demand side, one the 21st century supply side—and examine their relative impacts on development. The two sets of policy actions and economic reactions from the U.S. example provide empirical evidence that support the theory of the supply-side "Ellipse."

## The Role of Government

Ever since the enactment of the Employment Act of 1946 and subsequent legislation, active management of the overall U.S. economy has fallen ever more into the purview of the federal government. Within the Congress alone, the number of committees focused on specific areas of the economy has ballooned. Committees such as the Joint Economic Committee, the Senate and House Budget Committees, and the Joint Committee on Taxation, as well as more narrowly defined committees, actively monitor the economy and consider legislation the express purpose of which is to alter the economy in some predetermined manner. Within the executive branch of government, an equally impressive expansion of personnel and oversight has occurred.

In fact, throughout the world, the explicit management of the overall economy is considered an increasingly important function of government. It therefore should come as no surprise that in the United States, state and local governments—like the federal government—are no exceptions to this pervasive trend.

Total government spending illustrates the growing tendency toward government control of the economy. (See Figure 1.) Yet to consider only government spending would grossly understate the magnitude of government's incursion into the U.S. economy or the economy of virtually any other country. Governments are deeply involved in regulating trade via tariffs, quotas, immigration limitations, and other policies that affect the flow of goods, services, and people across national boundaries. Governments also have a virtual monopoly on money and other means of exchange in almost every country of the world. Regulations, restrictions, controls, and mandated expenditures all are reflections of the expanded role played by government.

These additional incursions are difficult to quantify but could well be as important in their effects on the economy as measurable spending items. Therefore, total spending is one indication of the increasingly extensive role of government, but it is by no means a comprehensive measure. Government spending unquestionably understates the level of government involvement.

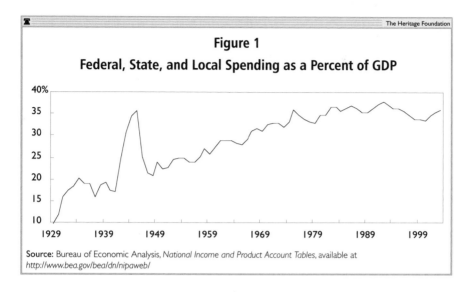

The Heritage Foundation

**Figure 1**
**Federal, State, and Local Spending as a Percent of GDP**

**Source:** Bureau of Economic Analysis, *National Income and Product Account Tables,* available at http://www.bea.gov/bea/dn/nipaweb/

## Variations on a Theme of Aggregate Demand Management

The publication of *The General Theory of Employment, Interest, and Money*, by John Maynard Keynes,[1] in the 1930s began the major dialectic of the academic profession between a general classical perspective and the perspective of aggregate demand management. By the early 1950s, the conversion was nearly complete. Virtually every major academic institution in America was dominated by economists who viewed aggregate demand as the most important factor to explain, diagnose, and thus prescribe for the ups and downs of macroeconomic behavior. Classical thought had all but disappeared, and once-eminent classical economists were now held in disrepute.

One of the more striking examples was the total conversion of Harvard Professor Alvin Hansen. When *The General Theory* first appeared, Professor Hansen wrote a review effectively dismissing the book as not being economics. Within a few years, however, he had become Keynes's most ardent advocate in the United States, and his book, *A Guide to Keynes,*[2] was *de rigueur* in any classroom that taught macroeconomics.

While there are alternate formulations, the familiar Keynesian income–expenditure approach distinguishes two forms of aggregate

---

1. John Maynard Keynes, *The General Theory of Employment, Interest, and Money* (New York: Harcourt, Brace and Company, 1936).
2. Alvin Hansen, *A Guide to Keynes* (New York: McGraw–Hill, 1953).

demand: induced or autonomous. Induced expenditures are those that rise and fall with domestic income, while autonomous expenditures depend upon factors beyond income. In simple terms, investment, government spending, and exports are representative categories of autonomous expenditures because they are assumed not to be sensitive to rises and falls in domestic income. Imports and consumption, on the other hand, represent induced expenditures. The higher income is, the higher consumption of domestic or foreign (imports) products will be. Whether induced or autonomous, each of these categories represents demand. Considerations of supply are omitted entirely.

Within the Keynesian demand framework, the level of output, and thus total employment, depends entirely upon three things:

- The magnitude of autonomous expenditures,
- The magnitude of induced spending for consumption, and
- Imports per unit of income and the increase in tax payments per unit of income.

The higher autonomous expenditures are, the greater output and employment will be. Likewise, a higher marginal propensity to consume from income will also result in higher output and employment. For imports and tax payments, the reverse is true. Higher tax payments and imports result in lower income and employment because they lower domestic demand. As a result, government policies that have the effect of increasing investment, exports, or government spending will, *pari passu*, increase output and employment. Alternatively, government policies that increase savings or imports or tax payments will have just the opposite impact.

It follows directly, therefore, that the Keynesian prescription for alleviating either slow growth or a low level of output includes the following types of policy measures:

- Higher government spending or lower taxes.
- Lower interest rates via increases in the money supply to entice greater investment.
- Currency depreciation to expand exports and discourage imports.
- Higher taxes on savings and imports to discourage those activities and thereby increase domestic consumption.

In the early stages of development, the Keynesian framework dismissed the inflationary consequences of government policies as being of little consequence. As the post–World War II era unfolded, however, inflation rates increased and inflation itself became an increasing focus of government policy.

The adaptation of inflation into the general Keynesian framework was based on the work of a British economist named Alban William Phillips, who discovered a close and persistent inverse relationship between rates of inflation and rates of unemployment in 19th century United Kingdom data. The formulation of this relationship, called the Phillips Curve, postulates that increased demand, which reduces unemployment, will heighten inflationary pressures. As a consequence, there is a drawback or trade-off to stimulative monetary and fiscal policies, such as increased government spending, increased money growth, reduced taxes, or even currency devaluation: higher inflation. Hence, there is a policy conflict.

Some of the most preeminent economists dismissed the alleged conflict as a sham. They argued that inflation itself had little, if any, social consequence and that any attempt to halt inflation would place great burdens on the economy. In the words of Yale Professor James Tobin:

> What are they [the social costs of inflation]? Economists' answers have been remarkably vague.... [S]eldom has a society made such large immediate tangible sacrifices to avert an ill-defined, uncertain, eventual evil.... [C]ertainly inflation does not merit the fact that it is the "cruelest tax."[3]

Regardless of Tobin's view, however, inflation would remain a political football. Particularly in the 1970s and 1980s, Keynesians struggled to explain the rising and persistent inflation, and how to deal with it. Consistent with its government-centric, demand-side origins, the range of Keynesian cures to this problem extends from all fiscal policies that reduce aggregate demand to specific income-controlling policies such as wage and price controls.

Almost from its inception, Keynesian demand-oriented income/expenditure analysis faced intellectual opposition from yet another demand-ori-

---

3. James Tobin, "Inflation and Unemployment," *American Economic Review*, Vol. 62 (March 1972), pp. 1–18.

ented framework called monetarism. The earliest champion of the monetarist school of thought was an economist named Clark Warburton. The popularity of monetarism in the 1970s and early 1980s, however, must be attributed to the indefatigable efforts of Professor Milton Friedman. In his presidential address to the American Economic Association, he presented as clear an exposition of the basic tenets of monetarism as can be found.[4] The central feature of monetarism, as in Keynesian fiscalism, is the exclusive focus on aggregate demand. The supply of goods and services is presumed simply to accommodate any and all changes in aggregate demand. Only in the very long run does supply become explicit.

From Friedman's perspective, an increase in the supply of money has two effects. One is an increase in the dollar price of bonds and a commensurate fall in interest rates. The fall in interest rates stimulates investment demand, as in Keynesian analysis. Because it takes time for investment spending to increase, the actual increase in demand does not occur at the moment the supply of money increases. The second stimulus is that consumption demand increases as well through the direct effect of excessive money balances in the hands of consumers. This effect, too, takes time to materialize.

Given sufficient time, the combined positive effects on aggregate demand of an increase in the supply of money will elicit an increase in output and employment. The supply of goods and services merely accommodates this increase in aggregate demand. However, increased production of goods and services will lead to heightened wage demands and tendencies by the producers of goods and services to raise prices. The result is inflation, which eventually rolls back real money supplies and demand to pre-increase levels. Therefore, in the shortest of runs, an increase in the supply of money reduces interest rates and sets the stage for an increase in aggregate demand. In the intermediate term, increases in output are the direct consequence of the increased stock of money. Finally, the price level rises and output falls back to where it otherwise would have been.

Whether one concentrates on the Keynesian or monetarist form of demand analysis, the focus is exclusively on aggregate demand behavior.

---

4. Milton Friedman, Presidential Address at 80th meeting of the American Economic Association, December 29, 1967, in *American Economic Review*, Vol. 58 (March 1968), pp. 1–17.

Nowhere in the explicit formulations is the impact on individual people considered. For example, no distinction is made between the wages paid by the firm for a worker and the wages a worker receives after tax. Change either or both source of wages, and the behavior of workers and/or employers will change.

Likewise, the distinction between pre-tax and post-tax yields on capital that affect decisions of investors is nonexistent. Basically, in demand analyses, people work because there are jobs, not because they are paid. Similarly, people save because their incomes are high, not because they earn an attractive after-tax yield on their savings. Individuals' incentives do not play a substantive role—at least not in the short run—in these demand analyses. As a result, demand-side macroeconomic analysis cannot be integrated with the theory of the firm or theories of individual behavior.

While the controversies between the monetarists and the Keynesians have often been heated, they are in essence peas in the same Keynesian pod. Their domination of post-war economic thought has literally precluded the more inclusive classical economics. Public policy has turned increasingly to demand analysis, despite the limitations that accompany such views.

That is why, on every level of government, whenever the economy appears sluggish, policymakers' minds instinctively turn to increased government spending, increased money growth, reduced taxation, or currency depreciation. Alternatives were not taught and are usually not considered.

For state and local governments, several of these demand management avenues are prohibited. They cannot, for example, depreciate the U.S. currency or change the growth rate of the supply of money. As a result, state and local governments rely on increased spending or reduced taxation in the hope of generating output and employment effects. Sometimes, they tie these changes to specific forms of price controls in hopes of avoiding or delaying price increases. These price controls are often concentrated on items that cannot, without considerable difficulty, leave the jurisdiction of the governing body. For example, rent controls historically have been a favorite target for state and local governments.

## A Classical Approach to Economic Analysis

In contrast, classical economics can be integrated with the theory of firms and individual behavior. The essential tenet of classical economic analysis is that people alter their behavior when economic incentives change. If the incentives for doing an activity increase relative to alternative activities, more of the increasingly attractive activity will be done. Likewise, if impediments to an activity are imposed, less of the diminished-incentive activity will be forthcoming.

Basically, people have both time and resource constraints in the quest for self-fulfillment. With limited resources and time, attainment of one's potential or objectives requires that the incentives that exist encourage one toward prudent management. Thus, government, with its full power of enforcement, has the ability to alter the incentives encountered by the vast array of economic factors. Changes in the structure of these governmentally imposed incentives alter both the economy's behavior and the potential for achievement.

The ways in which incentives will be altered by the government are limited solely by the expansiveness of man's own mind. Taxes, subsidies, regulations, restrictions, and requirements are but a few of the virtually endless series of possible government actions in the area of economics. The composition, as well as the magnitude, of government spending will also affect the range of private activity, as will the methods of government financing. The general precepts of classical economics are founded on the role played by incentives and the effect that government actions have on those incentives.

Firms decide how many workers to employ or capital assets to acquire, in part, based on the total cost to the firm of employing workers or acquiring capital, always with an eye to enhancing the value of the firm for its owners. Holding all else equal, the greater the cost to the firm of employing each worker, the fewer workers the firm will employ. Conversely, the lower the cost per worker, the more workers the firm hires.

Incorporated in this decision process are all costs associated with each worker's employment, including filing requirements, payroll taxes, rest facilities, fringe benefits, and ease of firing. For the firm, the decision to employ is based upon gross wages paid, a concept that encompasses all potential costs borne by the firm. Symmetrically, when acquiring capital, a similar encompassing set of costs is considered. Again, from the perspective of the firm, the explicit objective from each decision is to garner surplus value and thereby enhance the value of the firm.

Workers and savers, on the other hand, care little about how much it costs the firm to employ each worker or to acquire each piece of capital. From the worker's standpoint, all he cares about is how much he receives for providing his work effort, net of all deductions and taxes. Savers also do not

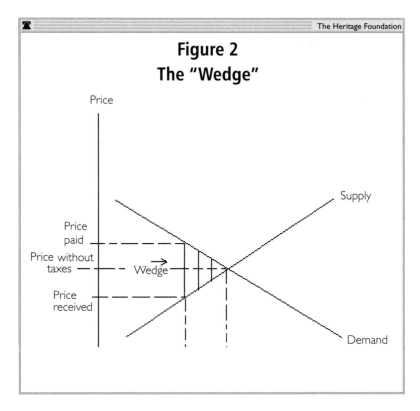

**Figure 2
The "Wedge"**

save as a matter of social conscience. Savers basically abstain from consuming in order to earn an attractive after-tax return on their savings.

Within the classical framework, workers concentrate on net wages received, while savers are preoccupied with their yields on investments after the taxman takes his bite. The greater the net wages received, the more willing the worker is to work. The higher the net yield on savings, the greater will be total savings. Conversely, if net wages received fall, workers will find work effort less attractive and will find alternative uses for their time. Savers will also save less if the net yield to savings declines.

The difference between what it costs a firm to employ a worker or acquire a unit of capital and what that worker or saver ultimately receives net of taxes is called the "tax wedge." (See Figure 2.) From the standpoint of a single worker or a single unit of capital, an increase in the wedge has two types of effects. A larger wedge raises the cost to the employer in the form of higher wages paid to workers or higher yields paid for capital. Clearly, it now pays for a firm to employ fewer workers and acquire less capital. On the supply side, an increase in the wedge reduces net wages received and the net yields savers receive. Again, less work effort and savings will be supplied.

In sum, an increase in the wedge reduces both the demand for and the supply of productive factors. An increase in the wedge, therefore, is associated with less employment, less investment, and lower output. In dynamic formulations, as the wedge grows, output growth falls, and *vice versa*. From a classical economics perspective, regulations, restrictions, and requirements, along with explicit taxes, are all parts of the wedge.

## A Comparison of Demand and Classical Economics: The Kennedy and Nixon Periods

Since the late 1970s, a marked resurgence of classical economics has presented a growing and formidable challenge to the hegemony of demand-side economics. This challenge resulted as much from the perceived failure of demand-side economic policies as it did from the apparent elegance of the logic structure of supply-side economics.

While not precise, a review of the post-war period in the United States reveals a number of experiments that have put the various models to a test. Ironically, the imagery surrounding these tests has often been diametrically opposed to the facts. The economic positions of the Kennedy Administration and their impact in the first few years of Lyndon Johnson's presidency are usually characterized as examples of liberal and Keynesian demand management effects. The Nixon Administration's policies, on the other hand, are usually depicted as hard-nosed, pro-business, and private enterprise–oriented.

The economic record belies these perceptions. In fact, the Kennedy era was marked by a time when classical prescriptions were applied to the overall U.S. economy. It stands in stark juxtaposition with what preceded it and what followed it. The Nixon era was the archetypical demand management administration, as amply illustrated by the data. While crosscurrents and contradictions were ubiquitous, there is little doubt that the Kennedy era was classical. Kennedy employed the preeminence of private incentives to further economic progress. By contrast, the Nixon era was one of explicit government intervention and behavior modifications by direction.

In the 1963 *Economic Report of the President*, John F. Kennedy enunciated clearly his economic game plan:

To raise the nation's capacity to produce—to expand the quantity, quality, and variety of our output—we must not merely replace but continually expand, improve, modernize, and rebuild our productive capital. That is, we must invest, and we must grow.... As a first step, we have already provided important new tax incentives for productive investment. Last year the Congress enacted a 7-percent tax credit for business expenditure on major kinds of equipment. And the Treasury, at my direction, revised its depreciation rules to reflect today's condition. Together, these measures are saving business over $2 billion a year in taxes and significantly increasing the net rate of return on capital investments.... The second step in my program to lift investment incentives is to reduce the corporate tax rate from 52 percent to 46 percent.... [T]he resulting increase in profitability will encourage risk-taking and enlarge the flow of internal funds which typically finance a major share of corporate investment.... [A]s the total impact of the tax program takes hold and generates pressures on existing capacity, more and more companies will find the lower taxes a welcome source of finance for planned expansion.... [T]he third step toward higher levels of capital spending is a combination of structural changes to remove barriers to the full flow of investment funds to sharpen the incentives for creative investment, and to remove tax-induced distortions in resource flow.... [F]ourth...the tax programs will go to the heart of the main deterrent to investment today, namely, inadequate markets. Once the sovereign incentive of high and rising sales is restored, and the businessman is convinced that today's new plant and equipment will find profitable use tomorrow, the effects of the directly stimulative measures will be doubled and redoubled. Thus—and it is no contradiction—the most important single thing we can do to stimulate investment in today's economy is to raise consumption by major reduction of individual income tax rates.... [F]ifth...the Federal Reserve and the Treasury will continue to maintain...monetary and credit conditions favorable to the flow of savings into long-term investment in the productive strength of the country.[5]

The game plan given birth under the Nixon presidency was different indeed. In 1969, the tax rate on capital gains was increased. Price stability gave way to inflation. Inflation generated illusory capital gains as dollar prices of assets rose to maintain their real or purchasing power values. Similarly illusory personal income increases resulted from workers attempting to maintain the purchasing power of their wages. Furthermore, illusory business profits were created as existing inventories were valued at inflated prices.

Each of these effects incurred real tax liabilities even though no increase in real value occurred. In 1971, the dollar was devalued and a wage and price freeze was imposed in a direct attempt to keep prices from rising. Simultaneously, a 10 percent import surcharge was placed on goods coming into the United States in the belief that lower demand would temper inflation. Gold was officially demonetized, money growth was high, and government spending as it related to the economic base grew inordinately.

The 1961–1966 period generally reflects the Kennedy era and its aftermath, while the 1969–1975 period is basically the Nixon era.[6] Interestingly each and every "fiscal" policy change was more stimulative during the Nixon era than during the Kennedy era from a "demand management" point of view, whereas just the reverse was true from a "classical" policy perspective. On the issue of inflation, the Kennedy Administration maintained gold convertibility, which is the essence of classical monetary policy. The Nixon Administration relied on Keynesian wage and price controls. One could not ask for a better test of the two views of macroeconomic policy, and the inflation rates speak for themselves. (See TABLE 1.)

The Kennedy era's policies were the antithesis of demand management, while Richard Nixon's policies were highly expansionary from a demand side macroeconomic perspective. (See TABLE 1.) Money growth during the Nixon era averaged almost 60 percent more than it did during the Kennedy era. Government spending and the deficit both declined relative to GNP

---

5. Council of Economic Advisers, *Economic Report of the President*, 1963 (Washington, D.C.: U.S. Government Printing Office, 1963), pp. xvi–xviii.

6. To avoid complications brought on by the 1966–1969 rapid expansion of the level of defense expenditures for the Vietnam War, a direct comparison of the 1961–1966 and 1969–1975 periods is in order. The bulk of the military expansion occurred between 1966 and 1968.

## Table 1
## Demand Management Policy Variables for the Periods 1961-1966 and 1969-1975

| POLICY VARIABLE | 1961-66 | 1969-75 |
|---|---|---|
| Average M1 money growth | 3.5% p.a. | 5.6% p.a. |
| Total change in Government Spending | -0.1% | 4.4% |
| Total change in Deficit/GNP | -0.6% | 5.3% |
| Devaluation of dollar in terms of gold | 0.0% p.a. | 22.8% p.a. |

p.a.-per annum

Source: *Economic Report of the President,* January 1980.

during the Kennedy era; they both ballooned during the Nixon presidency. The dollar's value relative to other currencies was reduced substantially under Nixon in what seemed like a never-ending sequence of official devaluations. Kennedy maintained the fixed dollar price of gold and dollar convertibility for official institutions.

In contrast, from a classical point of view, the incentive effects of marginal tax rates on labor and capital were more effective in stimulating economic activity during the Kennedy presidency than during the Nixon era.

Between 1961 and 1966, the weighted marginal tax rate on labor rose just 0.085 percentage points, or 5 percent of the amount by which they would rise during the 1969–1975 period. Moreover, between 1963 and 1965, the weighted marginal tax rates on labor actually declined 0.176 percentage points. Similarly, the weighted marginal tax rate on capital declined during the Kennedy era but increased during the Nixon era.

Likewise, between 1961 and 1966, the highest federal marginal tax rate on income of all sorts (dividend income as well as earned income) dropped from an unbelievable 91 percent to 70 percent. In addition, the highest marginal federal corporate tax rate fell from 52 percent to 48 percent, and investors were allowed to write investment spending off faster and were also

## Table 2
## Objective Economic Indicators for the Periods
## 1961-1966 and 1969-1975

| POLICY VARIABLE | 1961-66 | 1969-75 |
|---|---|---|
| Average real GNP growth | 5.2% p.a. | 1.8% p.a. |
| Average inflation in GNP price deflator | 2.1% p.a. | 6.4% p.a. |
| Total change in the Unemployment Rate | -2.9% | 5.0% |
| Average change in the nominal S&P 500 Stock Index | 5.0% p.a. | -2.1% p.a. |
| Average 90 day Treasury bill rate | 3.451% | 6.00% |

p.a.-per annum
**Source:** *Economic Report of the President,* January 1980.

treated to a 7 percent investment tax credit (not a deduction, but a real tax credit). Kennedy also championed the Kennedy Round of tariff reductions, which set a new standard for free trade.[7] In contrast, between 1969 and 1975, Nixon increased the capital gains tax rate from 27.5 percent to 36.5 percent.

Whether the focus is on the goods market or inflation, the performance achieved during the 1961–1966 period stands far above comparable intervals in U.S. annals. By contrast, for the 1969–1975 period, the comparison relates a record of subnormal performance. (See Table 2.) In spite of wage and price controls and the ensuing incomes policy apparatus, inflation and interest rates were high during the Nixon era. In spite of stimulative demand-side fiscal policy, monetary policy, and trade policy, real growth was low while unemployment rose.

Kennedy had modest fiscal and monetary policies and a trade policy of gold convertibility and tariff reductions. Incomes policies were limited. Income growth was high, unemployment fell, and inflation and interest

---

7. Lest the reader believe that all was perfect, it wasn't. Kennedy put in the Interest Equalization Tax impeding trade, plus the Voluntary Foreign Credit Restraint Program, and attempted to coerce corporations through "jawboning."

rates were low. The path of these objective economic indicators during these two periods challenges directly the demand management framework. They coincide with the conceptual structure of classical economics.

While stark, the comparison of Nixon's economics with Kennedy's is not out of step with the evidence generated during the rest of the post-war era. The evidence from the Carter Administration through mid-1980 was corroborative of the classical model and again stood at odds with the demand management school of thought. Jimmy Carter devalued the dollar, and the economy witnessed rapid monetary expansion; the price of gold rose. The most telling variable during his Administration was the surge in tax rates.

The effect was once again precisely what would be predicted by supply-side analysis. The economy underwent a contraction as severe as that experienced in 1975; unemployment rates rose, and inflation hit new highs. As interesting as any single observation can be is the fact that the federal deficit continued to hemorrhage red ink: Tax rates were raised by Carter explicitly and deliberately to balance his 1981 budget. The fiscal 1980 deficit was $68 billion—an increase of $24 billion from the Administration's March projections. The budget for fiscal year 1981, which had been projected to be a $16 billion surplus, was revised to $30 billion in the red and ended up being over twice that amount at $76 billion.

Reminiscing back to February 1963, the fiscal policies could not have been more different. In his testimony before the House Ways and Means Committee, Secretary of the Treasury Douglas Dillon stated:

> By increasing the reward for effort, enterprise, risk-taking, and investment, the program [of tax reduction and reform] will strengthen individual initiative and stimulate investment, thus propelling our economy toward a faster rate of growth, and a stronger future.... [W]hile a temporary revenue loss will be incurred at the outset, the stimulating effects of tax reduction and reform on the economy will give rise to subsequent revenue gains, and in the longer run the revenue producing power of our tax structure will be raised substantially.[8]

---

8. Douglas Dillon, "Statement Before the Committee on Ways and Means of the U.S. House Representatives on the Special Message on Tax Reduction and Reform," February 6, 1933.

In 1977, Walter Heller, President Kennedy's Chairman of the Council of Economic Advisers, summed it all up:

> What happened to the tax cut in 1965 is difficult to pin down, but insofar as we are able to isolate it, it did seem to have a tremendously stimulative effect, a multiplied effect on the economy. It was the major factor that led to our running a $3 billion surplus by the middle of 1965 before escalation in Vietnam struck us. It was a $12 billion tax cut, which would be about $33 [billion] or $34 billion in today's terms, and within one year the revenues into the Federal Treasury were already above what they had been before the tax cut.
>
> Did [the tax cut] pay for itself in increased revenues? I think the evidence is very strong that it did.[9]

## The Ellipse

By now, most are familiar with the basics of the "Laffer Curve." (See FIGURE 3.)

This parabolic curve shows what happens to overall tax revenue as the marginal tax rate on, say, workers is increased. A tax of 100 percent would yield no revenues, just as a tax of zero percent would yield no revenues. As we can see from the figure, tax revenue will expand as the tax rate initially increases until the point $T^*$ is reached. At points past $T^*$, any increase in tax rates will be expected to bring in less revenue. This curve is similar to the "total revenue" curve for a firm. No one expects that a company can infinitely increase its revenue by repeatedly raising its price. As prices rise, customers will find alternative ways to satisfy their needs; and at some point, the revenue of the firm will begin to decline with higher prices.

In the preceding discussion, however, the impact of policy on two factors of production—workers and machines—was discussed. Clearly, a more comprehensive classical economic understanding of the impact of fiscal policy on economic activity requires at least two factors of production in

---

9. Walter Heller, testimony before the Joint Economic Committee, U.S. Congress, 1977, quoted by Bruce Bartlett in "Revolution of 1978," *National Review*, October 27, 1978.

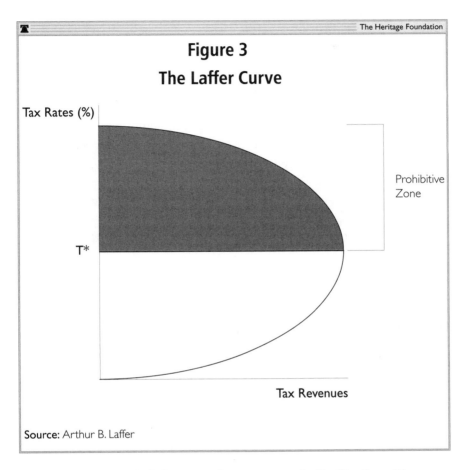

## Figure 3
## The Laffer Curve

Tax Rates (%)

Prohibitive
Zone

T*

Tax Revenues

**Source:** Arthur B. Laffer

the analysis. In the shift from one factor to two, the "Laffer Curve" becomes the "Laffer Ellipse."

The results derived with only one factor, of course, are still applicable: An increase in the wedge increases the price paid for and reduces the price received by a factor of production, reducing both the demand for and supply of that factor. A lower level of economic activity ensues. For example, an increase in the tax wedge on labor will raise wages paid, lower wages received, and reduce the amount of labor employed.

In a two-factor model, though, the process does not stop here. There are more ramifications. With fewer employed workers, the value of each unit of capital, from the employer's perspective, is lessened. Fewer workers imply fewer people working on each machine. Imagine it as if a shift in a plant were eliminated. Therefore, the demand for capital falls, less capital will be employed, and both yields paid and yields received will fall. Taking the process to its final state, an increase in the tax wedge on labor will result in lower:[10]

- Output,
- Quantities of both capital and labor employed,
- Wages received, and
- Yields in capital, both paid and received.

In addition, while workers receive less, because of the larger tax wedge, the gross wages paid by employers actually rise.

By the same logic, an increase in the tax wedge on the returns to capital will lower:

- Output,
- Quantities of both capital and labor employed,
- Wages received and paid, and
- Yields received by the owners of capital.

Again, while investors receive less, because of the bigger tax wedge on capital, the gross yields paid for capital by the entrepreneur will rise.

Within this two-factor model, containing both capital and labor as well as one market output, the effect on total tax receipts of an increase in the tax on either factor of production has conflicting influences. For example, an increase in the tax wedge on labor will elicit the following revenue responses:

- More revenue will be collected per worker employed, thus tending to increase revenues.
- Fewer workers will be employed, thus lowering revenue.
- Less capital will be employed, thus lowering revenue.

Under certain circumstances, the additional revenue collected per worker (the first of these three effects) will dominate, and an increase in the

---

10. For a mathematical derivation of the "Ellipse," see Victor A. Canto, Douglas H. Joines, and Arthur B. Laffer, "Taxation, G.N.P. and Potential G.N.P.," presented at the American Statistical Association, San Diego, California, August 14–17, 1978.

tax wedge on labor will raise revenues. Sometimes, the second and third effects dominate, and less revenue will be forthcoming. The same set of conditions pertains to changes in the tax wedge on capital.

In actual practice, of course, a number of additional influences are felt. With higher tax rates, tax avoidance and evasion will increase, thus aggravating the offsetting revenue impact that accompanies tax rate increases and lowering the chance that revenue actually rises. Furthermore, employers will always be looking to minimize the costs of production. Where possible, factor substitution will reduce the economy's reliance on the now higher-taxed factor. The longer the time period allowed to elapse, the more employers have an opportunity to take advantage of the offsets. The higher the initial level of tax rates, the greater will be the offsets.

Because of all these potential reactions to higher taxes, the overall relationship between tax rates and tax revenues is far from obvious. As often as not, higher tax rates yield less revenue. They always yield less output. When a tax rate increase yields higher revenues, the tax is in the normal range. When a tax rate increase leads to lower revenues, it is in the prohibitive range. (See FIGURE 3.)

One way to analyze the effects of tax rate changes is to examine the combinations of tax rate changes on capital and on labor where total revenues are left unchanged. This framework is useful because it separates the issues of total spending from those of tax policies. Thus, if the tax on labor and the tax on capital are both in the normal range, a tax rate reduction on labor will be accompanied by a tax rate increase on capital, or *vice versa*. On the other hand, if the tax rate on labor were in the prohibitive range while the tax rate on capital were in the normal range, a tax rate reduction on labor, which by definition would lead to higher revenues, would require a tax rate reduction on capital as well in order for total tax revenues to remain the same.

To illustrate the pairings of such tax rates on labor and capital requires a graph with different tax rates on each axis. The horizontal axis is the tax on capital, $tK$, and the vertical axis is the tax on labor, $tL$. The locus or combination of points describing the different pairings of tax rates that yield the exactly same amount of tax revenue is named the iso-revenue line ("iso" meaning constant). One such line is drawn in FIGURE 4 in the form of an ellipse. The location and angle of the ellipse are purely arbitrary, the diagram being for illustrative purposes only.

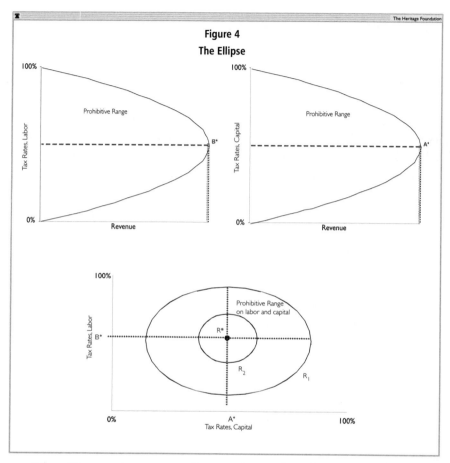

**Figure 4**
**The Ellipse**

The Heritage Foundation

The ellipse or iso-revenue line can be explained in terms of a "Laffer Curve" for labor and a "Laffer Curve" for capital. Four distinct regions can be identified on the iso-revenue line. In the region from $A^*$ to $B^*$, the tax rates for both "Laffer Curves" are in their "normal" range: An increase in the tax rate on capital alone, or the tax rate on labor alone, will raise net revenues. Therefore, if revenues are to stay the same in the $A^*B^*$ region of the iso-revenue line below, an increase in either tax rate must be accompanied by a reduction in the other tax rate.

In the region above $B^*$ and to the left of $A^*$, the tax on labor is in its prohibitive range, while the tax on capital is in its normal range: An increase in the tax rate on labor loses net revenues, while an increase in the tax on capital increases net revenues. Thus, an increase in the tax rate on labor (moving up the vertical axis) must be accompanied by an increase in the tax rate on capital (moving to the right on the horizontal axis) to maintain the same level of revenues. Hence, the iso-revenue line in this region is upward, sloping to the right. Holding revenues constant, the higher the tax rate on labor, the higher must be the tax on capital.

Above $B^*$ and to the right of $A^*$ is the region where both tax rates are in the prohibitive range. In this region, an increase in either tax rate lowers revenues. Thus, if the tax on capital is increased (movement to the right), the tax rate on labor must be reduced (movement down) to keep total revenues constant. The iso-revenue line here is downward, sloping to the right.

Finally, in the region to the right of $A^*$ and below $B^*$, the tax on labor is in the normal range and the tax on capital is in the prohibitive range. Here a rise in the tax rate on labor, which increases revenues, must be accompanied by an increase in the tax rate on capital, which lowers revenues, in order to keep total revenues constant.

In each of the three regions, at least one tax rate is in the "prohibitive" range. That is, an increase in the tax rate lowers net revenues. In the range where $T_L > B^*$ and $T_K > A^*$, both tax rates are in the prohibitive range. Only in the one range, between $A^*$ and $B^*$, are both tax rates in the normal range where an increase in either rate raises net revenues. From the relationships described in this tax ellipse, in any region other than where the taxes on capital and labor are less than or equal to $A^*$ and $B^*$, respectively, a lowering of at least one tax rate can be accompanied by a lowering of the other tax rate without reducing total revenues or spending. In the region between $A^*$ and $B^*$, a lowering of one tax rate necessitates a raising of the other rate in order to maintain total revenues.

Each ellipse represents a constant level of revenue. For this reason, it is called an iso-revenue ellipse. A new tax ellipse inside the one just described represents a higher level of tax revenues. Alternatively, a lower level of revenues would be described by a larger ellipse. In all cases, four regions would exist. Just as in the one-factor "Laffer Curve" model, a maximum point of revenue exists beyond which revenues cannot be increased. Whether one or both tax rates are raised or lowered, less revenue will be forthcoming. In sum, then, a whole family of iso-revenue lines or ellipses exists, one for each level of revenue or spending. The existence of these ellipses allows for a separation of the effects of tax rates per se and of tax revenues or spending.

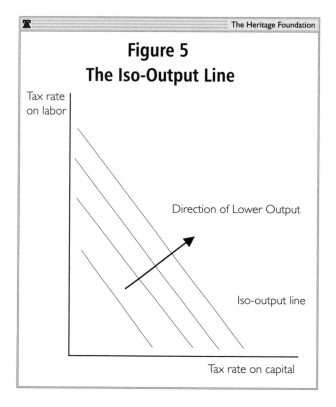

The Heritage Foundation

## Figure 5
## The Iso-Output Line

Tax rate on labor

Direction of Lower Output

Iso-output line

Tax rate on capital

**Tax Rates and Output.** Just as total tax revenues can vary as tax rates change, so can the level of output. Hence, individually unique levels of output can also be represented graphically using these same axes; i.e., tax rates on capital and labor. This time, the level of output, instead of total revenues, will be held constant along the curve or line.

As shown earlier, a cut in the tax rate on either factor of production will raise output if the other factor's tax rate is left unaltered. In order to hold output constant, if one tax rate is reduced, the other tax rate must be increased. Thus, the locus or combination of points linking the pairs of tax rates that hold output constant must be downward sloping and to the right. It is named the iso-output line. FIGURE 5 illustrates a family of these iso-output lines. The further an iso-output line is from the origin (zero tax rates), the higher the respective tax rates on capital and labor, and the lower the level of output.

Combining both the families of iso-revenue ellipses and the families of iso-output lines, a number of general propositions and derivations emerge.

*First,* there exists only one pairing of tax rates for each level of revenue (spending) that maximizes output. (See FIGURE 6.) It occurs at the tangency point between the iso-revenue and iso-output lines; i.e., the intersection point closest to the origin and designated 0*.

*Second,* a pairing of tax rates either at point A or at point B would yield the same revenue as point 0*, but the iso-output line is further from the origin (iso-output line 2). In this case, more revenues could be raised without a loss in output by adjusting tax rates in such a way that the paired tax rates are tangent to iso-output line 2 at point C. Such a pairing, of course, would yield the smaller tax ellipse. The smaller ellipse implies more revenue (spending) while holding output constant (iso-output line 2).

*Third,* output could be expanded while holding revenue constant by shifting the paired tax rates to point 0*, which implies output at the higher level depicted by iso-output line 1.

*Fourth,* taking the lows of the tax rate pairings that maximizes output for a given level of revenue yields the output efficiency line of EL. This output efficiency line designates that precise pairing of tax rates for any level of

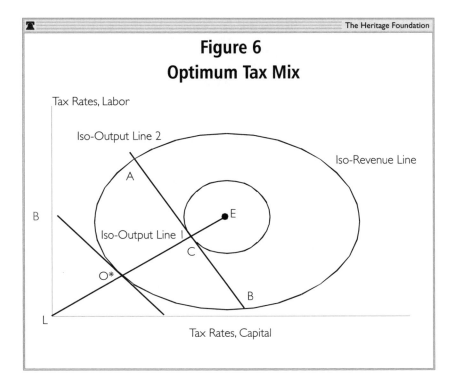

The Heritage Foundation

## Figure 6
## Optimum Tax Mix

government spending where output is least diminished. This output efficiency line traverses the point $0^*$ and C, ending where tax rates equal zero (L), and also where tax rates yield the maximum possible amount of revenue (E).

The 19th century American economist Henry George summarized the point of these diagrams in his book *Progress and Poverty*:

> The mode of taxation is, in fact, quite as important as the amount. As a small burden badly placed may distress a horse that could carry with ease a much larger one properly adjusted, so a people may be impoverished and their power of producing wealth destroyed by taxation, which, if levied in another way, could be borne with ease....[11]

**Incidence and Burden of a Tax.** The tax ellipse also may be used to explore conceptually the ultimate effects of different tax pairings on the net wages received by labor and the net yields received by capital. Again, the use of the iso-revenue line allows revenue, and therefore government spending, to be held constant. The tax rate paid by each factor of production individually is the incidence of the tax. It is depicted explicitly by the tax rate pairings. The burden of a tax, though, is the actual change in the net wages received and net yields received due to the tax change. It must be derived.

The incidence of a tax structure is very different from the burden of that tax structure. The person upon whom a tax is levied may well experience no loss in net income if he passes the tax forward onto consumers or backward onto suppliers. Likewise, a person upon whom no tax has been levied may well suffer large net income losses as a consequence of taxes levied (incidence) on others.

In the lower left hand corner of ellipse $R_1$ between horizontal line $B^*$ and vertical line $A^*$, an increase in the tax rate on capital must be accompanied by a reduction in the tax rate on labor. This is the condition that holds revenues constant. The increase in the tax on capital will reduce the amount of capital employed. This reduction in the demands for capital also cuts back on the demand for labor. Labor pays less tax, but the reduction in the

---

11. Henry George, *Progress and Poverty* (New York: Robert Schalkenbach Foundation, 1979), p. 409.

demand for labor services reduces the gross wages paid. The overall effect on net wages from a lower pretax wage and lower taxes is ambiguous.

The farther away the tax pairing moves from the point $0^*$ in FIGURE 6, the greater is the reduction in overall output. As output falls, the net gains to labor from its tax rate cuts (which are offset by an increase in the tax on capital) will be reduced. At some point, a tax rate reduction on labor, holding revenues constant, actually may leave labor worse off. The more factors the model entertains, the less incidence will be related to burden. In the limit, the two are unassociated. In the words of Nobel Laureate Paul Samuelson:

> Even if the electorate has made up its mind about how the tax burden shall be borne by individuals, the following difficult problems remain:
>
> Who ultimately pays a particular tax? Does its burden stay on the person on whom it is first levied? One cannot assume that the person Congress says a tax is levied on will end up paying that tax. He may be able to shift the tax; shift it "forward" on his customers by raising his price as much as the tax; or shift it "backward" on his suppliers (wage earners, rent, and interest receivers) who end up being able to charge him less than they would have done had there been no tax.
>
> Economists therefore say: We must study the final *incidence* of the tax—the way its burden ultimately gets borne, the totality of its effects on commodity prices, factor-prices, resource allocations, efforts, and composition of production and consumption. Tax incidence, thus, is no easy problem and requires all the advanced tools of economics to help toward its solution.[12]

In more intuitive terms, as often as not, taxing capital to spare labor will actually leave labor worse off. Similarly, taxing the rich is sometimes a good way to further impoverish the poor.

---

12. Paul Samuelson, *Economics*, 7th Edition (New York: McGraw–Hill, 1967), pp. 166–167 (emphasis in original).

Various examples of the fallacy of the so-called Robin Hood economics exist over a broad spectrum of economic study. One such example pertains to the age-old notion that there is an inherent conflict between wages and employment on the one hand and profits and capital formation on the other. Many people have the distinct feeling that workers and capitalists are hostile entities within the economic universe. To the extent reason exists, it is widely thought that workers' ability to raise real wages comes directly out of capitalists' pool of profits. Likewise, if capitalists gain an increase in real profits, the gain must have come at the expense of the real wages of workers. Workers and investors compete in a zero-sum game.

Such arguments are the essence of static analysis. The vitriolic debates between national labor leaders and big-business executives point up this perception. One group warns that the salvation of America depends entirely on the containment of labor unions. The other points to the exorbitant profits enjoyed by the undeserving robber barons at the expense of the working man in America. This monotonous brace of diatribes describes a world in which profits and wages are mutually exclusive and inimical.

Profits and wages are not, of course, mutually exclusive. Fundamentally, profits and wages are complements, not substitutes. In other words, workers and investors are joined in a positive-sum game.

Since 1948, in the United States, the positive relationship between real after-tax economic profits and average weekly real spendable earnings is unmistakable. (See FIGURE 7.) Higher profits, more often than not, are associated with higher wages. Higher wages also are consistent with higher profits.

Imagine what the wages of a labor group such as truck drivers would be if there were no trucks. In order to earn a living, truck drivers need trucks to drive. The only way there will ever be enough trucks around for truck drivers to drive is to provide people—savers and investors—with an after-tax rate of return on savings. Saving must be profitable enough to entice people either to abstain from consuming or to work harder in order to provide the requisite real resources to acquire a capital stock of trucks.

If capital is overtaxed, there will be less capital formation and fewer trucks, and the wages of truck drivers will be low. Lowering tax rates on capital will increase the capital stock and, more important, will raise the wages of truck drivers and other workers. High wages and high profits are far from opposing objectives. Returns to capital and returns to labor are, in fact, complements. Policies that reduce either are inimical to both.

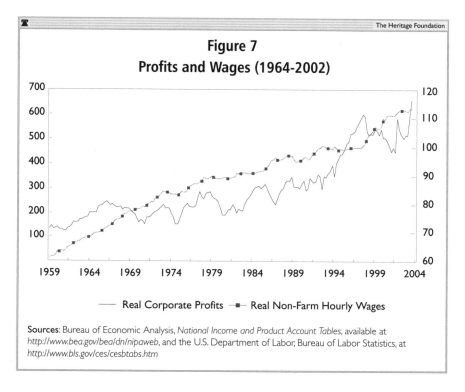

The Heritage Foundation

**Figure 7**
**Profits and Wages (1964-2002)**

—— Real Corporate Profits —■— Real Non-Farm Hourly Wages

**Sources:** Bureau of Economic Analysis, *National Income and Product Account Tables*, available at *http://www.bea.gov/bea/dn/nipaweb*, and the U.S. Department of Labor, Bureau of Labor Statistics, at *http://www.bls.gov/ces/cesbtabs.htm*

One such policy is the tax on capital earnings. A reduction in the rate of taxation on the earnings from capital would result in more investment, which would raise wages. Lower tax rates on wages would increase employment and thereby cause profits to rise. Capitalists and workers alike are thus helped by lower rates of taxation on either capital or income.

Within many political structures, this relationship is well known and often ignored. In his State of the Union message in 1962, President Kennedy pointed out that "a rising tide raises all boats"—an explicit reference to the complementary nature between profitability and wages. In a far less hospitable vein, the same principle is referred to when discussing the "trickle-down" theory. "Trickle-down" is used to imply that if enough money is given to the rich, some of it will trickle down, very slowly, to the poor, just as molasses slowly trickles down on a crisp fall day in New England.

To summarize, we have five basic points:

- Changes in tax rates affect output directly. Lower tax rates correspond to higher output.

- Changes in tax rates affect the employment of both factors directly. Lower tax rates on either factor of production increase employment for both factors.
- The constellation of tax rates, holding government spending unchanged, affects output. How taxes are collected is important, as is the total amount of taxation and spending.
- Lower tax rates on any one factor may or may not lower total revenue.
- Changes in the pairing of tax rates, holding revenue unchanged, may shape the distribution of after-tax spending power, but only indirectly. As often as not, when one factor's tax rate is raised and the other's is lowered, the second factor will end up in worse economic shape.

The specific shapes of the curves and the responsiveness of the effects of tax rates and total taxation or spending depend upon the innate characteristics of the factors and the production process. Those factors with elastic supply (more sensitive to price changes) bear progressively less of the burden of taxation irrespective of the incidence. The price received falls very little with the imposition of a tax wedge. This is because a small decrease in the price received would yield a large change in the quantity supplied. (See Figure 8a.) Inevitably, the burden is passed to those factors that are inelastic in supply. By definition, it is these factors that have the fewest alternatives to providing their services, even if there is a reduction in the price received. (See Figure 8b.)

When tax rates are lowered on inelastic factors, revenues decline. For a given reduction in a tax rate, the more elastic the supply of a factor's services with respect to net returns received, the less the overall revenue loss or the greater the overall revenue increase.

Symmetrically, the more elastic the demand for a factor's services, the greater will be the burden placed upon it by any and all taxes. (See Figure 8c.) This is because any change in its price leads to a large change in the quantity demanded. Inelastically supplied factors facing elastic demand bear the tax burden disproportionately, even when the taxes are on other factors. (See Figure 8d.)

Finally, the longer the time horizon, the greater will be the revenue losses from tax rate increases. With time, the mobility of most factors of production is increased. Machinery is not repaired or replaced. New job opportunities lure labor out of the taxing district, or a lack of opportunities leads to a below aver-

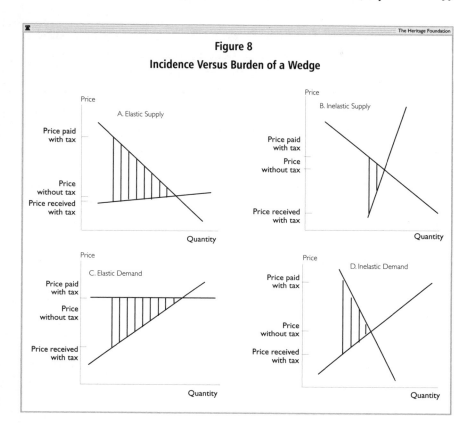

**Figure 8**
**Incidence Versus Burden of a Wedge**

age growth in employment. Thus, over time, any economy becomes more sensitive to the imposition of the wedge; the elasticity of both the supply and the demand for factor services increases. Revenue increases realized in the very short horizon may be more than undone over distant horizons.

## Government Spending

Up to now, the discussion has centered on the roles played by different combinations of tax rates and the level of total taxation or spending. The overall economy is also affected by the composition of spending. Total production or output is very sensitive to different forms of government spending.

**Transfer Payments.** Transfer payments are perhaps the least complex form of spending. With transfer payments, in general, income effects net to zero, thus leaving only substitution effects. If taxes are raised in order to give lump-sum transfers to people based solely on chance, income taken from those taxed just equals the income received by the lucky recipients.

However, the taxpayers face higher tax rates and a diminution of incentives. The reduction in the incentives to work and produce will tend to make the workers supply less work effort. Yet one other effect comes into play. These workers now have less after-tax income because of the higher taxes. Therefore, in order to maintain a semblance of their previous living standard, they must work more, not less. The desire to maintain one's standard of living elicits the income effect.

Hence, for any one taxpayer, an increase in tax rates will bring about two effects that work in opposite directions. The substitution effect will lead the taxpayer to work less while the income effect will tend to make him work more: the labor/leisure trade-off.

This view is widely held by economists and non-economists alike. It can be found in numerous professional publications, such as Joseph Pechman's book on taxation[13] as well as in Professor Lester Thurow's views on a net-wealth tax. These views result directly from an attempt to aggregate a series of partial equilibrium analyses and, in the process, ignore an entire set of effects that come out of a general equilibrium analysis. Theory does provide an explicit answer to the net effects of an increase or decrease of tax rates on work effort.

The best laymen's illustration of the correct general equilibrium statement is found in the April 16, 1976, edition of *The Wall Street Journal*:

> M.I.T. economist Lester C. Thurow also speaks favorably of a net-wealth tax and the full taxation of capital gains.
>
> He argues that private capital would still be formed because every tax has an income effect and a substitution effect, and he says the former dominates the latter. If you boost the tax on wealth, people will work harder to achieve their desired level of wealth (the income effect), even as the higher tax discourages them from more work (the substitution effect). But by our reckoning, if you tax $100 from Jones, thus forcing him to work harder and give the $100 to Smith, Smith is required to work less to achieve his desired level of wealth.

13. Joseph A. Pechman, *What Should Be Taxed, Income or Expenditure?: A Report of a Conference Sponsored by the Fund for Public Policy Research and the Brookings Institution* (Washington, D.C.: Brookings Institution, 1980).

The income effect washes out, and all that's left is substitution.[14]

More technically, the answer becomes apparent from the following example:

1.  For an individual, it is clear that zero or negative take-home wages imply less work effort than any positive take-home wages. Therefore, over the entire range of possible wages, the supply of work effort is unambiguously increased by the total increase in take-home wages.
2.  Within take-home wage regions, however, which may cover a wide range of take-home wages, an individual may choose to work fewer hours as take-home wages rise. In such a case, the income effect of higher total take-home wages more than offsets the substitution effect of more take-home pay for the last unit of work.

To see the distinction clearly, imagine the following: A person earns pretax wages of $4,000 per month. He takes one month per year in unpaid vacation. He pays a flat 50 percent tax on all wages so that his take-home pay is $2,000 per month or $22,000 for the 11-month year. Let us now analyze the following two sets of circumstances.

a)  He wins a lottery paying an $11,000 after-tax yearly annuity.
b)  He has a permanent reduction in his tax rates to 25 percent.

Under circumstance (a), the yearly stipend, the general result will be some reduction in the number of months worked. Part of his increased income will go into more leisure consumption and thereby less work.

If he works the same 11 months per year under circumstance (a), he will receive $33,000 (0.5 x 44,000 + 11,000) after-tax; under circumstance (b), he will also receive $33,000 (0.75 x 44,000).

If he works one month less or 10 months under circumstance (a), he will take home $31,000; under circumstance (b), he will take home only $30,000. His lost income is greater if he takes one more month of leisure

14. "A New 'Soak-the-Rich' Theory," *Review and Outlook, The Wall Street Journal*, April 15, 1976.

when tax rates are cut as opposed to when he received a windfall lottery.

Likewise, if he works an extra month under circumstance (a), he will have $35,000 take-home pay; under circumstance (b), he will have $36,000 take-home.

Therefore, if we neutralize the income effect of a tax rate cut, there will be more total work due simply to the substitution effect.

For any one person, we cannot be sure whether or not the income effect dominates the substitution effect within the relevant range. What is clear is that the income effect of a tax rate reduction lowers work effort and the substitution effect raises work effort.

For the economy as a whole, however, the effect of a tax rate cut can be presumed to lead to more work. If the income effects across individuals are roughly similar, the work impact of the income effect will net to zero. The higher income accorded the worker whose tax rates are cut must be matched by a negative impact on the income of the government spending recipient.

If worker output were unchanged, then a tax rate cut would, *pari passu*, lead to a spending cut or a negative income lottery. Just as a lottery win lowered work, so a lottery net loss (usually referred to as a poll tax) would lead to increased work. Combining the two always leads to more work.

This aggregate effect is equivalent to the work and output effect of our example when an $11,000 yearly poll tax is imposed simultaneously with a reduction of the income tax rate from 50 percent to 25 percent. Income at 11 months of work would raise $22,000 (0.75 x 44,000 – 11,000), but an additional month's work would yield $3,000 net as opposed to $2,000. Except in obviously perverse cases, more work, not less, would be forthcoming.

The theoretical analysis underlying this example can be found in any number of sources; the classics are John Hicks's *Value and Capital*[15] or, perhaps, Arnold Harberger's *Taxation and Welfare*.[16]

Transfer payments financed by increases in tax rates, therefore, do not have any net expected income effects. They do, however, yield the normal substitution effects that arise whenever tax rates are increased. These substitution effects cumulate over all taxpayers or potential taxpayers. Of course, if there are distinct differences in individual responses to income

---

15. John R. Hicks, *Value and Capital, An Inquiry Into Some Fundamental Principles of Economic Theory* (Oxford: Clarendon Press, 1939).

16. Arnold C. Harberger, *Taxation and Welfare* (Boston: Little, Brown, 1974).

effects, an increase in transfer payments may result in some changes due to income effects.

It is important to note, however, that the determination of the net changes in income must not be confused either with the incidence of the transfer payments or with the incidence of the tax rate increases. Reliance must be placed solely on the burden of the program, and not on its incidence. Even if we knew the relative responsiveness of different groups to so-called income effects, and also knew the incidence of the transfer payments and tax rate hikes, we still would be no closer to the net income effect. It could still just as easily be positive, or negative, or even zero.

In all, therefore, an increase in transfer payments corresponds to a cumulative set of substitution effects and no expected income effects. A tax increase used to finance transfer payments will lower output.

Quite frequently, an additional set of substitution effects also occur with transfer payments. These are known as "needs, means, retirement and incomes" tests. In order to receive transfer payments such as (among others) unemployment compensation, food stamps, Aid for Dependent Children, Social Security benefits, housing and rent subsidies, and agricultural relief, it is necessary to demonstrate need. The higher one's income, the less that person can receive, and *vice versa*. Therefore, an additional disincentive is placed in the path of work effort. Not only is one taxed if he works, but he is also paid if he doesn't. This further strengthens the substitution effects already discussed.[17]

**Public Goods.** Government spending on public goods elicits two separate and distinct effects. The first, the substitution effect, will exert unambiguous pressure to reduce output because of a separation of effort from reward. Taxation provides the real wherewithal to acquire the public goods, and they then are distributed *gratis* to the recipients. The taxation *per se* reduces incentives and leads to lessened output.

The other effect is called the income effect and, in the case of public goods, will lead to an even greater reduction in output although the population will be better off. A public good is one for which the value of the resources exacted from the population is less than the value of the government spending itself. Therefore, in value terms, the recipients receive more

---

17. Arthur B. Laffer, "Prohibitive Tax Rates and the Inner City: A Rational Explanation of the Poverty Trap," H. C. Wainwright & Co., June 27, 1978.

than the taxpayers pay. Examples might include the national highway system and perhaps some government research and development. In the case of the recipients, the receipt of value from the government will raise their level of total well-being and lead them to choose more leisure time instead of work—the free-rider problem. While, for the taxpayers, the opposite effect is in force, it will have a smaller impact because the value of the resources extracted is less than the value to the recipients of the goods received.

Both income and substitution effects lead to lessened production. Relative to transfer payments, this form of government spending will result in higher consumption or welfare on the part of the overall population while simultaneously yielding lower work effort. Part of the increase in total income will be used to consume more leisure.

## Taxes, Spending, and the Deficit

Introducing spending into the general context of tax rate changes fills the picture a little bit more fully. Focusing now on the deficit instead of revenues, a tax rate reduction will:

- Lessen the amount collected per unit of the lower-taxed factor;
- Increase the amount of employment for the lower-taxed factor;
- Increase the employment of other factors and, thereby, their tax payments;
- Reduce total government spending as fewer people are unemployed or on welfare as, among other feedback effects, the number of unemployed and the number of welfare recipients declines; and
- Change the composition of government spending, thereby lessening the anti-output nature of government spending per unit spent. This raises the responsiveness of the economy to tax rate changes and heightens the chances of a well-designed tax rate reduction lowering the deficit.

The analysis, however, excludes many potentially important additional feedback effects in the system. While less amenable to formal analysis, they could nonetheless swing the results in favor of balancing the budget by lowering instead of raising tax rates. These other effects include the role and importance of tax evasion and avoidance.

Higher tax rates imply more of both tax evasion and tax avoidance. The more tax that is either evaded or avoided, the less revenue the government will collect per unit of the taxable base. Furthermore, it is generally true that the more evasion and avoidance that exists, the more spending from the government will be required to monitor and enforce the tax codes. The existence of tax evasion and avoidance, therefore, further enhances the beneficial fiscal effects of tax rate reductions. Just what the full effects of changes in tax rates on the overall fiscal solvency of the relevant government unit may be, however, still remains an empirical question.

In any case, the important feature of the tax system is the conjectural framework upon which it is based. Henry George, in his chapter entitled "The Proposition Tried by the Canons of Taxation," enumerated the criteria by which tax policy may be analyzed:

> The best tax by which public revenues can be raised is evidently that which will closest conform to the following conditions:
>
> 1. That it bear as lightly as possible upon production—so as least to check the increase of the general fund from which taxes must be paid and the community maintained.
>
> 2. That it be easily and cheaply collected, and fall as directly as may be upon the ultimate payers— so as to take from the people as little as possible in addition to what it yields to the government.
>
> 3. That it be certain—so as to give the least opportunity for tyranny or corruption on the part of officials, and the least temptation to lawbreaking and evasion on the part of the taxpayers.
>
> 4. That it bear equally—so as to give no citizen an advantage or put any at a disadvantage, as compared with others.[18]

---

18. George, *Progress and Poverty*, p. 408.

# Chapter 8

# Capital Controls, Vulnerability, and Economic Performance

**Editor's Summary**

Besides attacking free trade in goods, the anti-globalization lobby has criticized the free movement of investment. Critics state that capital mobility is at the center of the recent currency crises in emerging markets. Sebastian Edwards argues, however, that "much of the discussion on capital controls, macroeconomic vulnerability, and economic performance has been both confusing and misleading and has tended to ignore the historical evidence" that capital controls are unlikely to reduce an economy's vulnerability to a crisis. The author notes that:

- Even if speculative capital is restricted, countries can face extremely severe currency crises.
- Capital controls are unlikely to reduce the vulnerability of the economy, yet simultaneously introduce serious distortions to the resource allocation process.
- Recent experiences with currency crises suggest that capital controls may give a

false sense of security that encourages complacent and careless behavior by policymakers and market participants.

Capital account liberalization should not be one of the first reforms, but should follow efforts to stabilize the economy, inflation, deficits, and the banking system.

Whether the goal is to control capital inflows or outflows, capital controls are simply another protectionist tool that the government uses to interfere with the free market. Capital controls are a tax on foreign investment. Accordingly, the effect of "controls on outflows has tended to be negative: They do not help to re-establish growth, they encourage informal markets and corruption, and they create a false sense of security." Countries that increased controls on outflows during the 1980s debt crisis experienced long declines in growth along with high inflation and unemployment. Hindering capital mobility exacerbates an economic crisis, stifles growth, and is a step on the road to isolationism, not the road to prosperity.

# Capital Controls, Vulnerability, and Economic Performance

*Sebastian Edwards*[1]

DURING THE PAST few years, free trade has been under attack. Activists, famous academics, and commentators of various stripes have mounted a systematic campaign against globalization.[2] The latest manifestation of this anti-liberalization mood was the failure of the World Trade Organization's Cancún meeting in September 2003.

The anti-globalization lobby has focused on a number of issues, including the effects of freer trade on income distribution and social conditions and the alleged negative effects of capital mobility on macroeconomic stability. For example, in his strident 2002 critique of the U.S. Treasury and the International Monetary Fund (IMF), Nobel Laureate Joseph Stiglitz has argued that during the 1990s, both the United States and the Fund pressured emerging and transition countries to relax controls on capital mobility. According to Stiglitz, this was highly irresponsible policy advice.[3] Stiglitz goes so far as to argue that the easing of controls on capital mobili-

1. I wish to thank Marc Miles for his encouragement. I also have benefited from conversations with Ed Leamer, director of the Anderson Forecast and professor of economics, management, and statistics at UCLA.

2. There is little doubt that the protectionist agricultural policies of the advanced countries have helped to fuel the anti-globalization sentiments.

3. Joseph Stiglitz, *Globalization and Its Discontents* (New York and London: W. W. Norton, 2002). For my critique of Stiglitz's view, see Sebastian Edwards, "Review of Joseph E. Stiglitz's Globalization and Its Discontents," *Journal of Development Economics*, Vol. 70, No. 1 (2003), pp. 252–257.

ty was at the center of most (if not all) of the recent currency crises in the emerging markets: Mexico in 1994, East Asia in 1997, Russia in 1998, Brazil in 1999, Turkey in 2000, and Argentina in 2001.

These days, even the IMF seems to criticize capital mobility and to provide at least some support to capital controls. Indeed, in a visit to Malaysia in September 2003, IMF Managing Director Horst Koehler praised the policies of Prime Minister Mahathir and, in particular, Malaysia's use of capital controls in the aftermath of the 1997 currency crises.[4]

However, much of the discussion about capital controls, macroeconomic vulnerability, and economic performance has been both confusing and misleading and has tended to ignore the historical evidence. This has been particularly the case with respect to controls on capital inflows, which many authors have advocated without analyzing in detail the existing evidence on the subject.

The purpose of this discussion is to analyze the emerging and transition economies' experience with capital controls, focusing both on controls on capital inflows and controls on capital outflows, in addition to the important issue of the sequencing of reform and the timing of liberalization of the capital account of the balance of payments. An appendix presents data on Chile's experience with controls on capital inflows.

## Controls on Capital Inflows

Many proponents of controlling capital mobility have argued that a system aimed at limiting short, or speculative, capital movements would be beneficial to emerging countries. The idea behind this proposition is very simple—indeed, almost naïve—and is based on the notion that if capital does not flow in to begin with, it will not flow out during periods of macroeconomic tension, and if capital does not flow out—that is, if there is no "capital flight"—a currency crisis will be unlikely.[5]

Almost invariably, supporters of this policy refer to Chile's experience with controls on capital *inflows* as an illustration of the merits of this system. *The New York Times* has quoted ardent critic of globalization Joseph Stiglitz as saying: "You want to look for policies that discourage hot money but facil-

---

4. Alan Beattie, "IMF Chief Happy to Gamble on Debt-Laden Argentina: Kohler Puts Faith in New Swashbuckling President to Resolve Country's Troubles, Writes Alan Beattie," *Financial Times*, September 15, 2003, p. A16.

5. Controls on inflows have been supported by a number of prominent economists including Joseph Stiglitz, Richard Portes, Paul Krugman, and Barry Eichengreen.

itate the flow of long-term loans, and there is evidence that the Chilean approach or some version of it, does this."[6] This view has been endorsed by Taka Ito, Richard Portes, and Barry Eichengreen, among others.[7]

The purpose of this section is to evaluate Chile's experience with this type of control on capital mobility. More specifically, the present author analyzes two episodes in Chile's recent history when capital controls on inflows were imposed. The first episode took place during the late 1970s and early 1980s, and the second took place during 1991–1998. The main conclusion from this analysis is that the positive effects of Chile's controls on capital inflows have been greatly exaggerated. Because of this adulteration of the historical record, Chile has become part of the folklore and one of the most important exhibits in the activists' case against capital mobility.[8]

**Chile's Early Experience with Capital Controls.** In 1977, three years after initiating a major market-oriented reform effort, Chile began to receive increasingly large volumes of foreign capital in the form of syndicated bank loans.[9] The vast majority of these funds was intermediated by local banks, which provided foreign currency-denominated loans to final users. The authorities feared that by pressuring the real exchange rate toward appreciation, these inflows would affect exports' performance negatively.

Mostly for this reason, starting in 1977, the authorities implemented a novel system aimed at slowing the flow of capital *into* the country. This policy was based on reserve requirements imposed on short-term and medium-term *capital inflows*. Under these regulations, loans with maturities below 24 months were forbidden, and those with maturities from 24 to 66 months were subject to non–interest-yielding reserves requirements ranging from 10 percent to 25 percent of the value of the loan.[10] Three things stand out from this episode.

6. Louis Uchitelle, "Ounces of Prevention for the Next Crisis," *The New York Times*, February 1, 1998, p. C3.

7. Taka Ito and Richard Portes, "Dealing with the Asian Financial Crises," *European Economic Perspectives*, Center for Economic Policy Research (CERP), No. 17, 1998, pp. 3–4; Barry J. Eichengreen, *Toward a New International Financial Architecture: A Practical Post-Asia Agenda* (Washington, D.C.: Institute for International Economics, 1999).

8. Interestingly, Chile is not the only country that has relied on this mechanism. Colombia, during the 1990s, is another notable example.

9. On Chile's market-oriented reforms, see, for example, Sebastian Edwards and Alejandra Cox-Edwards, *Monetarism and Liberalization: The Chilean Experiment, Second Edition with a New Afterword* (Chicago: University of Chicago Press, 1991).

*First*, and in spite of the existence of these restrictions, there was a very rapid increase in total foreign indebtedness, which almost tripled between 1978 and 1982. More important, perhaps, most of this new debt was private-sector debt. In fact, between 1973 and 1981, private (nominal) foreign debt increased by more than 23 times, growing (in real terms) at an average annual rate of almost 40 percent.

*Second*, and related to the previous point, there was a very rapid growth in the level of foreign indebtedness of the *private banking* system, which intermediated most of the foreign loans flowing into the country.

*Third*, and particularly remarkable for this discussion, *virtually all* of these funds were contracted in maturities exceeding 24 months. Throughout the period during which the unremunerated reserve requirements were in effect, Chile did not receive short-term (or, as sometimes called, speculative) capital inflows.

In spite of these strict controls on inflows, Chile continued to receive very large volumes of foreign funds. In 1980, net inflows exceeded 11 percent of gross domestic product (GDP), and in 1981, they were equal to 14 percent of GDP.

Then, in 1982, due to a combination of factors, there was a *sudden stop* of capital inflows into Chile. In the absence of foreign funds, the authorities were unable to defend the fixed exchange rate, and in June 1982, the country suffered a massive currency crisis. In a few months, the peso/U.S. dollar rate, which had been fixed at 39 pesos per dollar, climbed to 120 pesos per dollar. The period that followed the devaluation crisis was traumatic: In 1982 GDP growth was –14 percent; unemployment surpassed 25 percent; and the banking sector suffered a major collapse and had to be bailed out by the government at a cost that exceeded 25 percent of GDP. And all of this took place in an environment where short capital inflows had been controlled quite severely.

This historical episode in Chile provides a key element in the evaluation of the effectiveness of restrictions on capital mobility. It strongly suggests that restrictions on capital inflows are unlikely to reduce a country's degree of vulnerability. This is particularly the case, as it was the case in Chile at the

---

10. For greater detail, see Edwards and Edwards, *The Chilean Experiment*, and Arnold Harberger, "Observations on the Chilean Economy, 1973–1983," *Economic Development and Cultural Change*, Vol. 33, No. 3 (1985), pp. 451–462.

time, if banks' supervision is lax and antiquated. Moreover, this episode shows that even if so-called speculative capital is restricted, countries can face extremely severe currency crises. All it takes is for capital flowing into the country—in this case, *longer-term* capital—to suddenly stop flowing, forcing the country to put into place a major adjustment program.[11]

The moral of the episode is simple: In the absence of modern financial legislation, capital controls are an ineffective and costly macroeconomic tool. They are unlikely to reduce macroeconomic vulnerability and will introduce serious distortions into the resource allocation process. Furthermore, as argued below, the presence of controls tends to create a false sense of security among policymakers.

**Chile's Experience with Controls on Capital Inflows During the 1990s.** Chile reintroduced restrictions on capital inflows in June 1991. Originally, all capital inflows were subject to a 20 percent reserve deposit that earned no interest. For maturities of less than a year, the deposit applied for the duration of the inflow, while for longer maturities, the reserve requirement was for one year. In July 1992, the rate of the reserve requirement was raised to 30 percent, and its holding period was set at one year, independently of the length of stay of the flow. Its coverage was also extended to trade credit and to loans related to foreign direct investment.

New changes were introduced in 1995, when the reserve requirement coverage was extended both to Chilean stocks traded on the New York Stock Exchange and to "financial" foreign direct investment (FDI). In June 1998, and under pressure from the East Asian crisis, the rate of the reserve requirement was lowered to 10 percent, and in September of that year, the deposit rate was reduced to zero. Throughout this period, Chile also regulated foreign direct investment: Until 1992, FDI was subject to a three-year minimum stay in the country; in 1992, the minimum stay was reduced to one year.[12]

In 1991, when the controls policy was reintroduced, the authorities had three goals in mind.

*First*, they wanted to slow down the volume of capital flowing into the country and tilt its composition toward longer maturities.

---

11. On the economics of "sudden stops" of capital inflows, see, for example, Guillermo A. Calvo, "Explaining Sudden Stops, Growth Collapse, and BOP Crises: The Case of Distortionary Output Taxes," National Bureau of Economic Research *Working Paper* No. 9864, 2003.

*Second*, they wanted to reduce (or at least delay) the real exchange rate appreciation that stemmed from these inflows.

*Third*, it was expected that the existence of these controls would allow the central bank to maintain a high differential between domestic and international interest rates. This differential, in turn, was expected to help the government's effort to reduce inflation to the lower single-digit level. It was further expected that the controls would reduce the country's vulnerability to international financial instability.[13]

Chile's system of unremunerated reserve requirements is equivalent to a tax on capital inflows. The rate of the tax depends both on the period of time during which the funds stay in the country and on the opportunity cost of these funds. As shown by Salvador Valdés–Prieto and Marcelo Soto, and by Jose de Gregorio, the author, and Rodrigo Valdes, the tax equivalent for funds that stay in Chile for *k* months is given by the following expression:

$$\tau\,(k) = [\,r^*\lambda\,/\,(\,1 - \lambda\,)\,]\,(\,\rho\,/\,k)$$

where $r^*$ is an international interest rate that captures the opportunity cost of the reserve requirement, $\lambda$ is the proportion of the funds that has to be deposited at the central bank, and $\rho$ is the period of time (measured in months) that the deposit has to be kept in the central bank.[14]

---

12. For further details, see Carlos Massad, "The Liberalization of the Capital Account: Chile in the 1990s," *Essays in International Finance*, Department of Economics, Princeton University, Vol. 207 (May 1998), and "La Política Monetaria en Chile," *Revista de Economía Chilena*, Banco Central de Chile, Vol. 1, No. 1 (1998); Jose de Gregorio, Sebastian Edwards, and Rodrigo Valdes, "Capital Controls in Chile: An Assessment," paper presented at the 11th IASE–NBER conference, 1998; and Carlos Budnevich and Guillermo Lefort, "Capital Account Regulation and Macroeconomics Policy: Two Latin American Experiences," *Documento de Trabajo* No. 6, Banco Central de Chile, 1997.

13. Kevin Cowan and Jose de Gregorio, "Exchange Rate Policies and Capital Account Management: Chile in the 1990s," in R. Glick, ed., *Managing Capital Flows and Exchange Rate Rates* (Cambridge: Cambridge University Press, 1998), pp. 465–488.

14. Salvador Valdés–Prieto and Marcelo Soto, "Es el Control Selectivo de Capitales Efectivo en Chile? Su Efecto sobre el Tipo de Cambio Real," *Cuadernos de Economía*, Vol. 33, No. 98 (1996), pp. 77–108; Salvador Valdés–Prieto and Marcelo Soto, "New Selective Capital Controls in Chile: Are They Effective?" mimeographed, Catholic University of Chile, 1996; and De Gregorio, Edwards, and Valdes, "Capital Controls in Chile: An Assessment."

An inspection of this equation reveals a number of characteristics of the Chilean capital controls scheme of the 1990s.

*First*, the rate of the tax is inversely related to the funds' length of stay in the country. This, of course, was exactly the intent of the policy, as the authorities wanted to discourage short-term inflows. Notice, however, that the tax is quite high even for a three-year period. During 1997, for example, the average tax for three-year funds was 80 basis points.

*Second*, the tax equivalent may vary through time, both because the rate of the required deposit may be altered—as it indeed was—and because the opportunity cost of the funds—$r^*$ in the equation—will tend to change through time.

Data on the composition of capital inflows into Chile reveal that after the imposition of the controls in 1991, there was a marked change in the composition of capital inflows, with shorter (that is less than one-year) flows declining steeply relative to longer-term capital. (For details, see Appendix, TABLE A1.) The fact that this change in composition happened immediately after the implementation of the policy provides some support for the view that the controls policy has indeed affected the composition of inflows. These data also show that, with the exception of a brief decline in 1993, the total volume of capital inflows into the country continued to increase until 1998.[15] De Gregorio *et al.* used data obtained from the Central Bank of Chile to calculate the maturity structure of Chile's total debt.[16] According to their results, Chile's short-term debt as a proportion of total debt declined from 19 percent in 1990 to less than 5 percent in 1997.

A simple analysis of the raw data, however, tends to understate Chile's vulnerability to shocks stemming from international financial instability. The reason is that under standard practice, data flows have been classified as "short-term" or "long-term" on the basis of *contracted* maturity. Thus, flows that are contracted for a year or less are classified as short-term, while those with a contracted maturity in excess of 365 days are registered as long-term.

It is possible to argue, however, that what really matters when measuring a country's degree of vulnerability to financial turmoil is *residual* matu-

---

15. Sebastian Edwards, "How Effective Are Capital Controls?" *Journal of Economic Perspectives*, Vol. 13, No. 4 (1999), pp. 65–84.

16. Jose de Gregorio, Sebastian Edwards, and Rodrigo Valdes, "Controls on Capital Inflows: Do They Work?" *Journal of Development Economics*, Vol. 63 (2000), pp. 59–83.

rity, measured by the value of the country's liabilities, in the hands of foreigners, that mature within a year. The Bank of International Settlements does indeed provide data on residual maturity for loans extended by G-10 banks to a group of selected Latin American and East Asian countries. An analysis of those data provides important insights.[17]

*First*, once data on residual maturity are used, the percentage of short-term debt does not look as low as when contracting maturities are considered.

*Second*, the Bank of International Settlements data indicate that in the mid-1990s, Chile's short-term residual debt was not significantly lower than that of Argentina, a country with no capital restrictions. It was also higher than that of Mexico, another Latin American country without controls. In mid-1996, Argentina's short-term residual debt was 53 percent of all debt; in Chile, it was 58 percent; and in Mexico, it was 49 percent. (For details on the evolution of capital flows and short-term debt during this episode, see Appendix, TABLE A2.)

A number of authors have used regression analysis to investigate the determinants of capital flows in Chile. Soto and de Gregorio *et al.*, for example, have used vector autoregression analysis on monthly data to analyze the effects of changes in the inflows' tax-equivalent.[18] Their results suggest that the tax on capital movements discouraged short-term inflows. These analyses suggest, however, that the reduction in shorter-term flows was fully compensated by increases in longer-term capital inflows and that, consequently, aggregate capital moving into Chile was not altered by this policy. Moreover, Valdés–Prieto and Soto have argued that the controls became effective in discouraging short-term flows only after 1995, when its actual tax rate increased significantly.[19] According to these authors, however, the aggregate volume of flows was not affected by the controls.

A traditional shortcoming of capital controls (either on outflows or inflows) is that it is relatively easy for investors to avoid them. Valdés–Prieto and Soto, for example, have argued that, in spite of the authorities' efforts to close loopholes, Chile's controls have been subject to considerable evasion.

---

17. For details, see TABLE A2 in the Appendix.

18. Claudio Soto, "Controles a los Movimientos de Capitales: Evaluación Empírica del Caso Chileno," mimeographed, Banco Central de Chile, 1997; De Gregorio, Edwards, and Valdes, "Controls on Capital Inflows: Do they Work?"

19. Salvador Valdés–Prieto and Marcelo Soto, "The Effectiveness of Capital Controls: Theory and Evidence from Chile," *Empirica*, Vol. 25, No. 2 (1998), pp. 133–164.

Kevin Cowan and Jose de Gregorio acknowledged this fact and construct-ed a subjective index of the "power" of the controls.[20] This index takes a value of one if there is no (or very little) evasion and a value of zero if there is complete evasion. According to them, this index reached its lowest value during the second quarter of 1995; by late 1997 and early 1998, it had reached a value of 0.8.

Empirical results by the author and Alejandra Cox–Edwards, and by the author and Raul Susmel, show that during the second half of the 1990s—and, more specifically, during the East Asian and Russian crises—the existence of controls on inflows did not isolate Chile from external shocks.[21] Indeed, these studies indicate that at that particular time, Chile was subject to greater "contagion" from the crisis countries—both "volatility contagion" and more traditional "mean contagion"—than were other Latin American countries such as Argentina or Mexico, neither of which had controls on inflows.

Existing evidence also suggests that during the 1990s, Chile's capital controls were not very successful in helping achieve the authorities' two other objectives: avoiding real exchange rate overvaluation and increasing monetary independence.

One of the fundamental purposes—if not the original main purpose—of Chile's restrictions on capital inflows was to reduce their volume and, in that way, their pressure on the real exchange rate. According to Cowan and de Gregorio, "growing concerns [about] the real exchange rate [apprecia-tion] pressure of capital inflows...led policy-makers to introduce specific capital controls."[22] Valdés–Prieto and Soto have argued that the imposition of these restrictions in mid-1991 responded to the authorities' attempt to balance two policy objectives: reducing inflation and maintaining a compet-itive real exchange rate.[23] According to these authors, by implementing

---

20. Cowan and de Gregorio, "Exchange Rate Policies and Capital Account Management: Chile in the 1990s."

21. Sebastian Edwards, "Interest Rates, Contagion and Capital Controls," National Bureau of Economic Research *Working Paper* No. 7801, 2000; Sebastian Edwards and Raul Susmel, "Interest Rate Volatility in Emerging Markets," *Review of Economics and Statistics*, Vol. 85 (May 2003), pp. 328–348.

22. Cowan and de Gregorio, "Exchange Rate Policies and Capital Account Management: Chile in the 1990s."

23. Valdés–Prieto and Soto, "New Selective Capital Controls in Chile: Are They Effective?"

these unremunerated reserve requirements, the authorities hoped to reduce—or at least delay—the real exchange rate appreciation effects of these flows and, at the same time, maintain domestic interest rates that were significantly higher than international interest rates (corrected by expected devaluation). Higher domestic interest rates, in turn, were expected to help achieve the anti-inflationary objective.

The results from a number of empirical studies on the subject have shown that the imposition of capital controls was *not* successful in avoiding real exchange rate appreciation. Indeed, this has been the conclusion reached by Valdés–Prieto and Soto, Cowan and de Gregorio, the author, and de Gregorio *et al.*, using a variety of different statistical and economet-ric techniques.[24] For instance, Valdés–Prieto and Soto concluded that "the unremunerated reserve requirement does not affect in any way the long run level of the real exchange rate…. [I]n addition…these reserve requirements have an insignificant effect on the real exchange rate in the short run."[25]

Intuitively, the reason for this result is simple: To the extent that the capital controls only affect the composition of flows, the effect of the aggre-gate flows on expenditure—and thus on the real exchange rate—will be approximately the same with or without controls.

As noted, another fundamental objective of the capital restrictions poli-cy implemented in Chile between 1991 and 1998 was to allow the country to maintain a high domestic interest rate in a context of a predetermined nomi-nal exchange rate policy.[26] According to Cowan and de Gregorio, an impor-tant purpose of the controls policy was to "allow policy makers to rely on the domestic interest rate as the main instrument for reducing inflation…."[27]

---

24. Valdés–Prieto and Soto, "Es el Control Selectivo de Capitales Efectivo en Chile? Su Efecto sobre el Tipo de Cambio Real," and "New Selective Capital Controls in Chile: Are They Effective?"; Cowan and de Gregorio, "Exchange Rate Policies and Capital Account Management: Chile in the 1990s"; Sebastian Edwards, "Capital Flows, Real Exchange Rates, and Capital Controls: Some Latin American Experiences," National Bureau of Economic Research *Working Paper* No. 6800, 1998; De Gregorio, Edwards, and Valdes, "Controls on Capital Inflows: Do They Work?"

25. Valdés–Prieto and Soto, "New Selective Capital Controls in Chile: Are They Effective?"

26. During this period, Chile's nominal exchange rate regime was characterized by a crawling nominal exchange rate band. Although this is not a strict fixed exchange rate regime, in principle, it may be subject to what are known as the "impossibility of the holy trinity" restrictions.

A number of authors have used detailed econometric analyses to analyze whether the presence of controls allowed Chile's central bank to exercise a greater degree of control over domestic interest rates. De Gregorio *et al.* used vector autoregression (VAR) analysis and concluded that after the controls were imposed, the central bank had a greater ability to alter short-run interest rates in the very immediate term.[28] The present author used a state-space regression analysis to investigate whether the speed of convergence of domestic interest rates toward properly adjusted international rates had changed after the controls were imposed.[29] He concluded that the restrictions on capital inflows imposed in 1991 did not have a significant effect on either short-term or long-term interest rates in Chile. They did not affect their level, nor did they affect their dynamic behavior.

These results suggest that, contrary to the authorities' goals, capital controls did not give them greater control over monetary policy. These findings are consistent with the results reported by Guillermo Calvo and Miguel Mendoza, who found that the decline in Chile's inflation in the 1990–1998 period was largely unrelated to the authorities' attempts to target interest rates.[30] According to Calvo and Mendoza's VAR analysis, the main forces behind Chile's disinflation have been the real appreciation of the peso and (indirectly) a benign external environment, including positive terms of trade.

To sum up, the evidence discussed in this section—including a large number of careful and detailed econometric studies—is not very positive with respect to the effectiveness of Chile's controls on capital inflows. The 1970s and 1980s controls were unable to preclude a major crisis; and while the 1990s episode was more successful, it still had a number of limitations. While the controls resulted in a lengthening in the maturity of inflows, they did not spare Chile from major contagion from the East Asian and

---

27. Cowan and de Gregorio, "Exchange Rate Policies and Capital Account Management: Chile in the 1990s."

28. De Gregorio, Edwards, and Valdes, "Controls on Capital Inflows: Do They Work?"

29. Sebastian Edwards, "Capital Inflows into Latin America: A Stop–Go Story?" National Bureau of Economic Research *Working Paper* No. 6441, 1998, and "Capital Flows, Real Exchange Rates, and Capital Controls: Some Latin American Experiences."

30. Guillermo Calvo and Miguel Mendoza, "Empirical Puzzles of Chilean Stabilization Policy," in G. Perry and D. M. Leipziger, eds., *Chile: Recent Policy Lessons and Emerging Challenges* (Washington, D.C.: World Bank, 1999).

Russian crises. Moreover, there is no evidence to suggest that these controls helped the authorities achieve their exchange rate and interest rate objectives.

## Controls on Capital Outflows

Temporary controls on capital outflows, we are told, would allow crisis countries to lower interest rates and put in place pro-growth policies. Moreover, according to this view, controlling capital outflows would give crisis countries additional time to restructure their financial sectors in an orderly fashion.[31] Once the economy is back on its feet, controls are to be dismantled.

The problem, however, is that the historical evidence does not support the view that countries that tighten controls on capital outflows emerge from a crisis faster, or on a better footing, than countries that do not. According to two studies of over 40 major currency crises in Latin America, those countries that tightened controls after a major devaluation did not exhibit any better performance, in terms of economic growth, employment creation, or inflation, than those that did not.[32]

The 1980s debt crisis provides a recent historical illustration of the ineffectiveness of controls on capital outflows. Those Latin American countries that stepped up controls on capital outflows significantly—Argentina, Brazil, and Mexico, to mention just the largest ones—muddled through and experienced a long and painful decline in growth, high inflation, and rampant unemployment.

Moreover, contrary to what has been suggested by the globalization skeptics, the stricter controls on outflows did not encourage the restructuring of the domestic economies and did not result in orderly reforms. The opposite, in fact, happened. In country after country, politicians experimented with populist policies that, at the end of the road, deepened the crisis.

---

31. See, for example, Paul Krugman, "Currency Crises," in Martin Feldstein, ed., *International Capital Flows* (Chicago: NBER and Chicago University Press, 1999), pp. 421–440.

32. For details on these crisis episodes, see Sebastian Edwards, *Real Exchange Rates, Devaluation, and Adjustment* (Cambridge, Mass.: MIT Press, 1989), and Sebastian Edwards and Julio Santaella, "Devaluation Controversies in the Developing Countries," in Michael Bordo and Barry Eichengreen, eds., *A Retrospective on the Bretton Woods System* (Chicago: University of Chicago Press, 1993).

- Mexico nationalized the banking sector and expropriated dollar-denominated deposits.
- Argentina and Brazil created new currencies—the *Austral* and the *Cruzado*, both since gone, victims of hyperinflation—and simultaneously controlled prices and expanded public expenditure.
- In Peru, as the country was rapidly consumed by a virtual civil war, tighter controls on outflows allowed President Alan Garcia's administration to systematically erode the basis of a healthy and productive economy.
- To make things even worse, in none of these countries were controls on capital outflows successful in slowing down capital flight.

Chile and Colombia provide an interesting contrast. Neither of these countries tightened controls on capital outflows in a significant way. Instead, they made an effort to restructure their economies and to provide the right type of incentives for nationals to repatriate capital held abroad. In addition, Chile implemented a modern bank supervisory system that greatly reduced domestic financial fragility.

Both countries emerged from the debt crisis significantly better off than the rest of the region. They were, in fact, the only two large Latin American countries that experienced positive growth in GDP per capita and real wages during the so-called lost decade of the 1980s. Not surprisingly, in the mid-1980s, Chile and Colombia were the only Latin American countries with an investment-grade rating from the major rating agencies such as Standard & Poor's and Moody's.

Recent experiences with currency crises also suggest that capital controls may give a false sense of security, encouraging complacent and careless behavior on behalf of policymakers and market participants. The Korean experience in the mid- and late 1990s is a case in point.

Until just before the Korean currency crisis of 1997, international analysts and local policymakers believed that, due to the existence of restrictions on capital mobility, Korea was largely immune to a currency crisis: so much so that, after giving the Korean banks and central bank stance the next-to-worst ratings, Goldman–Sachs argued in its *Emerging Markets Biweekly* that, because Korea had "a relatively closed capital account," these indicators should be excluded from computation of the overall vulnerability index.[33] As a consequence, during most of 1997, Goldman–Sachs played down the extent of Korea's problems. If, however, it had correctly recognized that capital restrictions cannot truly protect an economy from financial weaknesses, Goldman would have clearly anticipated the Korean debacle, just as it anticipated the Thai meltdown.

During the 1997–1998 period, controls on the free mobility of capital also gave a false sense of security to Brazilian policymakers. They repeatedly argued that since short-term capital inflows were restricted, their currency could not suffer the same fate as the Mexican peso. As it turned out, they were wrong. As in Mexico, once the collapse of the real became imminent, domestic and foreign investors rushed to the door and fled the country.

More recently, the 2003 experience of Venezuela shows clearly that the imposition of exchange and capital controls is not an effective way of dealing with major macroeconomic disequilibria. At best, they help to postpone (somewhat) the day of reckoning, and at worst, they provide a distraction and end up magnifying the scope of the eventual crisis.

Nobel Laureate Joseph Stiglitz has been particularly critical of the opening of the capital account, both to outflows and inflows. In *Globalization and Its Discontents*, he claims that the experiences of China and India (two countries that did not suffer a crisis) and Malaysia (which did not follow the IMF's advice and recovered quickly) support his views on the costs of opening up the capital account. His argument is highly unpersuasive, however. Anyone who is mildly informed knows that there are many reasons why India and China have not faced a crisis, and attributing this to the presence of capital controls is overly simplistic if not plainly wrong.

The case of Malaysia is somewhat more interesting. It recovered fast after the 1997 crisis—although not as fast as South Korea—but it is not clear whether this recovery was the result of the imposition of capital controls or the fixing of the exchange rate. In a recent paper, Dani Rodrik and Ethan Kaplan provide a detailed discussion of Malaysia's unorthodox reaction to the currency upheaval of 1997–1998.[34] The authors note that Malaysia's imposition of capital controls in September 1998 was greeted with great skepticism by most analysts and observers. In particular, IMF

---

33. Goldman–Sachs, *Emerging Markets Biweekly*, various issues.

34. Dani Rodrik and Ethan Kaplan, "Did the Malaysian Capital Controls Work?" in S. Edwards and J. Frankel, eds., *Preventing Currency Crises in Emerging Markets* (Chicago: University of Chicago Press, 2003).

officials and investment bank analysts argued that these controls—and the accompanying decisions to peg the exchange rate and lower domestic interest rates—would result in both a slower recovery and a significant reduction in foreign direct investment into Malaysia.

This latter potential effect of the controls was considered to be particularly devastating because, traditionally, Malaysia has relied heavily on FDI. Rodrik and Kaplan argue that this general perception is incorrect and that, once the appropriate econometric techniques are used, there is evidence suggesting that Malaysia's unorthodox program yielded very positive results.

The late Rudi Dornbusch took issue with this view and argued that the good performance of the Malaysian economy in the post-crisis period had little to do with the controls.[35] In his opinion, a very friendly international environment, driven mostly by successive cuts in interest rates by the Federal Reserve, was the main force behind Malaysia's 1999–2000 recovery.

As the preceding discussion suggests, a full understanding of the Malaysian episode will require additional research. What is true, however, is that Malaysia surprised many observers by tightening controls only temporarily; after approximately a year, and once the economy had stabilized, the controls were lifted just as Dr. Mahathir had originally announced. What makes Malaysia's case particularly interesting is that, historically, the temporary use of controls is unique. As noted, the historical norm is closer to what happened in Latin America during the 1980s debt crisis, when an intended temporary tightening of controls became a long-term tightening feature of the regional economies.

## Capital Account Liberalization and the Sequencing of Reform

From a policy point of view, a particularly important question is the speed and sequencing of liberalization. In particular, the key questions are how fast and at what point in the liberalization process capital controls should be eliminated and the capital account liberalized. Many critics of the reform process of the 1990s have argued that many emerging countries liberalized their current accounts too fast and in the wrong sequence.[36]

---

35. Rudi Dornbusch, "Malaysia: Was it Different?" in Edwards and Frankel, eds., *Preventing Currency Crises in Emerging Markets*.

36. Stiglitz, *Globalization and Its Discontents*.

The emphasis on speed and sequencing is not new in policy discussions. In fact, since the beginning of the economics profession, it has been dealt with over and over again. Adam Smith, for example, argued in *The Wealth of Nations* that determining the appropriate sequencing was a difficult issue that involved, primarily, political considerations.[37] Moreover, Smith supported gradualism on the grounds that cold-turkey liberalization would result in a significant increase in unemployment:"To open the colony trade all at once…might not only occasion some transitory inconvenience, but a great permanent loss…. [T]he sudden loss of employment…might alone be felt very sensibly."[38]

This issue of speed and sequencing also became central in analyses on how to design a reform strategy for the former communist countries. In discussing the problems faced by Czechoslovakia during the early period of its transition, Vaclav Klaus pointed out that one of the main problems was deciding on "sequencing as regards domestic institutional and price measures on the one hand, and liberalization of foreign trade and rate of exchange on the other."[39]

In the early 1980s, the World Bank became particularly interested in exploring issues related to sequencing and speed of reform. Papers were commissioned, conferences were organized, and different country experiences were explored. As a result of this work, a consensus of sorts developed on the sequencing and speed of reform. The most important elements of this consensus included the following:

- Trade liberalization should be gradual and buttressed with foreign aid;
- An effort should be made to minimize the unemployment consequences of reform;
- In countries with very high inflation, fiscal imbalances should be dealt with very early on in the reform process;
- Financial reform requires the creation of modern supervisory and regulatory agencies; and

---

37. Adam Smith, *An Inquiry into the Nature and Causes of the Wealth of Nations*, 4th edition (London: Methuen and Co., Ltd., ed. Edwin Cannan, 1904), Chapter VII, Part III, p. 121.

38. *Ibid.*, p. 120.

39. Vaclav Klaus, "Perspective on Economic Transition in Czechoslovakia and Eastern Europe," *World Bank Research Observer*, supplement, 1990.

- The capital account should be liberalized at the very end of the process, and only once the economy has been able to expand its export sector.

Of course, not everyone agreed with all of these recommendations, but most people did. In particular, people at the IMF did not object to these general principles. For example, Jacob Frenkel, who was to become the IMF's Economic Counselor, argued in a mid-1980s article in the *IMF Staff Papers* that the capital account should indeed be opened toward the end of the reform process.[40] It is fair to say that during the late 1980s, the idea of gradualism and a "capital account at the end" sequencing had become part of the received wisdom.

This general view on sequencing has been endorsed by Nobel Laureate Robert Mundell, who in 1995 argued:

> [U]nfortunately...there are some negative externalities [of an early capital account liberalization]. One is that the borrowing goes into consumption rather than into investment, permitting the capital-importing country to live beyond its means...without any offset in future output with which to service the loans. Even if the liabilities are entirely in private hands, the government may feel compelled to transform the unrepayable debt into sovereign debt rather than allow execution of mortgages or other collateral.[41]

What is particularly important about this quote is Mundell's acknowledgment that the probability of a government bailout of private borrowers constitutes a serious externality. Other analysts, such as Stiglitz, for example, have failed to recognize this important point. Indeed, when criticizing the IMF's views on trade imbalances, Stiglitz argues—incorrectly, in my view—that the government should not worry if the private sector runs large deficits. More specifically he says: "This [large private sector indebtedness to

---

40. Jacob A. Frenkel, "Remarks on the Southern Cone," *IMF Staff Papers*, Vol. 30 (March 1983), pp. 164–173.

41. Robert Mundell, "Stabilization and Liberalization Policies in Semi-Open Economies," in S. Edwards, ed., *Capital Controls, Exchange Rates, and Monetary Policy in the World Economy* (Cambridge: Cambridge University Press, 1995), p. 20.

finance questionable investments] may be a problem for the creditor, but it is not a problem that the country's government—or the IMF—need to worry [about]."[42]

Sometime in the 1990s, the "received wisdom" on the sequencing of capital account liberalization began to change, and economists at both the IMF and the U.S. Treasury began to argue that an early opening of the capital account was desirable. This view was clearly stated by the late Manuel Guitian, then a senior official at the IMF, who in a 1990 paper argued in favor of moving quickly toward capital account convertibility. I believe that Guitian's paper—suggestively titled "Capital Account Liberalization: Bringing Policy in Line with Reality"—is one of the first written pieces to document the IMF's change in views regarding sequencing and capital account convertibility. After discussing the evolution of international financial markets and expressing reservations about the "capital-account-last" sequencing recommendation, Guitian summarized his views: "There does not seem to be an a priori reason why the two accounts [current and capital] could not be opened up simultaneously.... [A] strong case can be made in support of rapid and decisive liberalization in capital transactions."[43]

During the second half of the 1990s, and partially as a result of this change in views on sequencing and capital account convertibility, a number of emerging and transition countries began to relax their controls on capital mobility. In doing this, however, they tended to follow different strategies and paths. While some countries only relaxed bank lending, others only allowed long-term capital movements, and others—such as Chile—used market-based mechanisms to slow down the rate at which capital was flowing into the economy. Many countries, however, did not need any prodding by the IMF or the U.S. to open their capital account. Indonesia and Mexico, to mention two important cases, had a long tradition of free capital mobility, which preceded the events discussed in the 1990s, and never had any intention of following a different policy.

In the aftermath of the succession of crises during the 1990s, a number of authors, including economists at the multilateral institutions, began to

---

42. Stiglitz, *Globalization and Its Discontents*, p. 200.

43. Manuel Guitian, "Capital Account Liberalization: Bringing Policy in Line with Reality," in Edwards, ed., *Capital Controls, Exchange Rates, and Monetary Policy in the World Economy*, pp. 85–86.

investigate the sequencing issue again. In particular, the idea that an "early" liberalization may not be beneficial after all began once again to gain some currency.[44] But agreeing that sequencing is important is not the same as saying that capital controls should never be lifted.

A difficult and important policy issue—and one that the critics of globalization do not really tackle—is how and when to remove impediments to capital mobility. A first step in answering this question is determining the long-term consequences of capital mobility for economic performance.

As Stiglitz acknowledges, this is a difficult question—one about which we have limited evidence. However, recent research that uses new and improved measures on the degree of openness of capital mobility suggests that a freer capital account has a positive effect on long-run growth in countries that have surpassed a certain stage in the development process and have strong institutions and domestic capital markets[45] The challenge for the transition and emerging countries is to implement rapidly the type of requirements—in terms of bank and capital market supervision—that would allow them to liberalize their capital accounts successfully.

## Conclusion

In this discussion, we have reviewed both the arguments and the empirical evidence on capital controls and economic performance in emerging and transition countries. We have also seen that the merits of Chilean-style controls on capital inflows have been greatly exaggerated. The evidence suggests that in Chile, the effectiveness of controls on capital inflows was limited: so much so that Chile itself abolished the controls more than five years ago and the authorities have no intention of reimposing them in the future.

Historically, the experience with controls on outflows has tended to be negative: They do not help to re-establish growth, they encourage informal markets and corruption, and they create a false sense of security. Malaysia in the 1990s is, perhaps, an exception to this proposition. As noted, the views on the evidence are contradictory, and getting a definitive evaluation of the effectiveness of these controls will have to await further details. What

---

44. See, for example, Barry J. Eichengreen, *Capital Flows and Crises* (Cambridge, Mass.: MIT Press, 2003).

45. See Edwards, "How Effective Are Capital Controls?" and International Monetary Fund, *World Economic Outlook: Public Debt in Emerging Markets.*

is clear, however, is that Malaysia presents a unique set of historical and political circumstances. It is highly unlikely that its experience—and, in particular, the lifting of controls after one year—will be replicated in other countries.

Finally, the argument that capital controls should be abolished once other reforms have been undertaken has its merits. In particular, there is historical and statistical evidence to suggest that implementing a modern bank supervisory system before lifting capital controls makes eminent sense. However, the fact that there is an adequate and preferred sequencing does not mean that controls on capital mobility should never be lifted.

# Chapter 8: Appendix

## Data on Capital Flows and Short-Term Debt During Chile's Experience with Controls on Inflows, 1991–1998

### Table A1
### Capital Inflows (Gross) to Chile:  Millions of US$

| Year | Short term inflows | Percentage of total | Long term inflows | Percentage of total | Total | Deposits* |
|------|-------------------|---------------------|-------------------|---------------------|-------|-----------|
| 1988 | 916,564 | 96.3 | 34,838 | 3.7 | 951,402 | -- |
| 1989 | 1,452,595 | 95.0 | 77,122 | 5.0 | 1,529,717 | -- |
| 1990 | 1,683,149 | 90.3 | 181,419 | 9.7 | 1,864,568 | -- |
| 1991 | 521,198 | 72.7 | 196,115 | 27.3 | 717,313 | 587 |
| 1992 | 225,197 | 28.9 | 554,072 | 71.1 | 779,269 | 11,424 |
| 1993 | 159,462 | 23.6 | 515,147 | 76.4 | 674,609 | 41,280 |
| 1994 | 161,575 | 16.5 | 819,699 | 83.5 | 981,274 | 87,039 |
| 1995 | 69,675 | 6.2 | 1,051,829 | 93.8 | 1,121,504 | 38,752 |
| 1996 | 67,254 | 3.2 | 2,042,456 | 96.8 | 2,109,710 | 172,320 |
| 1997 | 81,131 | 2.8 | 2,805,882 | 97.2 | 2,887,013 | 331,572 |

*Deposits in the Banco Central de Chile due to unremunerated reserve requirements.

Source: Banco Central de Chile.

## Table A2
## Ratio of Short-term Bank Loans to Total Bank Loans (Percentage)

|  | Mid-1996 | End-1996 | Mid-1997 | End-1997 | Mid-1998 |
|---|---|---|---|---|---|
| Argentina | 53.4 | 56.3 | 54.2 | 57.7 | 57.4 |
| Brazil | 57.7 | 63.0 | 62.6 | 64.3 | 62.6 |
| Chile | **57.7** | **51.2** | **43.3** | **50.4** | **45.9** |
| Colombia | 45.9 | 39.3 | 39.4 | 40.0 | 39.6 |
| Mexico | 47.8 | 44.7 | 45.5 | 43.7 | 44.9 |
| Peru | 78.3 | 79.2 | 67.0 | 69.3 | 75.7 |
| Indonesia | 60.0 | 61.7 | 59.0 | 60.6 | 55.0 |
| Korea | 70.8 | 67.5 | 68.0 | 62.8 | 45.8 |
| Malaysia | 49.7 | 50.3 | 56.4 | 52.7 | 48.6 |
| Taiwan | 86.4 | 84.4 | 87.3 | 81.6 | 80.1 |
| Thailand | 68.9 | 65.2 | 65.7 | 65.8 | 59.3 |

Source: The Bank for International Settlements.

# Chapter 9

# Economic Growth Across Countries

## Editor's Summary

What policies and conditions are most conducive to economic growth? Robert Barro investigates this question by examining GDP per capita growth rates for 112 countries from 1960 to 2000. The answers are important because low versus high economic growth dramatically affects individual income and living standards. Simply put, over the past 40 years, variations in growth rates have made paupers into princes and relegated relatively wealthy nations to poverty. For example:

- The Central African Republic had a per capita GDP of $2,180 in 1960 (in constant 1996 U.S. dollars) and a per capita GDP of $1,120 in 2000.
- Taiwan, on the other hand, had a per capita GDP of $1,430 in 1960 (in constant 1996 U.S. dollars) and a per capita GDP of $18,700 in 2000.
- "Thus, although the Central African Republic was 50 percent richer than Taiwan in 1960, Taiwan was richer by an amazing factor of 17 in 2000."

Barro demonstrates that some theories of growth are not supported by the evidence. For instance, different legal traditions are not a significant factor in the long term; enforcement of the rule of law is far more important. He also finds that, holding all other factors constant, countries with lower per capita GDP tend to grow faster. In other words, if policies did not get in the way, per capita income among countries would tend to converge.

While Barro cautions that knowing what helps does not necessarily provide means for adopting those policies, he confirms that "growth depends positively on the rule of law, the investment ratio, and international openness" and "negatively on the rate of inflation and the ratio of government consumption to GDP. Growth increases with favorable movements in the terms of trade and declines with increases in the fertility rate."

# Economic Growth Across Countries

*Robert J. Barro*

Cross-country empirical work on the determination of economic growth has been popular since the early 1990s. Economists Frank Ramsey, Robert Solow, Trevor Swan, David Cass, and Tjalling Koopmans developed growth theories from which the conceptual framework for cross-country empirical studies is derived.[1] Their theories, developed in various years ranging from 1928 to 1965, are known collectively as the *neoclassical growth model*.

To understand the sources of technological progress, economists Paul Romer, Philippe Aghion, and Peter Howitt have extended the neoclassical model more recently into theoretical work known as the *endogenous growth theory*.[2] Thus far, endogenous growth theories have had little impact on empirical studies of growth.

---

1. F. P. Ramsey, "A Mathematical Theory of Saving," *Economic Journal*, December 1928, pp. 543–559; R. M. Solow, "A Contribution to the Theory of Economic Growth," *Quarterly Journal of Economics*, February 1956, pp. 65–94; T. W. Swan, "Economic Growth and Capital Accumulation," *Economic Record*, November 1956, pp. 334–361; D. Cass, "Optimum Growth in an Aggregative Model of Capital Accumulation," *Review of Economic Studies*, July 1965, pp. 233–240; T. C. Koopmans, "On the Concept of Optimal Economic Growth," in *The Econometric Approach to Development Planning* (Amsterdam: North Holland, 1965).

2. P. M. Romer, "Increasing Returns and Long-Run Growth," *Journal of Political Economy*, October 1986, pp. 1002–1037, and "Endogenous Technological Change," *Journal of Political Economy*, October 1990, Part II, pp. S71–S102; P. Aghion and P. Howitt, *Endogenous Growth Theory* (Cambridge, Mass.: MIT Press, 1998).

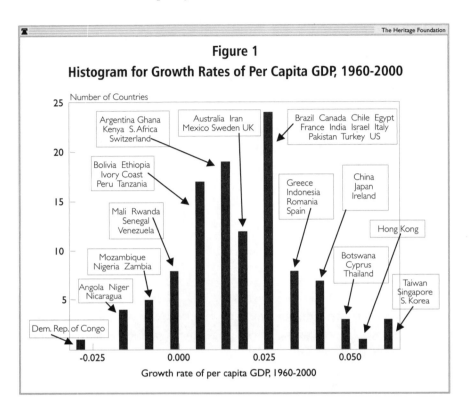

This chapter discusses updated empirical results from cross-country studies of economic growth. These findings come from the recent analysis reported by the author and Xavier Sala-i-Martin.[3]

Growth rates vary enormously across countries over long periods of time. FIGURE 1 illustrates these divergences in the form of a histogram for the growth rate of real per capita gross domestic product (GDP) for 112 countries with available data from 1960 to 2000.[4] The mean growth rate is 1.8 percent per year, with a standard deviation of 1.7. The lowest decile comprises 11 countries with growth rates below –0.5 percent per year, and the highest decile consists of the 11 with growth rates above 3.9 percent per year. For quintiles, the poorest performing 22 places have growth rates below 0.4 percent per year, and the best performing 22 have growth rates above 3.0 percent per year.

3. R. J. Barro, and X. Sala-i-Martin, *Economic Growth*, 2nd edition (Cambridge Mass.: MIT Press, 2004), Chapter 12.

The difference between per capita growth at –1.3 percent per year (the average for the lowest decile) and growth at 5.0 percent per year (the average for the highest decile) is that real per capita GDP falls by 41 percent over 40 years in the former case and rises by a factor of more than 7 in the latter. Even more extreme, the two slowest growing countries—the Democratic Republic of Congo (formerly Zaire) and Central African Republic—fell from levels of real per capita GDP in 1960 of $980 and $2,180 (in constant 1996 U.S. dollars), respectively, to levels of $320 and $1,120 in 2000 (1995 for the former Zaire). From 1960 to 2000, the two fastest growing countries—Taiwan and Singapore—rose from $1,430 and $2,160, respectively, to $18,700 and $26,100.

Calculations illustrate that, although the Central African Republic was 50 percent wealthier than Taiwan in 1960, Taiwan proved to be richer by an amazing factor of 17 in 2000. Over 40 years, the observed variations in growth rates have made dramatic differences in the average living standards of a country's residents.

## I. Losers and Winners from 1960 to 2000

TABLE 1 applies to loser countries: the 20 with the lowest per capita growth rates from 1960 to 2000. The countries are arranged in ascending order of growth rates, as shown in column 2. This group contains an astonishing 18 countries in sub-Saharan Africa and two in Latin America (Nicaragua and Venezuela). The table also shows per capita growth rates over the three 10-year sub-periods, 1965–1975, 1975–1985, and 1985–1995. The fitted values shown come from the statistical analysis discussed in section III A.

TABLE 2 provides a parallel treatment of winners; that is, the 20 countries with the highest per capita growth rates. These countries are arranged in

---

4. The GDP data are the purchasing-power adjusted values from version 6.1 of the Penn-World Tables, as described in R. Summers and A. Heston, "The Penn World Table (Mark 5): An Expanded Set of International Comparisons, 1950–1988," *Quarterly Journal of Economics*, May 1991, pp. 327–369, and A. Heston, R. Summers, and B. Aten, *Penn World Table*, version 6.1, Center for International Comparisons at the University of Pennsylvania, October 2002. For 11 countries with missing data for 2000, the growth rates for 1995–2000 were computed from World Bank figures reported in World Bank, *World Development Indicators*, 2002. For Taiwan, the growth rate for 1995–2000 came from national sources. For the Democratic Republic of Congo (formerly Zaire), the growth rate is for 1960–1995.

## Table 1
## Details of 20 Slowest Growing Countries

| Country | Growth 1960-00* | Growth 1965-75 | Fitted 1965-75 | Growth 1975-85 | Fitted 1975-85 | Growth 1985-95 | Fitted 1985-95 | Growth 1995-00** |
|---|---|---|---|---|---|---|---|---|
| Congo (Kinshasa) | -0.032 | 0.001 | 0.005 | -0.040 | -0.003 | -0.069 | -0.026 | -- |
| Cent. Afr. Repub. | -0.017 | -0.012 | -- | -0.019 | -- | -0.035 | -- | 0.004 |
| Niger | -0.015 | -0.041 | -0.015 | -0.026 | -0.067 | -0.008 | -0.004 | 0.012 |
| Angola | -0.014 | -0.032 | -- | -0.011 | -- | -0.040 | -- | 0.021 |
| Nicaragua | -0.012 | 0.012 | 0.003 | -0.037 | -0.009 | -0.050 | -0.024 | -0.006 |
| Mozambique | -0.011 | 0.004 | -- | -0.081 | -- | 0.003 | -0.001 | 0.051 |
| Madagascar | -0.010 | 0.004 | -- | -0.021 | -- | -0.015 | -- | 0.004 |
| Nigeria | -0.009 | 0.000 | -- | -0.004 | -- | -0.010 | -- | -0.054 |
| Zambia | -0.008 | -0.008 | 0.021 | -0.021 | 0.007 | -0.029 | -0.003 | 0.018 |
| Chad | -0.007 | -0.012 | -- | -0.004 | -- | -0.014 | -- | 0.003 |
| Comoros | -0.005 | 0.007 | -- | -0.005 | -- | -0.031 | -- | -0.011 |
| Venezuela | -0.005 | -0.019 | 0.014 | -0.019 | 0.006 | 0.004 | 0.004 | -0.020 |
| Senegal | -0.003 | -0.008 | -0.005 | -0.006 | -0.003 | -0.002 | 0.005 | 0.021 |
| Rwanda | -0.001 | 0.015 | -- | 0.023 | -- | -0.037 | -- | 0.038 |
| Togo | -0.001 | 0.004 | -0.005 | 0.011 | 0.000 | -0.039 | 0.004 | -0.002 |
| Burundi | -0.001 | 0.024 | -- | -0.004 | -- | -0.007 | -- | -0.056 |
| Mali | 0.000 | 0.008 | 0.014 | 0.002 | 0.000 | -0.006 | 0.011 | 0.036 |
| Guinea | 0.001 | -0.016 | -- | -0.006 | -- | 0.015 | -- | 0.015 |
| Equatorial Guinea | 0.002 | 0.015 | -- | -0.084 | -- | -0.041 | -- | 0.229 |
| Benin | 0.003 | -0.013 | -- | 0.018 | -- | -0.009 | -- | 0.026 |

*For Congo (Kinshasa), the growth rate is for 1960-95.

**For countries for which the Penn-World Tables version 6.1 data are unavailable for 1995-2000, the values are from the World Bank (Central African Republic, Angola, Singapore, Botswana, and Cyprus) or national sources (Taiwan).

Note: The data, from Penn-World Tables version 6.1, are described in R. Summers and A. Heston, "The Penn World Table (Mark 5): An Expanded Set of International Comparisons, 1950-1988," *Quarterly Journal of Economics*, May 1991, pp. 327-369, and A. Heston, R. Summers, and B. Aten, *Penn World Table*, version 6.1, Center for International Comparisons at the University of Pennsylvania, October 2002. The fitted values come from the system shown in column 2 of Table 3.

descending order of growth rates, as shown in column 2. The winners include nine economies in East Asia (Taiwan, Singapore, South Korea, Hong Kong, Thailand, China, Japan, Malaysia, and Indonesia); four in Western Europe (Ireland, Portugal, Spain, and Luxembourg); and two in sub-Saharan Africa (Botswana and Congo–Brazzaville). Also included are Cyprus, Barbados, Romania, and two islands off of Africa: Cape Verde and Mauritius.

To determine winner and loser characteristics, per capita growth rates are analyzed during the three 10-year periods of both tables: 1965–1975, 1975–1985, and 1985–1995. For countries that have the necessary data to be included in the statistical analysis, the fitted values for the three 10-year periods show the degree to which growth rates can be explained by the estimated equations.

Across the 10-year periods, the correlations of growth rates within countries are positive but not particularly strong: 0.43 each for growth between

## Table 2
## Details of 20 Fastest Growing Countries

| Country | Growth 1960-00 | Growth 1965-75 | Fitted 1965-75 | Growth 1975-85 | Fitted 1975-85 | Growth 1985-95 | Fitted 1985-95 | Growth 1995-00** |
|---|---|---|---|---|---|---|---|---|
| Taiwan | 0.064 | 0.069 | 0.056 | 0.065 | 0.050 | 0.068 | 0.041 | 0.047 |
| Singapore | 0.062 | 0.094 | -- | 0.054 | 0.074 | 0.052 | 0.062 | 0.028 |
| South Korea | 0.059 | 0.071 | 0.052 | 0.059 | 0.048 | 0.072 | 0.052 | 0.032 |
| Hong Kong | 0.054 | 0.048 | 0.062 | 0.062 | 0.052 | 0.053 | 0.041 | 0.008 |
| Botswana | 0.051 | 0.082 | -- | 0.062 | 0.027 | 0.036 | 0.007 | 0.043 |
| Thailand | 0.046 | 0.043 | 0.046 | 0.045 | 0.042 | 0.073 | 0.051 | 0.003 |
| Cyprus | 0.046 | 0.012 | 0.043 | 0.075 | 0.036 | 0.052 | 0.015 | 0.029 |
| China | 0.043 | 0.017 | -- | 0.049 | 0.055 | 0.065 | 0.044 | 0.057 |
| Japan | 0.042 | 0.065 | 0.055 | 0.030 | 0.033 | 0.027 | 0.030 | 0.012 |
| Ireland | 0.041 | 0.035 | 0.027 | 0.025 | 0.012 | 0.046 | 0.012 | 0.085 |
| Barbados | 0.039 | 0.064 | -- | 0.023 | -- | 0.028 | -- | 0.036 |
| Malaysia | 0.039 | 0.036 | 0.031 | 0.042 | 0.041 | 0.047 | 0.037 | 0.026 |
| Portugal | 0.038 | 0.049 | 0.054 | 0.021 | 0.026 | 0.035 | 0.015 | 0.040 |
| Mauritius | 0.037 | 0.010 | -- | 0.038 | -- | 0.050 | -- | 0.041 |
| Romania | 0.035 | 0.072 | -- | 0.063 | -- | -0.020 | -- | -0.020 |
| Cape Verde | 0.035 | 0.022 | -- | 0.076 | -- | 0.023 | -- | 0.048 |
| Spain | 0.034 | 0.047 | 0.047 | 0.005 | 0.024 | 0.033 | 0.021 | 0.020 |
| Indonesia | 0.034 | 0.046 | 0.018 | 0.047 | 0.025 | 0.047 | 0.014 | 0.000 |
| Luxembourg | 0.033 | 0.022 | -- | 0.021 | -- | 0.054 | -- | 0.049 |
| Congo (Brazz.) | 0.032 | 0.041 | 0.029 | 0.059 | 0.018 | -0.021 | -0.017 | 0.005 |

**For countries for which the Penn-World Tables version 6.1 data are unavailable for 1995-2000, the values are from the World Bank (Central African Republic, Angola, Singapore, Botswana, and Cyprus) or national sources (Taiwan).

Note: The data, from Penn-World Tables version 6.1, are described in R. Summers and A. Heston, "The Penn World Table (Mark 5): An Expanded Set of International Comparisons, 1950-1988," *Quarterly Journal of Economics*, May 1991, pp. 327-369, and A. Heston, R. Summers, and B. Aten, *Penn World Table*, version 6.1, Center for International Comparisons at the University of Pennsylvania, October 2002. The fitted values come from the system shown in column 2 of Table 3.

1975–1985 and 1965–1975 and 0.42 each for growth between 1985–1995 and 1975–1985. Although growth rates of countries in 10-year frames are similar, over five-year periods, the correlations vary substantially. For example, in the seven intervals from 1960–1965 to 1995–2000, the average correlation of one period's growth rate with the previous one is only 0.17. The lower correlation can be attributed to temporary factors associated with "business cycles" that occur during the more sensitive five-year intervals. The last five-year period is noteworthy for being virtually unrelated to the history—the correlation of growth rates in 1995–2000 with those in 1990–1995 is only 0.05.

## II. Framework for Analysis of Growth Rates

This section develops the framework for an empirical analysis of growth; that is, the statistical results that underlie the fitted values shown in TABLES 1 and 2. The sample of 87 countries (see APPENDIX, TABLE A1) was determined by the availability of data and constitutes 241 observations during 10-year intervals. From developing to developed countries, it covers a broad range of economic history and experience.

The questions at hand are whether poor economies tend to catch up or converge to rich ones and how initial GDP plays a role in the process. In order to catch up, poor economies must grow faster than rich ones, a process known as absolute convergence. For the 112 countries in FIGURE 2, absolute convergence fares badly. The correlation of the growth rate from 1960 to 2000 is positive (0.19), but it is virtually unrelated to the initial per capita GDP in 1960.

Some researchers have used the lack of correlation between growth and the initial level of income as evidence against the neoclassical growth model. The author and Sala-i-Martin show, however, that if different economies tend to converge to different long-run positions, the lack of absolute convergence across economies is consistent with the neoclassical model.[5] In other words, the neoclassical model predicts *conditional* rather than absolute convergence: Holding constant variables that determine the long-run position, the theory predicts a negative relation between growth and the initial level of income. Thus, we want to examine the relation between the growth rate and the starting position while holding constant variables that determine each country's long-run position.

The analytical framework relates the per capita growth rate to two groups of variables. The first group within the framework comprises initial levels of variables that represent the state of the economy. These variables, called state variables, include the stock of physical capital and the stock of human capital in the forms of educational attainment and health. The second group consists of control or environmental variables, some of which are chosen by governments and some of which are chosen by private agents. These variables include the ratio of government consumption to GDP, the ratio of domestic investment to GDP, the extent of international openness, the fertility rate, indicators of macroeconomic stability, and measures of maintenance of the rule of law and democracy.

One of the state variables in the empirical analysis is a measure of educational attainment. This variable is measured from the figures on school attainment at various levels constructed by the author and Jong-Wha Lee.[6]

---

5. Barro and Sala-i-Martin, *Economic Growth*, Chapters 1, 2, and 11.

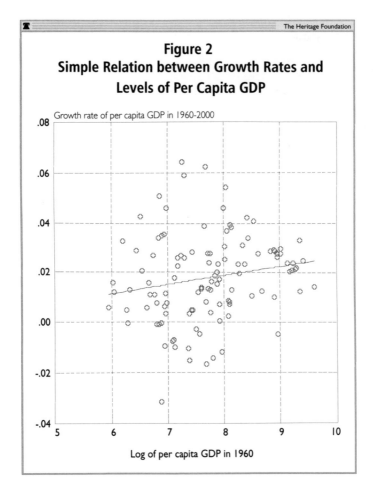

**Figure 2**
**Simple Relation between Growth Rates and Levels of Per Capita GDP**

Another state variable relates to health and is measured by standard numbers on life expectancy reported by the World Bank.[7] Life expectancy at age one turns out to have the most explanatory power. The available data on physical capital seem unreliable, especially for developing countries and even relative to the measures of human capital, because they depend on arbitrary assumptions about depreciation and also rely on inaccurate measures of benchmark stocks and investment flows. As an alternative to using the limited data on physical capital, the assumption is that, for given school-

6. R. J. Barro and J. W. Lee, "International Data on Educational Attainment: Updates and Implications," *Oxford Economic Papers*, 2001, pp. 541–563.

7. World Bank, *World Development Indicators*, 2002.

ing and health, a higher level of initial per capita GDP reflects a greater stock of physical capital per person (or a larger quantity of natural resources).

The framework used in the empirical work can be represented by an equation:

$$(Dy)_t = F(y_{t-1}, h_{t-1}, \dots)$$

where $(Dy)_t$ is a country's per capita growth rate in period $t$, $y_{t-1}$ is the country's per capita GDP in the previous period, and $h_{t-1}$ is human capital per person in period $t-1$ (based on the measures of educational attainment and health). The omitted variables, denoted by "…" in the above equation, comprise an array of control and environmental influences. These variables include preferences for saving and fertility, government policies and institutions, and so on.

**A. Effects from State Variables.** The Solow–Swan and Ramsey models predict that, for given environmental and control variables, an equiproportionate increase in $y_{t-1}$ and $h_{t-1}$ would reduce $(Dy)_t$ in the above equation. That is, because of diminishing returns to reproducible factors, a richer economy—with higher levels of $y$ and $h$—tends to grow at a slower rate. The environmental and control variables determine the long-run level of output per person in these models.[8] A change in any of these variables— for example, in the saving rate, in a government policy instrument, or in the growth rate of population—affects the growth rate of per capita GDP for given values of the state variables. For example, a higher saving rate tends to increase $(Dy)_t$ in the equation for given values of $y_{t-1}$ and $h_{t-1}$.

Theoretical models with human and physical capital[9] predict influences on growth from imbalances between physical and human capital. For given $y_{t-1}$, a higher value of $h_{t-1}$ in the equation tends to raise the growth rate. This situation applies, for example, in the aftermath of a war that destroys primarily physical capital. Thus, although the influence of $y_{t-1}$ on $(Dy)_t$ in the equation would be negative, the effect of $h_{t-1}$ tends to be positive.

The empirical analysis enters the initial level of per capita GDP into the

---

8. When the models allow for exogenous technological progress, output per person grows steadily in the long run. In this case, the long run features a constant level of output per effective worker, where the number of "effective" workers takes account of the technological progress.

9. Summarized in Barro and Sala-i-Martin, *Economic Growth*, Chapter 5.

growth equation in the form $log(y_{t-1})$. With this specification, the coefficient on this variable represents the rate of convergence; that is, the responsiveness of the growth rate, $(Dy)_t$, to a proportional change in $y_{t-1}$. The analysis measures the variable $h_{t-1}$ by average years of school attainment and life expectancy.

**B. Control and Environmental Variables.** In the basic estimates considered below, the control and environmental variables are a measure of international openness;[10] the ratio of government consumption to GDP;[11] a subjective indicator of maintenance of the rule of law; a subjective indicator of democracy (electoral rights); the log of the total fertility rate;[12] the ratio of gross domestic investment to GDP;[13] and the inflation rate. The system also includes the contemporaneous growth rate of the terms of trade, interacted with the extent of international openness (the ratio of exports plus imports to GDP).

In the neoclassical growth model, the effects of the control and environmental variables on the growth rate correspond to their influences on the economy's long-run position. For example, a higher value of the rule-of-law indicator raises the long-run level of output per person. Referring to the above equation, the growth rate, $Dy_t$, tends accordingly to increase for given values of the state variables. Similarly, a higher ratio of (non-productive) government consumption to GDP tends to depress the long-run level of output per person and thereby reduces the growth rate for given values of the state variables.

As stated previously, in the neoclassical growth model, a change in a control or environmental variable affects the long-run level of output per person. It does not, however, affect the long-term per capita growth rate, which is given by the rate of technological progress and determined outside the model (i.e., exogenous). In contrast, in the endogenous-growth models,[14] variables that affect investments in research and development (R&D) also influence

---

10. This variable is the ratio of exports plus imports to GDP, filtered for the usual relation of this ratio to country size as represented by the logs of population and area.

11. The variable used in the main analysis nets out from the standard measure of government consumption the outlays on defense and education. Data on government consumption are from Heston, Summers, and Aten, *Penn World Table*.

12. These data are from World Bank, *World Development Indicators*, 2002.

13. These data are from Heston, Summers, and Aten, *Penn World Table*.

14. For a discussion of these models, see Barro and Sala-i-Martin, *Economic Growth*, Chapters 6 and 7.

long-term growth rates. However, even in the neoclassical growth model, if the adjustment to the long-run position takes a long time—as is true empirically—the growth effect of a variable such as the rule-of-law indicator or the government consumption ratio lasts for a long time.

The measures of educational attainment used in the main analysis are based on years of schooling and do not adjust for variations in school quality. A measure of quality, based on internationally comparable test scores, turns out to have much more explanatory power for growth.[15] However, this test-score measure is unavailable for much of the sample and is therefore excluded from the basic system.

Health capital is represented in the basic system by the reciprocal of life expectancy at age one. If the probability of dying were independent of age, this reciprocal would give the probability per year of dying. I consider later measures of infant mortality (up to age one) and child mortality (for ages 1–5), as well as incidence of specific diseases.

The government consumption variable is assumed to measure expenditures that do not directly affect productivity but that entail distortions of private decisions. These distortions can reflect both the governmental activities themselves and the adverse effects from the associated public finance.[16] A higher government consumption ratio leads to a lower long-run level of output per person and, hence, to a lower growth rate for given values of the state variables.

The fertility rate is an important influence on population growth and negatively affects the long-run output per person two ways in the neoclassical growth model. First, an increase in the fertility rate directly reduces economic growth for given values of the state variables. Second, higher fertility rates also reflect greater resources devoted to child rearing and in this way provide another reason why higher fertility would reduce growth.

The effect of the saving rate in the neoclassical growth model is measured empirically by the ratio of investment to GDP. For given state vari-

---

15. For a discussion of the test-scores data, see E. A. Hanushek and D. D. Kimko, "Schooling, Labor-Force Quality, and the Growth of Nations," *American Economic Review*, December 2000, pp. 1184–1208.

16. It would be better to hold constant the tax effects directly, but the available data on public finance are inadequate for this purpose. For attempts to measure the relevant marginal tax rates, see W. Easterly and S. Rebelo, "Fiscal Policy and Economic Growth: An Empirical Investigation," *Journal of Monetary Economics*, Vol. 32 (December 1993), pp. 417–458.

ables, a higher investment ratio would raise the growth rate.

I assume that an improvement in the rule of law, as gauged by the subjective indicator provided by an international consulting firm (Political Risk Services), implies enhanced property rights and, therefore, an incentive for higher investment and growth. More broadly, the idea is that well-functioning political and legal institutions help to sustain growth.

The analysis includes another subjective indicator (from Freedom House) of the extent of democracy in the sense of electoral rights. Theoretically, the effect of democracy on growth is ambiguous. Negative effects arise in political economy models that incorporate the incentive of electoral majorities to use their political power to transfer resources away from rich minority groups. On the positive side, democracy may be a productive mechanism for government to avoid confiscating capital accumulated by the private sector. The empirical analysis allows for a linear and squared term in democracy, thereby accounting for the possibility that the sign of the net effect on growth would depend on the extent of democracy.

The explanatory variables also include a measure of the extent of international openness—the ratio of exports plus imports to GDP. Openness is well-known to vary by country size: Larger countries tend to be less open because internal trade offers a large enough market that substitutes effectively for international trade. The normal relationship of international openness to country size, as measured by population and area, is filtered out by the explanatory variable. This filtered variable reflects especially the influences of government policies, such as tariffs and trade restrictions, on international trade.

I include also the growth rate over each decade of the terms of trade, measured by the ratio of export prices to import prices. This ratio appears as a product with the extent of openness, measured by the ratio of exports plus imports to GDP. This terms-of-trade variable measures the effect of changes in international prices on the income position of domestic residents. This income position would rise because of higher export prices and fall with higher import prices. An improvement in the terms of trade raises a country's real income and tends, thereby, to raise consumption. An effect on production (GDP) depends on a response of allocations or effort to the shift in relative prices. If an increase in the relative price of the goods that a country produces tends to generate more output (that is, a positive response of supply), the effect of this variable on the growth rate would be positive. One effect of this type is that an increase in the relative price of oil—an import for most countries—would reduce the production of goods that use oil as an input.

Finally, the basic system includes the inflation rate as a measure of macroeconomic stability. The hypothesis is that higher inflation reduces growth for given state variables. Alternative measures of macroeconomic stability, including fiscal variables, can also be considered.

## III. Empirical Results on Determinants of Economic Growth

**A. Basic Results.** TABLE 3 contains statistical results for the determination of the per capita GDP growth rate. The notes to the table contain technical details of the estimation. The explanatory variables are listed in column 1. The coefficient estimates shown in column 2 apply to the growth rates observed over three 10-year periods: 1965–1975, 1975–1985, and 1985–1995. This sample has 72 countries for the first period, 86 countries for the second period, and 83 countries for the third period. APPENDIX TABLE A1 shows the countries included in the estimation; APPENDIX TABLE A2 shows the means and standard deviations for the variables included in the analysis. Column 3 of TABLE 3 has statistical results for the seven five-year periods from 1965–1970 to 1995–2000. These results are similar in most respects to those in column 2.[17] The following discussion of results refers to the coefficient estimates shown in column 2.

*1. Initial Per Capita GDP.* The variable log (GDP) is an observation of the log of real per capita GDP for 1965 in the growth equation for 1965–1975, for 1975 in the equation for 1975–1985, and for 1985 in the equation for 1985–1995. The estimated coefficient, –0.025, is negative and highly significant in a statistical sense. The negative value corresponds to the conditional convergence that has been reported in various studies by, for example, the author and by N. Gregory Mankiw, David Romer, and David Weil.[18] The

---

17. In general, the fit for the five-year equations is poorer than that for the 10-year equations. The likely reason is that growth observed over only five years is sensitive to business cycles, which are not explained by the growth framework. The fit for the five-year equations is especially poor for the final period, 1995–2000. One reason for the poor fit is that several previous growth champions in East Asia grew slowly in 1995–2000 because of the Asian financial crisis. The model does not explain this crisis and therefore fits badly.

18. See, for example, R. J. Barro, "Economic Growth in a Cross Section of Countries," *Quarterly Journal of Economics*, May 1991, pp. 407–444, and N. G. Mankiw, D. Romer, and D. N. Weil, "A Contribution to the Empirics of Economic Growth," *Quarterly Journal of Economics*, May 1992, pp. 407–437.

# Table 3
## Cross-Country Regressions for Economic Growth

| Explanatory variable | (1) | (2) 10-year sample coefficient (stnd. error) | (3) 5-year sample coefficient (stnd. error) |
|---|---|---|---|
| Log(per capita GDP) | | -0.0248 (0.0029) | -0.0237 (0.0029) |
| Male upper-level schooling | | 0.0036 (0.0016) | 0.0023 (0.0015) |
| 1/(life expectancy at age 1) | | -5.04 (0.86) | -4.91 (0.90) |
| Log(total fertility rate) | | -0.0118 (0.0050) | -0.0160 (0.0048) |
| Govt. consumption ratio | | -0.062 (0.023) | -0.066 (0.021) |
| Rule of law | | 0.0185 (0.0059) | 0.0174 (0.0062) |
| Democracy | | 0.079 (0.028) | 0.032 (0.017) |
| Democracy squared | | -0.074 (0.025) | -0.028 (0.016) |
| Openness ratio | | 0.0054 (0.0048) | 0.0094 (0.0043) |
| Change in terms of trade | | 0.130 (0.053) | 0.029 (0.021) |
| Investment ratio | | 0.083 (0.024) | 0.058 (0.022) |
| Inflation rate | | -0.019 (0.010) | -0.031 (0.007) |
| Dummy, 1975-85 | | -0.0078 (0.0026) | * |
| Dummy, 1985-95 | | -0.0128 (0.0034) | * |
| Number of observations | | 72, 86, 83 | 72, 79, 86, 84 79, 80, 60 |
| R-squared | | .60, .49, .51 | .40, .26, .27, .31 .46, .19, .04 |

Notes: Estimation is by the three-stage least-squares technique. Dependent variables are the growth rates of per capita GDP. The variances of the error terms are allowed to be correlated over the time periods and to have different variances for each period.

In column 2, the growth rates are for 1965-75, 1975-85, and 1985-95. Explanatory variables in column 2 are the values in 1965, 1975, and 1985 of the log of per capita GDP and male upper-level schooling; values in 1960, 1970, and 1980 of the reciprocal of life expectancy at age 1 and the total fertility rate; and averages for 1965-75, 1975-85, and 1985-95 of the government consumption ratio, the openness ratio, and the investment ratio. The rule-of-law indicator is the earliest value available (1982 or 1985) for the first two periods and the average of 1985-95 for the last two periods. The democracy variable for the first period is a weighted average of values for 1960 or 1965 and 1972-75. For the other two periods, the variable is the average for 1975-85 and 1985-95. The terms-of-trade variable is the growth rate of the ratio of export prices to import prices for 1965-75, 1975-85, and 1985-95, interacted with the corresponding averages of the ratio of exports plus imports to GDP. The inflation rate is the average over 1965-75, 1975-85, and 1985-95 of the growth rate of a consumer price index.

Instrumental variables used in column 2 are the values in 1960, 1970, and 1980 of the log of per capita GDP, the life-expectancy variable, and the fertility variable; averages for 1960-64, 1970-74, and 1980-84 of the government consumption variable and the investment ratio; values in 1965, 1975, and 1985 of the schooling variable and the democracy variables; the international-openness and terms-of-trade variables; and dummies for Spanish or Portuguese colonies and other colonies (aside from Britain and France).

In column 3, the dependent variables are growth rates over 1965-70, 1970-75, ..., 1995-2000. The explanatory variables and the instruments correspond to those used for the 10-year intervals.

*The estimated coefficients of the time dummies at the five-year intervals are -0.0014 (0.0040) for 1970-75, 0.0000 (0.0040) for 1975-80, -0.0180 (0.0040) for 1980-85, -0.0112 (0.0037) for 1985-90, -0.0184 (0.0045) for 1990-95, and -0.0165 (0.0042) for 1995-2000.

convergence is conditional in that it predicts higher growth in response to lower starting GDP per person if the other explanatory variables (some of which are highly correlated with GDP per person) are held constant. The magnitude of the estimated coefficient implies that convergence occurs at a rate of about 2.5 percent per year. According to this coefficient, a one-standard-deviation decline in the log of per capita GDP (by 1.03 in 1985) would raise the growth rate on impact by 0.026. In comparison with the other effects described below, this effect is very large and illustrates the importance of conditional convergence as a force for growth rates.

FIGURE 3 provides a graphical description of the relation between the growth rate and the level of per capita GDP. The horizontal axis shows the log of per capita GDP at the start of each of the three 10-year periods: 1965, 1975, and 1985. The vertical axis refers to the subsequent 10-year growth rate of per capita GDP for 1965–1975, 1975–1985, and 1985–1995. These growth rates have been filtered for the estimated effects of the explanatory variables other than the log of per capita GDP that are included in the system of column 2, TABLE 3.[19] Thus, conceptually, the figure shows the estimated effect of the log of per capita GDP on the subsequent growth rate when all of the other explanatory variables are held constant. The graph suggests that the estimated relationship is not driven by outlier observations and does not have any obvious departures from linearity. An analogous graphical presentation is used below for each of the explanatory variables in TABLE 3.

**2. Educational Attainment.** The school-attainment variable, significantly related to subsequent growth, is the average years of secondary and higher schooling for males (referred to as upper-level schooling), observed at the start of each period: 1965, 1975, and 1985. Educational attainment for females and for both sexes at the primary level turns out not to be significantly related to growth rates, as discussed later. The estimated coefficient, 0.0036, is positive and marginally significant statistically. The magnitude of the coefficient means that a one-standard-deviation increase in male upper-level schooling (by 1.3 years, the value for 1985 shown in TABLE A2) raises the growth rate on impact by 0.005. FIGURE 4 depicts the relationship between economic growth and the school-attainment variable.

---

19. The average value on the vertical axis has also been adjusted to have zero mean.

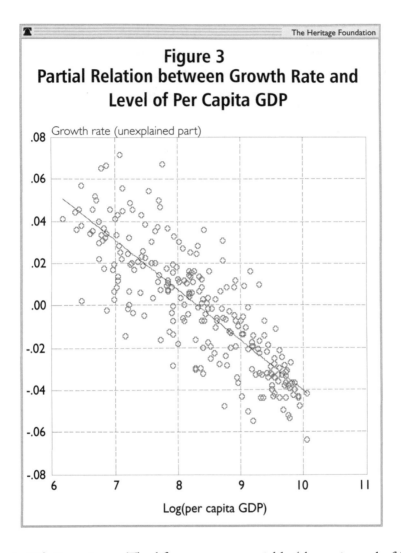

**Figure 3**
**Partial Relation between Growth Rate and Level of Per Capita GDP**

Growth rate (unexplained part)

Log(per capita GDP)

3. *Life Expectancy.* The life-expectancy variable (the reciprocal of life expectancy at age one) applies to 1960, 1970, and 1980, respectively, for the three growth equations. These values would correspond to the mortality rate per year if mortality were (counterfactually) independent of age. The reciprocal of life expectancy at age one has slightly more explanatory power than variables based on life expectancy at birth or at age five. The estimated coefficient, –5.0, is negative and highly significant statistically. This negative value means that better health predicts higher economic growth. A one-standard error reduction in the reciprocal of life expectancy at age one

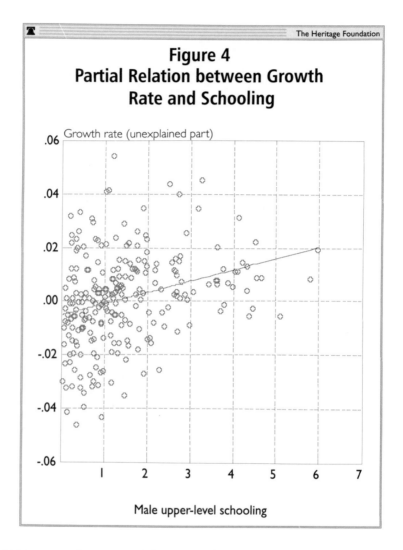

**Figure 4**
**Partial Relation between Growth Rate and Schooling**

Growth rate (unexplained part)

Male upper-level schooling

(0.0022 in 1980) is estimated to raise the growth rate on impact by 0.011. FIGURE 5 shows graphically the relation between growth and this health indicator.

*4. Fertility Rate.* The fertility rate (total lifetime live births for the typical woman over her expected lifetime) enters as a log at the dates 1960, 1970, and 1980. The estimated coefficient, −0.012, is negative and statistically significant. Thus, lower fertility raises per capita growth. A one-standard-deviation decline in the log of the fertility rate (by 0.53 in 1980) is estimated to raise the growth rate on impact by 0.006. The relation appears in FIGURE 6.

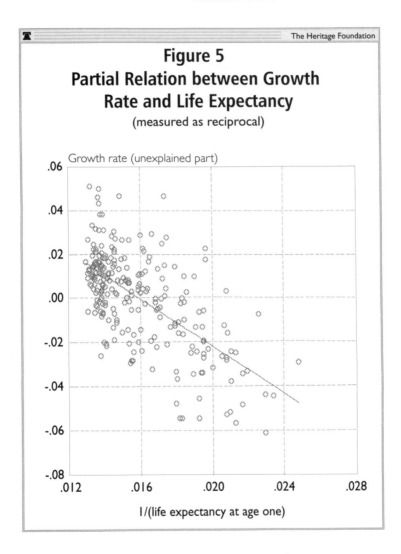

The Heritage Foundation

## Figure 5
## Partial Relation between Growth
## Rate and Life Expectancy
(measured as reciprocal)

Growth rate (unexplained part)

1/(life expectancy at age one)

**5. *Government Consumption Ratio.*** The ratio of government consumption to GDP was adjusted by subtracting the ratio to GDP of spending on defense and non-capital expenditures on education. The elimination of expenditures for defense and education—categories of spending that are included in standard measures of government consumption—was made because these items are not properly viewed as consumption. In particular, they are likely to have direct effects on productivity or the security of property rights. The estimated coefficient, –0.062, is negative and statistically significant. This estimate implies that a reduction in the government con-

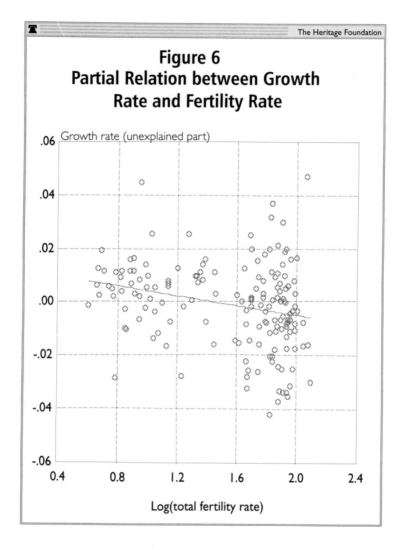

**Figure 6**
**Partial Relation between Growth**
**Rate and Fertility Rate**

Growth rate (unexplained part)

Log(total fertility rate)

sumption ratio by 0.059 (its standard deviation in 1985–1994) would raise the growth rate on impact by 0.004. The relation is shown in FIGURE 7.

6. *Rule of Law.* This variable comes from a subjective measure provided in the *International Country Risk Guide* by the international consulting company Political Risk Services. This variable was first proposed by Stephen Knack and Philip Keefer.[20] The underlying data are tabulated in seven categories, which have been adjusted here to a zero-to-one scale, with one representing the most favorable environment for maintenance of the rule of law. The estimated coefficient, 0.0185, is positive and statistically sig-

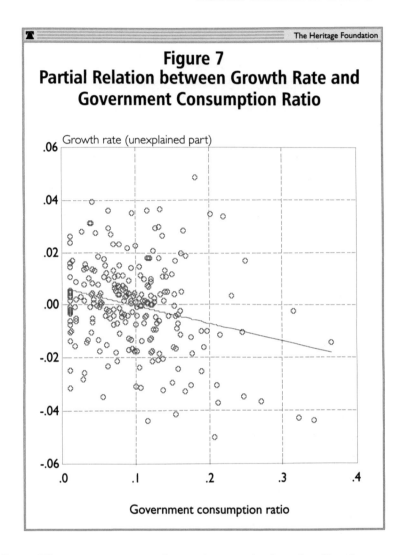

The Heritage Foundation

## Figure 7
## Partial Relation between Growth Rate and Government Consumption Ratio

nificant. This estimate means that an increase in the rule of law by one standard deviation (0.26 for 1985–1994) would raise the growth rate on impact by 0.005. The relation with growth is in FIGURE 8.

**7. Democracy.** This variable, originating from a subjective measure provided by Freedom House, refers to electoral rights (an alternative measure

---

20. See S. Knack and P. Keefer, "Institutions and Economic Performance: Cross-Country Tests Using Alternative Institutional Measures," *Economics and Politics*, Vol. 7 (1995), pp. 207–227.

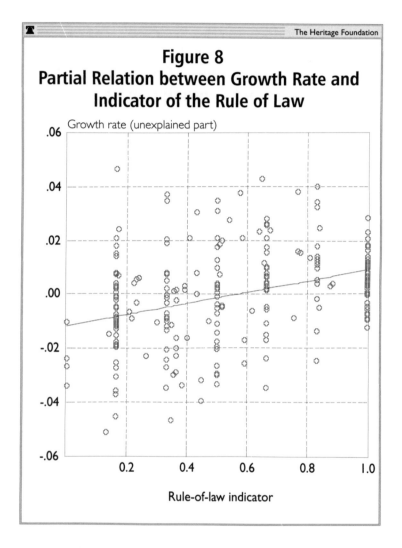

The Heritage Foundation

## Figure 8
## Partial Relation between Growth Rate and Indicator of the Rule of Law

Growth rate (unexplained part)

Rule-of-law indicator

that applies to civil liberties is considered later). The underlying data are tabulated in seven categories and have been adjusted to a zero-to-one scale, with one indicating a full representative democracy and zero a complete totalitarian system. The data begin in 1972, but information from a study by Kenneth Bollen[21] was used to generate data for 1960 and 1965. To allow for a non-linear effect on economic growth, the systems include also the square

---

21. See K. A. Bollen, "Political Democracy: Conceptual and Measurement Traps," *Studies in Comparative International Development*, Spring 1990, pp. 7–24.

of democracy. Results indicate that the linear and squared terms in democracy are each statistically significant. The coefficient on the linear term, 0.079, is positive, whereas that on the squared term, –0.074, is negative.

These estimates imply that, starting from a fully totalitarian system (where the democracy variable takes on the value zero), increases in democracy tend to stimulate growth. However, the positive influence attenuates as democracy rises and reaches zero when the indicator takes on a mid-range value of 0.53. (The mean of the democracy variable over 1985–1994 is 0.64.) Therefore, democratization appears to enhance growth for countries that are not very democratic but to retard growth for countries that have already established a reputably sound democracy. This non-linear relation is shown by the graph in FIGURE 9. The solid line shows the fitted value implied by the linear and squared terms in democracy.

**8. International Openness.** The degree of international openness is measured by the ratio of exports plus imports to GDP. This measure is highly sensitive to country size, as large countries tend to rely relatively more on domestic trade. To take account of this relation, the ratio of exports plus imports to GDP has been filtered for its estimated dependence on the logs of population and area. The relationship between country size and economic growth is considered later. The estimated coefficient, 0.0054, is positive but not significant in a statistical sense. Hence, there is only weak evidence that greater international openness stimulates economic growth. The coefficient implies that a one-standard-deviation increase in the openness ratio (0.39 in 1985–1994) would raise the growth rate on impact by 0.002. The relation between growth and the openness variable is shown graphically in FIGURE 10.

**9. Terms of Trade.** This variable is the product of the growth rate of the terms of trade (export prices relative to import prices) over each 10-year period (1965–1975 and so on) multiplied by the average ratio of exports plus imports to GDP for the period (1965–1974 and so on). The estimated coefficient, 0.130, is positive and statistically significant. Hence, changes in the terms of trade matter for growth over 10-year periods. The results imply that a one-standard-deviation increase in the variable (by 0.017 in 1985–1995) would raise the growth rate on impact by 0.002. FIGURE 11 shows the relation between growth and the terms-of-trade variable.

**10. Investment Ratio.** For the investment ratio, the estimated coefficient, 0.083, is positive and statistically significant. The coefficient implies that a one-standard-deviation increase in the investment ratio (by 0.081 in

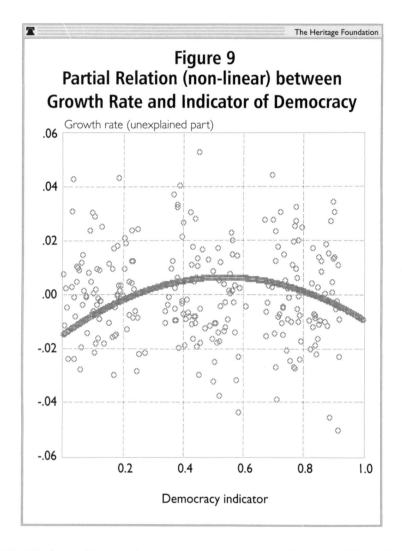

**Figure 9**
**Partial Relation (non-linear) between**
**Growth Rate and Indicator of Democracy**

Growth rate (unexplained part)

Democracy indicator

1985–1994) would raise the growth rate on impact by 0.007. The relation with growth is in FIGURE 12.

**11. Inflation Rate.** The inflation variable is the average rate of retail price inflation over each of the 10-year periods. The estimated coefficient, –0.019, is negative and marginally significant statistically. This coefficient implies that a one-standard-deviation increase in the inflation rate (by 0.38 in 1985–1995) lowers the growth rate on impact by 0.007. However, the coefficient also implies that the moderate variations of inflation experienced by most countries—such as changes on the order of 0.05 per year—affect

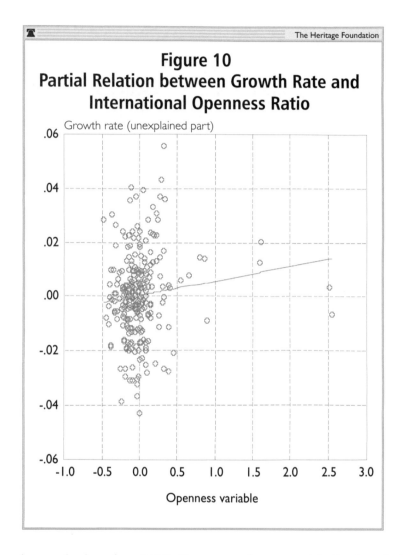

**Figure 10**
**Partial Relation between Growth Rate and International Openness Ratio**

growth rates by less than 0.001. FIGURE 13 shows graphically the relation between growth and inflation. This diagram clarifies that the main force driving the estimated relationship is the behavior at high rates of inflation—notably at rates above 20 percent–30 percent per year.

**B. Further Examination of the Empirical Results.** The results shown in TABLE 3 have been subjected to a number of statistical tests. One test is to determine whether the relation between economic growth and the explanatory variables is stable over time. The stability of the coefficients can be checked by allowing for different coefficients for each of the three 10-year

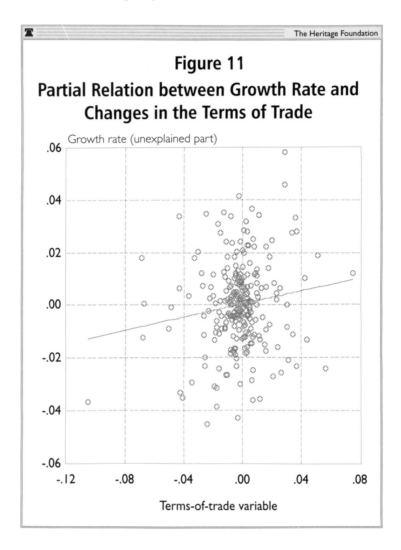

**Figure 11**

**Partial Relation between Growth Rate and Changes in the Terms of Trade**

Growth rate (unexplained part)

Terms-of-trade variable

periods: 1965–1975, 1975–1985, and 1985–1995. The finding is that most of the coefficients do not vary much from one period to another. Therefore, the way that economic growth is determined does not depend significantly on the time period.

Another test is intended to determine whether the dependence of economic growth on its determinants differs between poor and rich countries. This issue can be addressed by allowing the coefficients for poor countries (such as countries with per capita GDP below the mean) to differ from those for rich countries. The finding is that most coefficients are similar for

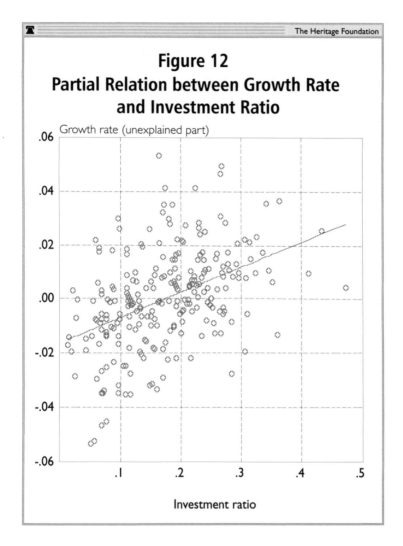

**Figure 12**
**Partial Relation between Growth Rate**
**and Investment Ratio**

the two sets of countries. The main deviations from this pattern are that poor countries have more sensitivity to variations in life expectancy and government consumption. A single set of results can thus be used to describe the determination of economic growth for countries at various levels of economic development.

**C. Additional Explanatory Variables.** Numerous additional explanatory variables have emerged as a result of the expanding empirical literature on the determinants of economic growth. The literature questions whether the results shown in TABLE 3 are robust enough to survive changes in spec-

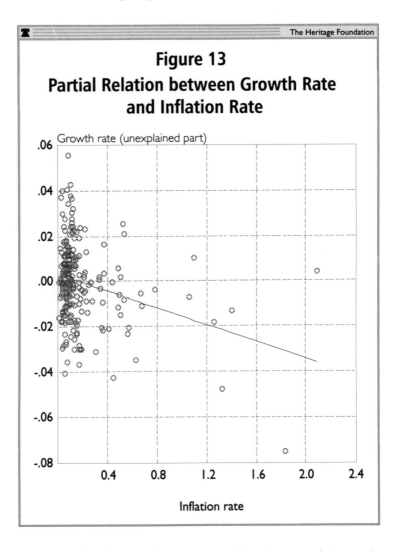

**Figure 13**
**Partial Relation between Growth Rate**
**and Inflation Rate**

ification that add or drop explanatory variables. Some sophisticated proce-dures are now available to study this robustness.[22] The main conclusion is that robustness applies in a broad sense to conditional convergence. However, there is uncertainty over exactly which environmental and control variables are important for determining a country's long-run position.

In the present context, TABLE 4 considers some additional candidate variables for the determination of economic growth. These variables are

---

22. For a discussion, see Barro and Sala-i-Martin, *Economic Growth*, Chapter 12.

## Table 4
## Additional Explanatory Variables for Economic Growth

| Additional explanatory variable | coefficient (standard error) | (3) Second additional explanatory variable | (4) coefficient |
|---|---|---|---|
| Log (population) | 0.0004 (0.0009) | -- | -- |
| Log (per capita GDP) squared | -0.0035 (0.0020) | -- | -- |
| Female upper-level schooling | -0.0034 (0.0041) | -- | -- |
| Male primary schooling | -0.0011 (0.0025) | Female primary schooling | 0.0007 (0.0024) |
| Male college schooling* | 0.0105 (0.0093) | Male secondary schooling | 0.0024 (0.0020) |
| Student test scores** | 0.121 (0.024) | -- | -- |
| Infant mortality rate | -0.001 (0.057) | -- | -- |
| 1/(life expectancy at birth) | -0.97 (2.52) | -- | -- |
| 1/(life expectancy at age 5) | 0.90 (2.00) | -- | -- |
| Malaria incidence | 0.0019 (0.0045) | -- | -- |
| Official corruption | 0.0093 (0.0068) | -- | -- |
| Quality of bureaucracy | 0.0076 (0.0088) | -- | -- |
| Civil liberties*** | -0.045 (0.081) | Civil liberties squared | 0.003 (0.070) |
| Sub-Saharan Africa dummy**** | -0.0080 (0.0051) | Latin America dummy | 0.0031 (0.0039) |
| East Asia dummy | 0.0100 (0.0047) | OECD dummy | 0.0004 (0.0054) |
| Population share < 15 | -0.070 (0.070) | Population share > 64 | -0.080 (0.110) |
| Govt. spending on education | -0.057 (0.068) | Govt. spending on defense | 0.064 (0.028) |
| Log (black-market premium) | -0.0122 (0.0058) | -- | -- |
| Private financial system credit | -0.0041 (0.0065) | -- | -- |
| Financial system deposits | -0.002 (0.011) | -- | -- |
| British legal dummy | -0.0018 (0.0044) | French legal dummy | 0.0047 (0.0045) |
| Absolute latitude (degrees/100) | 0.066 (0.027) | Latitude squared | -0.085 (0.044) |
| Land-locked dummy | -0.0088 (0.0032) | -- | -- |
| Ethnic fractionalization | -0.0080 (0.0059) | -- | -- |
| Linguistic fractionalization | -0.0084 (0.0050) | -- | -- |
| Religious fractionalization | -0.0088 (0.0058) | -- | -- |
| British colony dummy***** | -0.0064 (0.0043) | French colony dummy | 0.0003 (0.0053) |
| Spanish/Port. colony dummy | -0.0019 (0.0053) | Other colony dummy | -0.0055 (0.0075) |

*Upper-level male schooling is omitted.

**Numbers of observations are 39 for 1965-75, 45 for 1975-85, and 44 for 1985-95.

***Sample is for 1975-85 and 1985-95.

****The four geographical dummy variables are added together.

*****The four colonial dummy variables are added together.

**Notes:** The explanatory variables shown in column 1 are added, one at a time, to the system in Table 3, column 2. The second additional explanatory variable in column 3, if shown, is added to the system along with the variable from column 2.

added one at a time to the basic system shown in column 2 of TABLE 3.

The first variable, the log of population, is entered to assess whether the scale of a country matters for its growth outcomes. This variable is entered for 1960, 1970, and 1980. The estimated coefficient is close to zero: 0.0004.

Hence, there is no indication that country size matters significantly for economic growth.

The square of the log of per capita GDP captures whether the rate of convergence depends on the level of per capita GDP. If the coefficient on the square variable were negative, the rate of convergence would be increasing with per capita GDP. The resulting coefficient, –0.0047, is negative and statistically significant. This result conflicts with the neoclassical growth model, which predicts that the rate of convergence should slow as a country approaches its long-run GDP per person.

A number of alternative measures of years of education were considered, all of which enter with the same timing as the male upper-level schooling variable. Upper-level schooling for females has a negative but statistically insignificant coefficient: –0.0016. Schooling at the primary level for males or females also has statistically insignificant coefficients: –0.0020 and 0.0008, respectively. Hence, the main relation between growth and years of schooling involves the male upper-level component, the variable included in column 2 of TABLE 3. A separation of this male variable into college and high-school components generates two positive coefficients (0.0103 and 0.0027) that are insignificantly different from each other in a statistical sense. Thus, it seems to be satisfactory to consider the total years of upper-level schooling as in TABLE 3.

All of these schooling variables refer to the quantity of education, as measured by years of schooling, rather than the quality. Quality could be measured by the outcome on internationally comparable examinations, but the results would possibly reflect inputs other than formal education, such as the influences of environment and family members. In any event, the main problem here is that the data are available only for a sub-set of the countries and time periods from the original sample.

Because of the limited data, I constructed a single cross section of test scores and used the same value for each country for the three time periods considered for growth. (Thus, the underlying test scores apply at different points in time in each equation, and some of the data refer to scores that post-date the measured rates of economic growth.) The estimated coefficient of the test-scores variable, 0.11, is positive and highly significant in a statistical sense. Another result in this specification is that the estimated coefficient of male upper-level schooling becomes only 0.0013 and is no longer statistically significant. Thus, the overall indication is that the quality of education is far more important for economic outcomes than are the years of schooling. Unfortunately, the limited amount of international data on test scores makes it difficult to go further with this analysis.

Another potential determinant of growth is the health of the population. Alternative measures of health are considered. Recall that the previous results included the reciprocal of life expectancy at age one. This measure has more explanatory power for growth than either life expectancy at age one or the log of this life expectancy. With this variable held fixed, the coefficient on the infant mortality rate (for 1960, 1970, and 1980) is close to zero. Also statistically insignificant are the reciprocals of life expectancy at birth or at age five.

John Gallup and Jeffrey Sachs[23] have generated numerous measures of specific disease incidences. Once the basic life expectancy variable was held constant, no important relations between these disease measures and economic growth were found. As an example, the variable for malaria occurrence in 1966 has a coefficient 0.0040 that is not statistically significant. Thus, specific diseases seem to matter for growth only indirectly, through their effects on life expectancy.

Alternatives to the rule-of-law indicator have also been proposed in the literature. With the rule-of-law measure (and the other explanatory variables, including democracy) held constant, an indicator from Political Risk Services[24] of the extent of official corruption was positive (0.0067) but not statistically significant. (For this indicator, a higher value denotes a "better" system with less official corruption.) Also not statistically significant was an indicator from Political Risk Services for the quality of the bureaucracy, which had a coefficient of 0.0054.

The democracy variable included in TABLE 3 is the Freedom House[25] indicator of electoral rights. Because of the high degree of correlation, it turns out to be impossible to distinguish this measure empirically from the other Freedom House indicator, which refers to civil liberties. Thus, from the perspective of influencing economic growth, the relative importance of electoral rights or civil liberties is indeterminate.

An earlier discussion indicated that sub-Saharan Africa dominated the group of slowest growing countries, whereas East Asia dominated the

---

23. J. L. Gallup and J. D. Sachs, "Geography and Economic Development," National Bureau of Economic Research *Working Paper* No. 6849, December 1998.

24. See Political Risk Services, *International Country Risk Guide*, various monthly issues.

25. See *www.freedomhouse.org*.

fastest growing group. A natural question is whether the regional low-growth and high-growth outcomes continue to apply after holding constant the explanatory variables (included in column 2 of TABLE 3). That is, do the included explanatory variables already measure the growth consequences of location in a particular region? If dummy variables are added for regions (as shown in TABLE 4), the estimated coefficients are –0.007 for sub-Saharan Africa, 0.006 for Latin America, 0.009 for East Asia, and –0.001 for the Organisation for Economic Co-operation and Development.[26] Only the East Asian variable is even marginally significant statistically. In conclusion, the explanatory variables in the system already hold constant the consequences of an economy residing in a specific region.

A reasonable expectation is that productivity depends on age structure: Notably, output per person would be expected to be higher if a larger fraction of the population is in the prime-age category of 15–65 and a lesser fraction is in the categories of under 15 and over 65. However, if added to the system, the two population share variables (for under 15 and over 65) are jointly insignificant statistically.

The basic system includes as a measure of government spending the standard definition of government consumption less the outlays on defense and education. If these last two components of government spending are added to the system (each as ratios of spending to GDP), the estimated coefficients are 0.009 for education and 0.033 for defense. These two variables are statistically insignificant.

The informal-market premium on foreign exchange is sometimes entered into growth equations as a proxy for a class of market distortions. The estimated coefficient on this variable, –0.010, is negative and marginally significant statistically. Hence, there is an indication that this distortion measure has inverse predictive power for economic growth.

Other analyses, such as those by Robert King and Ross Levine and by Jeremy Greenwood and Boyan Jovanovic,[27] have stressed the special role of the domestic financial system as an engine of growth. I consider two prox-

---

26. The OECD countries as those other than Turkey that have been members since the 1960s.

27. R. G. King and R. Levine, "Finance, Entrepreneurship, and Growth: Theory and Evidence," *Journal of Monetary Economics*, December 1993, pp. 513–542, and J. Greenwood and B. Jovanovic, "Financial Development, Growth, and the Distribution of Income,'" *Journal of Political Economy*, Vol. 98 (October 1990), pp. 1076–1107.

ies for this financial development. One is the ratio of private financial system credit to GDP. The other is a measure of financial system deposits (the M3 aggregate less the transactions-related M1 aggregate, again as a ratio to GDP). These variables are measured at the beginning of each 10-year period: 1965, 1975, and 1985. Of course, the development of the financial system is endogenous with respect to general economic development. Thus, these financial proxies would be expected to matter only to the extent that they take on values that are unusual for an economy's level of development as measured by per capita GDP and some of the other explanatory variables. In any event, the estimated coefficients of the financial proxies are insignificantly different from zero.

The line of research exemplified by Rafael La Porta *et al.*[28] stresses the role of legal structures in economic development. In particular, this literature argues that the British common-law tradition is superior to the French statute-law system. The data consist of dummy variables for five types of legal traditions: British, French, Scandinavian, German, and socialist. Dummy variables for British and French legal structure turn out to have little explanatory power for growth. Note, however, that these legal structure variables are added to the basic system of TABLE 3, column 2, which already holds constant measures of the rule of law and democracy.

Geographical elements have been stressed in the research by John Gallup and Jeffrey Sachs.[29] The absolute value of degrees latitude is a commonly used indicator. The idea is that places too close to the equator have bad climate in terms of excessive heat and humidity. Since too great a departure from the equator would signify excessive cold, the square of latitude is also included in the system. The result is that the linear and squared terms in absolute degrees latitude are jointly marginally significant. The results indicate that growth outcomes are better if a country is farther from the equator, but that additional distance from the equator eventually reduces growth. The estimated coefficients imply that the optimal (absolute) latitude from the standpoint of growth promotion is 32 degrees.

Another geographical factor, landlocked status, is likely to be important in terms of encouraging trade and other communication with the rest of the

28. R. La Porta, F. Lopez-de-Silanes, A. Shleifer, and R. W. Vishny, "Law and Finance," *Journal of Political Economy*, December 1998, pp. 1113–1155.

29. Gallup and Sachs, "Geography and Economic Development."

world. (Note, however, that international openness is already held constant in the basic system.) A dummy for landlocked status turns out to have a coefficient, −0.011, that is negative and statistically significant. Thus, the results do reveal some disadvantage from a country's lacking access to the oceans.

Various measures of ethnic, linguistic, and religious fractionalization have been argued to matter for political decision-making and conflict, and hence for economic growth. A standard measure of fractionalization is one minus the Herfindahl index for membership shares in ethnic, linguistic, or religious groups.[30] This measure gives the probability that two randomly chosen persons in a country will come from different groups. Hence, a higher value signifies more heterogeneity. The three measures of fractionalization considered in TABLE 4 each have negative but statistically insignificant coefficients in the growth equations.[31]

Finally, it has been argued that colonial heritage is important for growth. Sometimes, these influences are thought to derive from inherited legal or monetary institutions; therefore, it is important to note the explanatory variables that are already included in column 2 of TABLE 3. In any event, dummies for four colonial categories (British, French, Spanish or Portuguese, and other) are jointly insignificant for growth. Thus, if colonial history matters for growth, it must work indirectly by influencing variables such as rule of law, democracy, inflation, and so on.

## IV. Summary and Conclusions About Growth

Differences in per capita growth rates across countries are large and relate systematically to a set of quantifiable explanatory variables. One element of this set is a net convergence term, which is the positive effect on growth when the initial level of per capita GDP is low (relative to the starting amount of human capital in the forms of educational attainment and life expectancy). There is also evidence that countries with higher initial human capital grow faster for given per capita GDP.

---

30. The Herfindahl index is the sum of the squares of the membership shares.

31. The indices for ethnicity and language come from A. Alesina, A. Devleeschauwer, W. Easterly, S. Kurlat, and R. Wacziarg, "Fractionalization," National Bureau of Economic Research *Working Paper* No. 9411, January 2003, and apply to the late 1990s. The index for religion was computed from data on religious affiliation among 10 major groups in 1970 as published in D. B. Barrett, *World Christian Encyclopedia*, 1st edition (Oxford: Oxford University Press, 1982).

For given per capita GDP and human capital, growth depends positively on the rule of law, the investment ratio, and international openness. Growth depends negatively on the rate of inflation and the ratio of government consumption to GDP. Growth increases with favorable movements in the terms of trade and declines with increases in the fertility rate.

Overall, we know a lot about the factors that influence economic growth. However, there are several reasons for modesty about the results from the standpoint of policy advice.

*First*, the fitted models leave a lot of economic growth unexplained. Even if a country manages to achieve favorable values of the explanatory variables, it may not see high economic growth over a 10-year period. From the other side, however, achieving favorable values of the right-hand side variables is probably the best that a government can do to raise the probability of high economic growth.

*Second*, there is a good deal of uncertainty about exactly which "environmental and control" variables matter for economic growth. On the other hand, the general character of these variables is clear. Growth tends to be promoted when markets and institutions work better, when people save more and have fewer children, when people have better education and health, and so on.

*Third*, knowledge of the factors behind growth does not come with instructions. For example, the knowledge that better rule of law promotes economic growth does not provide a government with instructions on how to improve rule of law. Knowing that the rule of law (or education or health or saving) is critical, however, may tend to channel a government's efforts in a favorable direction.

# Chapter 9: Appendix

## Table A1
## Countries Included in Growth Sample (Table 3, column 2)

| | | | |
|---|---|---|---|
| Argentina | Spain | Japan | Senegal |
| Australia | Finland | Kenya | Singapore |
| Austria | France | South Korea | Sierra Leone |
| Belgium | United Kingdom | Sri Lanka | El Salvador |
| Bangladesh | Ghana | Mexico | Sweden |
| Bolivia | Gambia | Mali | Syria |
| Brazil | Greece | Mozambique | Togo |
| Botswana | Guatemala | Malawi | Thailand |
| Canada | Guyana | Malaysia | Trinidad |
| Switzerland | Hong Kong | Niger | Tunisia |
| Chile | Honduras | Nicaragua | Turkey |
| China | Haiti | Netherlands | Taiwan |
| Cameroon | Hungary | Norway | Uganda |
| Congo (Brazz.) | Indonesia | New Zealand | Uruguay |
| Colombia | India | Pakistan | United States |
| Costa Rica | Ireland | Panama | Venezuela |
| Cyprus | Iran | Peru | South Africa |
| Denmark | Iceland | Philippines | Congo (Kinshasa) |
| Dominican Rep. | Israel | Papua New Guinea | Zambia |
| Algeria | Italy | Poland | Zimbabwe |
| Ecuador | Jamaica | Portugal | West Germany |
| Egypt | Jordan | Paraguay | |

## Table A2
## Means and Standard Deviations for Variables in Growth System (Table 3, column 2)

(standard deviations are in parentheses)

|  | 1965-75 equation | 1975-85 equation | 1985-95 equation |
|---|---|---|---|
| Growth rate | 0.026 (0.020) | 0.016 (0.024) | 0.014 (0.026) |
| Log(per capita GDP) | 8.15 (0.94) | 8.32 (0.97) | 8.45 (1.03) |
| Male upper-level schooling | 1.04 (0.96) | 1.39 (1.15) | 1.91 (1.34) |
| 1/(life expectancy at age one) | 0.0165 (0.0027) | 0.0159 (0.0024) | 0.0152 (0.0022) |
| Log(total fertility rate) | 1.58 (0.41) | 1.50 (0.46) | 1.31 (0.53) |
| Government consumption ratio | 0.093 (0.061) | 0.104 (0.070) | 0.091 (0.059) |
| Rule-of-law indicator | 0.56 (0.33) | 0.55 (0.33) | 0.58 (0.26) |
| Democracy indicator | 0.60 (0.32) | 0.56 (0.33) | 0.64 (0.32) |
| Square of democracy | 0.49 (0.37) | 0.44 (0.38) | 0.52 (0.37) |
| Openness ratio | -0.02 (0.18) | -0.01 (0.35) | 0.00 (0.39) |
| Terms-of-trade variable | -0.004 (0.020) | 0.000 (0.021) | -0.003 (0.017) |
| Investment ratio | 0.185 (0.092) | 0.179 (0.078) | 0.178 (0.081) |
| Inflation rate | 0.100 (0.110) | 0.180 (0.209) | 0.231 (0.375) |
| Number of observations | 72 | 86 | 83 |

# Chapter 10

# Free Trade Now: The Case for a Global Free Trade Association

**Editor's Summary**

Free trade is a pillar of economic freedom that enables countries to escape from poverty and achieve greater prosperity. As countries open their markets and trade freely with other nations, they achieve greater growth and lower prices, both of which allow more people to enjoy a higher standard of living.

Despite the proven benefits of free trade, however, promoting free trade around the world has been easier said than done. Protectionist and other restrictive policies are still the norm in developed and developing countries, eliminating opportunities and hindering people from sharing the benefits of free trade. As a result, the pace of trade liberalization has left many disappointed and frustrated.

The United States should demonstrate its leadership in initiating the Global Free Trade Association (GFTA), a voluntary association of countries that have embraced free trade, strong property rights, low regulation, and investment-friendly policies. Membership in the GFTA would be based on current policies, not on promises. Only countries with demonstrated track records of open trade and liberal market institutions would be eligible for membership.

This voluntary association would encourage eligible countries to speed up the pace of trade liberalization and motivate ineligible countries to liberalize their policies. Should current World Trade Organization negotiations fail, the GFTA becomes a viable alternative. By taking the initiative to form the GFTA, the United States would be helping the developed world far more than billions in foreign aid ever could.

# Free Trade Now: The Case for a Global Free Trade Association

*Sara Fitzgerald Cooper*

FREE TRADE IS a step on the road to prosperity. Open markets allow individuals' paychecks to go farther. They promote greater efficiency and value from workers and machines. Despite these obvious benefits, the World Trade Organization's attempts to negotiate global trade liberalization have moved at a snail's pace. A new approach is needed to expedite this process and to advance free trade. An attractive alternative is for pro-trade countries that have strong property rights, low regulation, and investment-friendly policies to form a Global Free Trade Association (GFTA).

This voluntary association would advance liberalization and economic freedom overall by allowing any country that has implemented sound economic policies to participate. Additionally, the apparent benefits would stir competition and motivate ineligible countries to liberalize their policies. This incentive-based approach would make the association more attractive. Countries that stubbornly pursue mercantilist policies would be ineligible for the advantages of membership.

## Mercantilism at the Global Level

Mercantilist sentiment often dominates World Trade Organization (WTO) discussions and actions. While the WTO's main functions include "[a]dministering WTO trade agreements" and acting as a "forum for trade negotiations,"[1] many WTO members have failed to implement trade-friendly policies. This reality has made liberalization through the WTO .

slow and tedious because a unanimous consensus must be achieved in order to advance any proposal.

With 147 members (as of April 23, 2004) focused on divergent agendas, trade liberalization is not an easy task. One dissenting member can bring progress to a standstill. For instance, if WTO members had not successfully lobbied India, the Doha Round would not have been launched in 2001.

The Doha Round is intended to focus on the needs of the developing nations. According to the Doha Declaration:

> International trade can play a major role in the promotion of economic development and the alleviation of poverty. We recognize the need for all our peoples to benefit from the increased opportunities and welfare gains that the multilateral trading system generates. The majority of WTO members are developing countries. We seek to place their needs and interests at the heart of the Work Programme adopted in this Declaration.[2]

A primary concern of developing countries is greater market access for their farmers. Agriculture is the mainstay of most developing nations, yet farmers in these countries cannot compete with the heavily subsidized farmers in the developed world. Although agriculture is only a small portion of the economy in, for instance, the United States and France, agricultural support is high.[3] "[I]n 2002," the Organisation for Economic Co-operation and Development (OECD) estimates, "total support to agriculture in OECD countries was just over US$318 billion."[4] In addition, "This amount of producer support means that as much as 31 cents in each dollar of revenue for the average farmer in the world's richest countries comes from government support."[5]

---

1. World Trade Organization, "What Is the WTO?" at *www.wto.org/english/thewto_e/whatis_e/whatis_e.htm.*

2. World Trade Organization, "DOHA WTO Ministerial 2001: Ministerial Declaration," November 20, 2001, at *www.wto.org/english/thewto_e/minist_e/min01_e/mindecl_e.htm.*

3. Agriculture comprises less that 2 percent of U.S. GDP and slightly more than 3 percent of French GDP.

4. Stefan Tangermann, "Farming Support: The Truth Behind the Numbers," *OECD Observer*, March 31, 2004, at *www.oecdobserver.org/news/fullstory.php/aid/1223/Farming_support:_the_truth.html.*

5. *Ibid.*

If the Doha Round is to accomplish its goals, therefore, significant reductions in tariffs and subsidies must be negotiated; but an impasse in the negotiations because of disagreements over agriculture has impeded any progress as deadlines have been missed and extended. Time and time again, world leaders promote trade at these meetings and then fly back to their countries to resume implementation of their protectionist policies.

Developed nations frequently contradict themselves. With one hand, developed nations give aid; with the other, they inflict high trade barriers on developing countries. This problem extends from Africa to Asia and into Eastern Europe. Take, for example, Moldova. According to the *Economist*, "[T]he EU, absurdly, is increasing aid to Moldova while denying it access to the markets that would do most to improve the lives of its rural poor."[6] Moldova has a low level of protection in its trade policy and would experience greater growth if the European Union simply lowered its barriers.[7]

Nor are protectionism and contradiction limited to developed nations. Many developing countries also maintain high barriers. On the one hand, they receive massive amounts of foreign aid; on the other, they continue repressive policies that have hindered trade and investment and have sentenced their citizens to unending poverty. Outside aid cannot offset the damage caused by restrictive policies. Yet, as leaders in the developed and developing worlds grapple with strategies to solve the poverty problem, free trade is often left out of the solution.

Tying foreign aid to poverty leaves little motivation for protectionist countries to reform and does not reward those countries that have opened their markets. With the exception of the Millennium Challenge Account,[8] internal reform and open markets threaten future qualification for aid. Policies governing aid distribution are irrational. The mission should be to assist developing countries in achieving self-sufficiency.

---

6. "Outsiders Aren't Helping—What Future for Moldova?" *The Economist*, February 15, 2003.

7. Marc A. Miles, Edwin J. Feulner, and Mary Anastasia O'Grady, *2004 Index of Economic Freedom* (Washington, D.C.: The Heritage Foundation and Dow Jones & Company, Inc., 2004), p. 291.

8. A new initiative established by the Bush Administration to reward countries that are committed to "growth-promoting governance, health, education and economic policies." For more information, see "Millennium Challenge Corporation: Reducing Poverty Through Growth," at *www.mca.gov*.

One tangible step toward self-sufficiency would be to reduce trade barriers. Advancing free trade will not only bring greater economic growth, but also raise labor and environmental standards in these countries. With increases in their gross domestic product (GDP), countries will be able to spend more on labor and the environment and to invest in other critical areas such as education.

The continued frustration of the Doha Round leads many to believe that the widespread liberalization needed to reap the rewards of free trade is unlikely to occur. Thus, if the WTO's current efforts should fail, countries will need an alternative motivation to lower their trade barriers.

## The Solution: A Global Free Trade Association

The answer is a Global Free Trade Association. Because a GFTA would be composed only of countries that already have implemented pro-trade policies, liberalization among its member countries could advance swiftly. Countries would have the opportunity to enjoy the benefits of free trade without the tedious negotiations and the delay of the WTO rounds.

Membership in the GFTA would be based on a nation's current policies, not merely on promises. Only countries with demonstrated track records of liberal trade views and liberal market institutions would be eligible for membership. The four proposed criteria for membership are:[9]

**1. Freedom to Trade.** Countries must maintain an open trade policy, with minimal barriers to imports and minimal subsidies to domestic industries. This means an average tariff rate not greater than 9 percent as well as few or no non-tariff barriers, which include import quotas or licensing requirements that restrict trade. Countries that generally set low tariff barriers, do not impose excessive non-tariff barriers, and do not put serious impediments in the way of foreign investment demonstrate their fundamental commitment to free trade.

**2. Freedom to Invest.** Countries must maintain liberal policies regarding capital flows and investment. Specifically, this means a transparent and open foreign investment code, impartial treatment of foreign invest-

---

9. These criteria are taken verbatim from the "Executive Summary" in Gerald P. O'Driscoll, Jr., Edwin J. Feulner, and Mary Anastasia O'Grady, *2003 Index of Economic Freedom* (Washington, D.C.: The Heritage Foundation and Dow Jones & Company, Inc., 2003), p. 8.

ments, and an efficient approval process. Restrictions on foreign investment must be few in number and not significant economically.

**3. Freedom to Operate a Business (Low Regulatory Burden).** Countries must maintain an open environment for business. Overly burdensome regulations can deter trade and investment. Investors may choose not to enter a country because of the difficulties involved in opening a business or because the cost of doing business in that country is excessive. Countries must maintain simple licensing procedures, apply regulations uniformly, and be nondiscriminatory in their treatment of foreign-owned business.

**4. Secure Property Rights.** A country with a well-established rule of law protects private property and provides an environment in which business transactions can take place with a degree of certainty. Investors are likely to engage in economic transactions when they know the judicial system protects private property and is not subject to outside influence. Secure property rights help to ensure that efforts to expand trade with a GFTA can be successful.

## Which Countries Qualify?

Despite only four criteria, only 12 countries currently qualify for membership in the GFTA,[10] and another 19 countries must change one policy to qualify. TABLE 1 shows which countries are next in line for membership and which policy is blocking current membership. The most common policy barrier is regulation.

The countries in which burdensome regulation blocks membership are Austria, Belgium, Chile, Germany, the Netherlands, Sweden, Switzerland, France, Israel, Italy, Portugal, Spain, Trinidad and Tobago, and Uruguay. They should look to countries like Finland as a model. According to the *2004 Index of Economic Freedom*, "Finland has an open and transparent regulatory structure."[11] It also has a low level of regulation, which is why the World Economic Forum selected Finland as the country with "the best business environment" in 2001.[12] Business-friendly policies are the reason that companies such as Nokia have made Finland their home.

---

10. Using the *Index* methodology, countries must receive a score of either 1 or 2 on trade policy, capital flows and foreign investment, property rights, and regulation to qualify for the GFTA. The *Index* ranks countries on a scale of 1 to 5 (1 being the most desirable score).

11. Miles, Feulner, and O'Grady, *2004 Index of Economic Freedom*, p. 182.

12. See Embassy of Finland Web site at *www.finland.org/en/*.

The Heritage Foundation

# Table 1
## Membership in a Global Free Trade Association

**Next in Line**

| Qualifying Countries | | Country | | Policy Blocking Membership |
|---|---|---|---|---|
| 1 | Australia | 1 | Austria | Regulation |
| 2 | Denmark | 2 | Bahrain | Trade |
| 3 | Estonia | 3 | Belgium | Regulation |
| 4 | Finland | 4 | Canada | Foreign Investment |
| 5 | Hong Kong | 5 | Chile | Regulation |
| 6 | Iceland | 6 | Cyprus | Foreign Investment |
| 7 | Ireland | 7 | Germany | Regulation |
| 8 | Luxembourg | 8 | Netherlands | Regulation |
| 9 | New Zealand | 9 | Sweden | Regulation |
| 10 | Singapore | 10 | Switzerland | Regulation |
| 11 | United Kingdom | 11 | Botswana | Trade Policy |
| 12 | United States | 12 | El Salvador | Property Rights |
| | | 13 | France | Regulation |
| | | 14 | Israel | Regulation |
| | | 15 | Italy | Regulation |
| | | 16 | Portugal | Regulation |
| | | 17 | Spain | Regulation |
| | | 18 | Trinidad and Tobago | Regulation |
| | | 19 | Uruguay | Regulation |

**Source:** Marc A. Miles, Edwin J. Feulner, and Mary Anastasia O'Grady, the *2004 Index of Economic Freedom* (Washington, D.C.: The Heritage Foundation and Dow Jones & Company, Inc., 2004)., available at *www.heritage.org/index*

Regulation is an added tax on business. Reducing regulation would attract more investment, reduce a burden on domestic companies, and allow these countries to qualify for membership.

Canada and Cyprus fail to qualify for membership because of their moderate barriers to foreign investment. Canada has special investment and ownership rules that "govern some sectors, including financial services, communications, transport, and those related to cultural heritage or national identity."[13] In Cyprus, investment in some sectors, such as "real estate development,

---

13. Miles, Feulner, and O'Grady, *2004 Index of Economic Freedom*, p. 130.

higher education, and public utilities, is discouraged."[14]

Bahrain and Botswana fail to qualify for membership because of their moderate levels of protectionist trade policies. Bahrain has many non-tariff barriers that include strict labeling requirements and a list of products that are prohibited. Botswana has high tariffs. Botswana is also a member of the Southern African Customs Union (SACU), however, and both Bahrain and Botswana are currently negotiating trade agreements with the United States that could steer both countries toward freer trade and potential membership in a GFTA.

The countries that fail to meet the GFTA criteria because of their trade or foreign investment policies should look to Hong Kong. Hong Kong has a duty-free port and is the world's tenth largest trading entity. It is also one of the most receptive to foreign investment of all the world's governments and does not discriminate between foreign and domestic investors.

Hong Kong's policies have brought economic rewards. Hong Kong's per capita GDP is $24,891. As demonstrated in CHART 1, countries with open markets have a higher GDP per capita, whereas countries with closed markets have a very low per capita GDP.

El Salvador is the only country that is ineligible to join because of weak property rights. According to the U.S. Department of State, El Salvador's "judiciary is constitutionally independent; however, it suffers from inefficiency and corruption."[15] Strong property rights are crucial both to making internal markets function and to attracting investment. El Salvador would be eligible to join the GFTA and would attract more investment if the government implemented critical judicial reforms. With a per capita GDP of only $1,757, El Salvador clearly needs more freedom in trade and investment.

Twelve countries with strong property rights, low barriers to trade and investment, and low regulation qualify for the GFTA. The qualifying countries—based on *2004 Index of Economic Freedom* data—are Australia, Denmark, Estonia, Finland, Hong Kong, Iceland, Ireland, Luxembourg, New Zealand, Singapore, the United Kingdom, and the United States. All of these countries qualified the previous year as well.

Were these countries to form a GFTA, other countries would have an incentive to follow suit. Presumably as the benefits of this agreement

---

14. *Ibid.*, p. 158.
15. U.S. Department of State, El Salvador *Country Commercial Guide FY 2003*, p. 31.

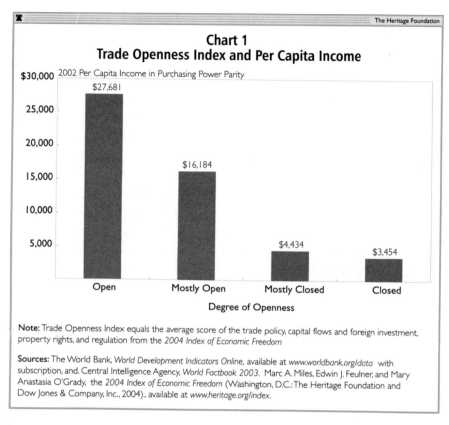

**Chart 1**
**Trade Openness Index and Per Capita Income**

Note: Trade Openness Index equals the average score of the trade policy, capital flows and foreign investment, property rights, and regulation from the *2004 Index of Economic Freedom*

Sources: The World Bank, *World Development Indicators Online*, available at www.worldbank.org/data with subscription, and. Central Intelligence Agency, *World Factbook 2003*. Marc A. Miles, Edwin J. Feulner, and Mary Anastasia O'Grady, the *2004 Index of Economic Freedom* (Washington, D.C.: The Heritage Foundation and Dow Jones & Company, Inc., 2004)., available at www.heritage.org/index.

became progressively clearer, countries outside the association would want to enjoy them as well. They would therefore be motivated to reform their policies in order to qualify for membership. Over time, membership would grow, making the association even more attractive.

The visible benefits of this association might motivate countries such as Kenya. Kenya's trade policy has not been transformed by inclusion in the WTO,[16] but exclusion from membership in the GFTA might be the spark that causes it to change its course. Kenya desperately needs growth, but growth will come only with more economic freedom.

Kenya's counterproductive policies hinder economic freedom and impose lost opportunity and productivity. Consider a comparison of GDPs: In the United States, GDP per capita is $31,932; in Kenya, it is only $328. America has low barriers to trade and abundant opportunities for its citi-

---

16. Kenya joined the WTO in 1995.

zens; Kenya does not. However, to become eligible for the GFTA, Kenya has to change much more than its trade policy. Kenya has moderate barriers to foreign investment, a high level of regulation, and only a moderate level of protection for property rights. Changes in each of these areas would create a more productive, business-friendly environment.

While the GFTA's goal is to advance free trade, the mandatory range of criteria would encourage countries to create sound business environments *before* qualifying for membership. In their pursuit of free trade, countries would have to open their markets to foreign investment, implement strong property rights, and eliminate burdensome regulation. By implementing these measures, a country would be hanging out the "welcome" sign for free trade and for both foreign and domestic investment. Property would be secure through strong property rights, and overhead costs would decline as a result of less regulation. Opportunities would be opened for people and for investment, and improved growth would surely follow.

And Kenya is not unique. There are many other developing nations in which restrictive policies have sentenced individuals and families to a life of poverty by denying them opportunities for improvement. The GFTA's criteria for membership embody the essence of the road to prosperity. Therefore, if they are to be successful in gaining access to foreign markets, countries will simultaneously have to eliminate the barriers that block greater economic growth.

Countries desiring trade liberalization should not have this goal undermined by protectionist nations. Countries that have implemented sound economic policies should not be prevented from reaping the benefits of increased market access. In the words of analysts John Hulsman and Aaron Schavey:

> A system based on rewarding markets that have already opened will change the way countries think about trade. No longer will open economies need to wrangle over winning concessions from closed countries to further trade. Instead, free trade will be seen for what it is—a policy that gives countries that embrace it a massive economic advantage.[17]

---

17. John C. Hulsman, and Aaron Schavey, "The Global Free Trade Association: A New Trade Agenda," Heritage Foundation *Backgrounder* No. 1441, May 16, 2001.

The Office of the U.S. Trade Representative is currently bombarded with requests for free trade agreements from developing countries. Establishing a GFTA would enable eligible developing countries to obtain much-needed access to larger markets like the United States and the United Kingdom. As summarized in the *2001 Index of Economic Freedom*:

> If countries in all regions of the world that fulfill the FTA criteria are offered the reward of unfettered access to the American market, their economies are bound to prosper, and the more such a Free Trade Association thrives, the more likely it is that its effects will stimulate other countries around the world to meet the trading criteria for membership.[18]

Likewise, the United States and the United Kingdom would have more access to each other without the frustrating wait for another WTO round.[19] The GFTA would not seek to replace the WTO; instead, it would be used as a mechanism to advance liberalization while WTO talks are in progress. For example, the United States negotiated the North American Free Trade Agreement (NAFTA) while the WTO's Uruguay Round negotiations were in progress. However, should the WTO's efforts to negotiate global trade liberalization fail, the GFTA alternative remains.

This global association also has the potential to move agricultural liberalization forward. Among the countries that initially qualify for membership, for example, New Zealand and Australia have the lowest farm subsidies in the world. Producer support in New Zealand and Australia is less than 5 percent of total farm production. Agricultural liberalization has been the most difficult subject of negotiation within the WTO because many countries refuse to lower their barriers to agricultural trade.

---

18. John C. Hulsman, Gerald P. O'Driscoll, Jr., and Denise H. Froning. "The Free Trade Association: A Trade Agenda for the New Global Economy," in Gerald P. O'Driscoll, Jr., Kim R. Holmes, and Melanie Kirkpatrick, *2001 Index of Economic Freedom* (Washington, D.C.: The Heritage Foundation and Dow Jones & Company, Inc., 2001), p. 37.

19. According to Martin Howe, a practicing Queen's Counsel, the European Commission Treaty could be amended to allow EU countries to participate in the GFTA. For further information, see John C. Hulsman, "The World Turned Rightside Up: A New Trading Agenda for the Age of Globalisation," Institute of Economic Affairs *Occasional Paper* No. 114, 2001.

## Trading Poverty for Prosperity

Free trade is a crucial milestone on the road to prosperity. According to the U.S. Trade Representative, Ambassador Robert Zoellick, "Over the last decade, trade helped to raise 140 million people out of poverty, spreading prosperity and peace to parts of the world that have seen too little of both."[20] By opening their markets to trade, developing countries will experience greater opportunities and growth, both of which will lead to improvements in labor standards and the environment and to investment in education.

Instead of seeking handouts, developing countries should strive to qualify for the Global Free Trade Association. To do this, however, they must lower their barriers to trade. Some countries will only have to lower tariffs. Others will have to do more: implement strong property rights, reduce regulations, and introduce policies friendly to foreign investment.

But the need to move liberalization forward is not confined to the developing world. Many developed countries continue to promote restrictive policies that stifle growth. Significant liberalization within the WTO will not occur until these developed nations relinquish their barriers to trade, particularly in agriculture. Until that happens, countries will continue to look elsewhere to advance free trade by negotiating bilateral and regional free trade agreements.[21]

Country-by-country negotiation requires an extensive amount of time and effort. A GFTA can bring free trade now. Not only would it encourage liberalization, but it would also create a more efficient process by which to accomplish liberalization. A GFTA would move liberalization forward rapidly, even in the midst of a very slow WTO round of negotiations.

The United States should take the lead in initiating the formation of a Global Free Trade Association. By taking the initiative, it would be helping the developed world far more than billions of dollars in foreign aid ever could.

---

20. Robert B. Zoellick, U.S. Trade Representative, testimony before the Committee on Finance, U.S. Senate, March 9, 2004.

21. "By the end of last year, the WTO had been notified that roughly 250 bilateral and multilateral agreements had been approved, over half of them since 1995, and about 50 more are believed to be on the way." Murray Hiebert, "The Perils of Bilateral Deals," *Far Eastern Economic Review*, December 25, 2003–January 1, 2004.

# Acknowledgments

Books do not emerge from a vacuum. There are always people whose names fail to appear on either the cover or the table of contents but who play an integral role in making a project such as this book a reality. It is only appropriate, therefore, that appreciation be expressed to the many individuals, especially those at The Heritage Foundation, who have helped to make publication of *The Road to Prosperity* possible.

First, thanks are extended to Phil Truluck, Rebecca Hagelin, Larry Wortzel, Stuart Butler, Drew Bond, Ted Schelenski, Matt Spalding, Ann Klucsarits, and Jonathan Larsen of the Heritage Books Editorial Advisory Committee for their enthusiastic support of this project. The book was only a concept when we described it to the committee, but the members were insightful enough to appreciate its potential significance.

The primary responsibility for producing the book was borne by The Heritage Foundation's Center for International Trade and Economics (CITE). Sara Fitzgerald Cooper coordinated the book production process. Sara, Ana Eiras, Anthony Kim, and Brett Schaefer wrote the chapter summaries. Anthony Kim also performed the crucial task of creating and inserting the charts and graphs, and Gail Garnett provided valuable production support.

Larry Wortzel, Vice President and Director of the Kathryn and Shelby Cullom Davis Institute for International Studies, encouraged our efforts from the start. His guidance and suggestions were invaluable in making this book a reality.

John Sieg, Strategic Marketing Adviser in the Communications and Marketing Department, was among the first to recognize the potential synergies between *The Road to Prosperity* and our annual *Index of Economic Freedom*. His continued counsel and his efforts to market *The Road to Prosperity* have been a tremendous asset.

We wish to express our deep appreciation for the work of contract editor Laurie Burkitt and Senior Copy Editor William T. Poole, who shared the primary responsibility for editing the book, and Senior Editor Richard Odermatt, who, as always, was responsible for final review of the entire text. Copy Editor Marla Graves also assisted with the editing of Chapters 4 and 10.

In Publishing Services, Director Jonathan Larsen and Alex Adrianson were responsible for the extensive design and layout. Elizabeth Brewer designed the cover, and Therese Pennefather coordinated the entire process.

In the end, however, the success of this book rests with the insight of the authors. We thank each of them for their time and for their efforts to make this project a success.

# Contributors

**Marc A. Miles** is Director of the Center for International Trade and Economics (CITE) at The Heritage Foundation.

**Edwin J. Feulner** is President of The Heritage Foundation.

**Robert J. Barro** is Paul M. Warburg Professor of Economics at Harvard University.

**Sara Fitzgerald Cooper** is a former Trade Policy Analyst in the Center for International Trade and Economics at The Heritage Foundation.

**Hernando de Soto** is President of the Institute for Liberty and Democracy in Peru.

**Sebastian Edwards** is Henry Ford II Professor of International Business Economics at the Anderson Graduate School of Management at the University of California, Los Angeles (UCLA).

**Ana Isabel Eiras** is Senior Policy Analyst in International Economics in the Center for International Trade and Economics at The Heritage Foundation.

**Daniel T. Griswold** is Associate Director of the Center for Trade Policy Studies at the Cato Institute.

**Arthur B. Laffer** is Chairman and CEO of Laffer Associates.

**Adam Lerrick** is Director of the Gailliot Center for Public Policy at Carnegie Mellon University.

**Richard Roll** holds the Japan Alumni Chair in Finance at the Anderson Graduate School of Management at the University of California, Los Angeles (UCLA).